Women's Studies Quarterly

An Educational Project at the Feminist Press at the City University of New York in Cooperation with Rochester Institute of Technology

Guest Editors for Current Issue
Cheryl J. Fish and Yi-Chun Tricia Lin, Borough of Manhattan Community College, The City University of New York (CUNY)

Editor
Diane Hope, Rochester Institute of Technology

Publisher
Jean Casella, the Feminist Press and the Graduate School and University Center, CUNY

Poetry Editor
Edvige Giunta, New Jersey City University

Editorial Board
Lynne Derbyshire, University of Rhode Island
Jean Douthwright, Rochester Institute of Technology
Lisa Freeman, Kansas State University
Edvige Giunta, New Jersey City University
Dorothy O. Helly, emerita, Hunter College and the Graduate School, CUNY
Barbara Horn, Nassau Community College, SUNY
Florence Howe, *Editor Emerita,* the Feminist Press
Alice Kessler-Harris, Columbia University
Wendy Kolmar, Drew University
Linda Layne, Rensselaer Polytechnic Institute
Tobe Levin, University of Maryland, European Division, and J.W. Goethe University, Frankfurt am Main, Germany
Kit Mayberry, Rochester Institute of Technology
Carol J. Pierman, University of Alabama
Nancy Porter, *Editor Emerita,* Portland State University
Lee Quinby, Hobart and William Smith Colleges
Carol Richardson, Rochester Institute of Technology
Deborah S. Rosenfelt, University of Maryland, College Park
Sue V. Rosser, Georgia Institute of Technology
Carole Anne Taylor, Bates College
Mari Boor Tonn, University of Maryland
Janet Zandy, *Editor Emerita,* Rochester Institute of Technology
Bonnie Zimmerman, San Diego State University

Managing Editors
Molly Vaux and Livia Tenzer

Copy Editor
Margaret A. Hogan

Editorial Assistant
Jesse Quillian

Administrative Assistant to the Editor
Cassandra Shellman

Contents

WOMEN'S STUDIES NOW: ACROSS THE GREAT DIVIDES

READING, WRITING, AND ASYNCHRONICITY

POETRY

TEACHING, LIFE, AND WORK: CRITICAL PEDAGOGIES

BOOK REVIEW

Editorial

Cheryl J. Fish and Yi-Chun Tricia Lin

On the morning of 11 September 2001, we were en route to a meeting to discuss our plans for editing this issue of *Women's Studies Quarterly* at our Borough of Manhattan Community College offices, four short blocks north of the former World Trade Center. What ensued need not be detailed here, but the tragic events that followed have cast deep shadows on this project. In fact, the impact of that day has heightened our desire to transform and reexamine our role as educators, scholars, and citizens from a perspective we can call "women's studies then and now." For in crisis, isn't it especially meaningful to ask questions related to the construction of knowledge and information, and the use and misuse of representations? History and our current predicaments demand sensitivity in investigating the intersections of global and local events. We hope that the actions this issue chronicles shed some light on recent conflicts and turmoil—on our campuses, in our communities, and in our struggles to gain influence—that can tear at us emotionally and intellectually.

Karla Jay's essay "Teaching as Healing at Ground Zero" points out that while fear is a great equalizer, "not all people were treated equally in the aftermath of the attacks." That harkens back politically to the continued sense of righting wrongs and fighting for justice in times of chaos that has marked the history of women's struggles. This issue of *Women's Studies Quarterly* continues conversations raised at the conference "Then and Now: The Politics of Women's Studies," which was held at the City University of New York's Graduate Center in December 2000 to celebrate the launching of the Feminist Press's Women's Studies History Series and the publication of the first volume in that series, *The Politics of Women's Studies: Testimony from Thirty Founding Mothers.* The opening section of this issue of the quarterly includes essays based on talks given at that conference and is dedicated to "looking back" at particular moments that form a backdrop and connection to where we are now—always a necessity so as not to assume easily, in Florence Howe's words, an "urgency of . . . new vision" that would erase or fail to acknowledge accomplishments of the past (28). How important, then, to draw on Annis Vilas Pratt's

"pedagogical bequest" to the "now" generation of women's studies
professors, and to listen to the wisdom of Inez Martinez who reminds
us that "the best part of women's studies' heritage [is that] from the
beginning, however imperfectly conceived . . . the goal of social justice for all informed our vision."

So, how do women's studies programs fare thirty years after the
founding mothers' work? And what role does social justice now play?
To go beyond "looking back" and to provide space for our examination of some of the "now" aspects of women's studies, we have
included a section of case studies from various campuses. These six
reports are a partial examination of the status of women's studies
today in the United States representing a range of institutions: the
community college, the four-year college/university, the technical
institute, and the state university. These reports are from the South
and North, and rural and urban institutions. In particular, the varied representation speaks to our work as committed women's studies faculty at a community college. Far too often, the realities of life
and work at community/junior colleges are left out of surveys and
studies in prestigious journals and conferences. Two-year campuses
educate many of the nation's college students. Elizabeth Clark and
Katie Hogan's essay illustrates how "teaching women's studies on the
sly" at a two-year campus without formal women's studies can be a
frustrating but ingenious way of teaching theory and critical texts,
and connecting intellectual work with women's lived experiences.
Nevertheless, the real struggles involved in the lives of students and
faculty and the sense of urgency for bringing particular issues and
questions into the classroom make it especially frustrating when we
see questions like "Are there any real feminists in academe" posited
in a tabloid manner on the cover of The Chronicle of Higher
Education (Patai). This volume testifies to the lively debate and commitment to feminist praxis that exist and evolve in many quarters of
our campuses today.

Distinctions notwithstanding, these narratives from the campuses
reveal how important it is to have institutional support to ensure the
longevity of women's studies, whether in the form of a department,
a program, a center, or faculty lines. Even with administrative support, however, women's studies often does not get the attention that
institutionalization might guarantee. In fact, it often gives the sem-
blance that the work is "done" and, hence, over. The case of
Greenfield Community College (GCC), in the account here by Anne
M. Wiley, describes how GCC at first sustained and then disbanded
its women's studies program. It is a rather poignant reminder of the

peril that comes without consistent administrative support and expansive energies. From other campus narratives we see exciting possibilities yet to be fully realized. The lesson from Scarlet Bowen and Emma Pérez's piece on the University of Texas at El Paso (UTEP) is that the field is full of untapped possibilities, interdisciplinary in nature and simultaneously global and local. At UTEP, women's studies continues the tradition of our foremothers in raising consciousness and activism, but, befitting its position on the border of two nations, is a bilingual, binational program focused on the needs of women and girls in the community. Likewise, in their account of developing women's studies at Georgia Institute of Technology, Sue V. Rosser, Mary Frank Fox, and Carol Colatrella point to other possibilities—in this case, the intersection between women's studies and science and technology disciplines—as a particularly fertile ground and one that has increasingly mustered institutional support.

Tensions and polarizations have always been a reality in women's studies; the sisterhood of the early days was fraught with unacknowledged divisions along racial, sexual, generational, and class-based lines. Now, as back then, we must be concerned with what happens when fragmentation, identity politics, and in-fighting over scarce resources are taken to the extreme. There are still many out there who would like to set us back. So it is encouraging then that some of the most lively and provocative scholarship in women's and gender studies is emerging out of the spaces in, around, and between "great divides" that can propel us to build stronger and more inclusive constituents. Emerging writers continue the feminist tradition of building on and criticizing their predecessors, pushing us to recognize the limits of various institutional, pedagogical, and epistemological practices. In this issue, for instance, we have included essays that examine the position of women of color within women's studies, as Patti Duncan's article does, and the lived experiences of intersex persons within the study of the construction of gender and sexuality, as in the essay by Emi Koyama and Lisa Weasel. Cathryn Bailey analyzes how feminist practices in college classrooms "produce feminist subjects"; it is her attempt to interrogate the generational "impasse" between the waves. The boom in online education raises the following question: How does communicating via advanced technologies affect the learning experience of women? Women's studies, after all, emerged out of a desire to share face-to-face experiences and to challenge patriarchal hierarchies—so (how) does the learner embody asynchronous cyberspace? Pamela Whitehouse addresses some of these questions in "Women's Studies Online: An Oxymoron?" Another aspect of cyberspace, the playful space of jouissance for feminists who "embrace the dynamics—the impossibilities of technology"—is set down in print here by Julie O'Neill Kloo and Laurie McMillan.

The most vital aspect of women's studies, then as now, lies in its constant revitalizing of academia by challenging disciplinary scholarship, infusing critical pedagogies, and disturbing boundaries between life, work, and teaching. In the past thirty years, since the introduction of the first women's studies courses on U.S. campuses, we have witnessed the advent and establishment of new areas of research. As such, sharing syllabi is one way for scholar-activists to witness the vitality of feminist scholarship. In the tradition of *Women's Studies Quarterly*, therefore, this volume includes a syllabus from Lynne Derbyshire that reminds us that service learning rose out of the desire to link feminist theory and practice. Jodi Vandenberg-Daves's syllabus is an appendix to her narrative on the construction of the history of motherhood. Barbara Omolade's essay, "Women and Work: Class Within the Classroom," further examines the scope of women's work in various "spheres." Most significantly, she addresses class consciousness, the central but often invisible focus in writing on the lives of working women of color. Activism and academic work is addressed by Berenice Malka Fisher, who reflects on the need for critically educating those preparing to enter the professions of nursing, human services, and other women-predominant fields.

Finally, we'd like to conclude on a personal note as this project marks the completion of one of many collaborations on our part. We wanted to briefly explore here how various personal, political, and circumstantial events have brought us to consider women's studies and feminism as our home—even as what *home* means is a constantly contested process. When Maryanne Dever studies the goals and expectations for today's generation of students who consciously choose women's or gender studies as their primary field, it greatly contrasts with the way we found ourselves invested in these spaces. As young women, neither of us could have possibly made such a choice. We often feel we're the "in-between" generation, not boomers, not pioneers, and not "postfeminist." We flirted with women's studies in graduate school as nontraditional students. Cheryl, from a working-class Jewish family in Queens, took a course in the sociology of gender at Michigan State University that blew off the top of her head, so to speak. However, it was in activist work for many causes during the 1980s that she first encountered feminist politics and leadership, and as a poet found feminist poetics. Graduate school at the City University of New York brought her into contact with leading feminist scholars and a tradition of students facing constant struggle during ongoing budget crises.

Tricia, on the other hand, growing up in conservative Nationalist Taiwan in the 1960s and 1970s, had all the feminist ideas and anything of women's studies neatly packed away from her. Her education, both at home and in school, was meant to prepare her for her housewifely duties, yet she traveled oceans and a continent to sneak into women's studies—via her reading of poststructuralism and Asian American literature for her doctoral degree in comparative literature—and could never find her way back. Today we have long-standing and more recent role models, and see mentoring and being mentored as an ongoing negotiation.

Different as our paths were, we met and bonded in our struggles toward—and found home in—women's studies in an institution with no formal women's studies. At our urban community college, we take our place among dedicated faculty and staff who use myriad strategies outside of formalized women's studies to support our students, primarily working class and of color, who work, go to school, and raise families. (Six perished in the World Trade Center disaster.) Therefore, although we are struck that many of the "now" models for women's or gender studies assume a certain level of acceptance and sophistication in the form of dedicated faculty lines, grant support, and Ph.D. programs, our work on this issue is part of a larger effort to reach out to colleagues and to create new models that can help the neediest—as well as the brightest—students to thrive.

Co-editing this volume through the year after 11 September seemed incredibly daunting. However, this process taught us the value of searching past and present accomplishments for insights and to come face–to–face with frightening new realities. We thank our contributors and the staff of the Feminist Press who have amazingly sustained us.

Works Cited

Howe, Florence, ed. *The Politics of Women's Studies: Testimony from Thirty Founding Mothers*. New York: Feminist, 2000.
Patai, Daphne. In "The Chronicle Review." *Chronicle of Higher Education* 6 Oct. 2000: B7–B9.

Cheryl J. Fish *is the coeditor, with Farah Griffin, of* A Stranger in the Village: Two Centuries of African-American Travel Writing *(Beacon Press, 1999) and is completing a study, "Going Mobile: The Body at Work in Black and White Women's Travel Writing in the Antebellum Americas." She is associate professor of English and cochair of the Women's Studies Project Committee at Borough of Manhattan Community College of the City University of New York (CUNY). A fifth-generation daughter of Taiwan,* **Yi-Chun Tricia Lin** *is associate professor of English and cochair of the Women's Studies Project Committee at Borough of Manhattan Community College, CUNY. She is currently working on a comparative studies project, "Re-Mapping the Other: Cultural Translation in Asian/Pacific and Caribbean American Writing."*

Then and Now in Women's Studies

My Pedagogical Bequest

Annis Vilas Pratt

The first thing it takes to survive is friends. The second thing it takes to survive is friendly people in high places.

—Electa Arenal, "Then and Now: The Politics of Women's Studies" Conference, 2 December 2000

We need to get perspective on a university by looking inside it as outsiders in a one thousand year old medieval structure with an entrenched hierarchy. The engaged campus, in contrast, is focused on its students with a democratic pedagogy and experiential learning.

—Yolanda Moses, "Then and Now: The Politics of Women's Studies" Conference, 1 December 2000

I have reached a season in my life when, retired from academe and swiftly approaching sixty-five years old, people ask me to write an article here, a chapter there about being a feminist in the 1960s and 1970s; or, as Florence Howe so cogently put it, about my experiences as a "founding mother" of women's studies. Not content with our writing a chapter each for *The Politics of Women's Studies*, in December 2000 Howe asked us each to invite a younger colleague and gather at a conference called "Then and Now: The Politics of Women's Studies" to discuss what parts of our heritage from Then had relevance for women's studies Now. To answer that question I thought back about my career as a university professor, and it seemed that my bequest for today's women's studies teachers would be an account of the classroom techniques with which I implemented our vision of an experiential, student-centered pedagogy.

So it was that I brought my Rip van Winkle-ish self back from my midwestern home to my native New York City to join a panel of wise old feminist pioneers, noting down in my travel diary what it felt like to arrive as a "Then" in the Christmas-in-Manhattan "Now."

1 December 2000

Go out onto 81st to catch crosstown and transfer down Fifth Avenue to attend Feminist Press signing and conference in old B. Altman building. At 35th I get off onto crowded, jostling avenue, walk half block down to familiar facade of B. Altman's. Is institutional vapidity of entry hall worsened by recollection of gold and silver bells, pine swags garlanded with red velvet ribbons, aroma of perfumes and cosmetics at Christmastime in the fifties, or is grimness just typical of college buildings, however jolly their origins?

Whichever, editor with familiar white stripe across black hair bustles up to greet me before bustling off to greet others, find "Now" younger feminist I have invited and several "Then" acquaintances, so warm friendliness not absent as we repair into auditorium. Editor arises to greet us, dampening jollity of reunion with catalogue of founding mothers suddenly ill—Annette suffering from chemo, Nellie suddenly struck down with flu and can't attend, ditto Jane. Then, mourned by all, Shauna, Betty, Elaine, Judith, Carol and Juanita are dead.

Feeling of ephemerality washes over me: check arms and legs to make sure I am still here, as current of death's dark river, into which I may vanish at any moment, laps about my feet.

Sensation of insubstantiality mitigated when one feminist pioneer after another rises at podium to become radiantly energized—face brightens up, tired eyes glow, every white hair sparkles—as she tells her story about standing up against tweedy male authorities shouting at her that women have written no literature worth including in curriculum, women haven't made history, there are no women in politics, there are no women mathematicians, etc., etc., etc., while she found her courage to speak out in the same lucent precision with which she is recounting her saga of resistance and courage for us now.

Listening to those panelists, I felt enormously satisfied that we *had* done all that, to the extent that women's literature, politics, history, and scientific contributions are now widely included in college and university curricula. And there are a lot more women professors, aren't there? Unfortunately not: However much I wish that the "Then" of the stubborn territorial patriarchate had given away to the "Now" community we founding mothers envisioned, Virginia Valian is unfortunately right on when, in *Why So Slow: The Advancement of Women*, she reminds us that "in almost every field and subfield, in almost every cohort and at almost every point in their teaching and research careers, women [still] advance more slowly and earn less money than men. The history of the profession in the past few decades suggests that the problem of women's lower status in academe will not dissipate in the fullness of time" (217). Which is why we *still* do all that, we tenured and retired women faculty who advise academic women who are being discriminated against and raise legal funds for them when the academic patriarchate holds them back from tenure and devises all kinds of crude retaliations should they engage in the "uncolleagial" behavior of protesting.

2 December 2000

Panels at CUNY building go on all day on topics of "Sustaining Energy, Then and Now," "Gains and Losses, Then and Now," making me feel definitely more Then than Now, doubtful if I can sustain energy to get through all of them until my own turn on four o'clock panel. Panelists waiting turn at table on stage seem pale and wan until they rise to speak, at which each perks up, ablaze with intelligence and passion, to tell about obdurate departments subverted, scurrilous deans outfoxed, whole academic disciplines stood on their heads.

Have impression of academic institutions weighing down upon backs of raconteurs like patriarchal granite of courts and temples under which caryatids hunch. Am worried, also, that valiant efforts may be ignored at their peril by rising generation blithely unaware of academe's enduring enmity and perfidious plans against women.

The Now generation of women's studies faculty need to analyze the lines of power on their campuses and face the fact that they are unlikely to advance merely on their merits. Gloria de Sole, who had a long career as the affirmative action officer at the State University of New York at Albany, points out that the more gains we make, the worse academic men behave: "Many feminists thought we would meet with resistance until we were understood. We didn't expect that once we were understood, we would meet with even more resistance because we would be challenging male definitions of academic disciplines and the university" (qtd. in Sidhu 38).

As coordinator of the Academic Discrimination Advisory Board of the National Women's Studies Association (NWSA), I receive case after case of women viciously held back in academe, and I frequently remind junior faculty in our newsletter (*The Strategist: Tips and Tactics for Women Faculty*) that one of the most serious mistakes they can make is to assume that academics are motivated by rationality, equity, common sense, collegiality, or concern for their students, rather than a sometimes clever and often brutal territoriality.

It is not at all surprising that in such a competitive atmosphere a lot of women should try to get ahead by assimilating the norms around them. One of the questions that Florence Howe had asked us to address in our *Politics of Women's Studies* chapters was what our regrets were: Where did we perhaps take a false turn? My regret was that we confused the equality we longed for with sameness, trying to be the same kind of college professors men were, striving to use our intellects in the exact way they did. Right in the middle of mainstreaming women's materials into our courses, right in the middle of documenting women's daily as well as public history in intricate detail, many women academics thought the way to get ahead was to assimilate the norms and mores of the dominant (male academic) culture. Some succeeded in rising through the ranks by pursuing this gender equivalent of passing for white: Assimilation was how getting along and moving up had always been done in America, and that was the way they were going to get ahead in academe. Our gender difference was to be left behind at the gates of academe, wasn't it? Who really needed Mary Daly's "Cosmosis of Sisterhood" when, by bending a bit here, squashing our personalities there, we might one day secure a deanship?

My chief regret was that this impossible and disempowering task absorbed so much of our energies that we had little left for sisterhood in an alien world where we needed each other most of all. We were like the blackbirds baked in a pie and set to sing before the king: Our song might be saddened by our constriction in the patriarchal oven, sticky masculine filling, and hot sexist crust but we were still blackbirds at heart, singing a countermelody derived from our ornithological identity. Although women's studies faculty were often tempted to cook ourselves into the patriarchal pie, it could never entirely engulf us. It wasn't just that we persisted in mainstreaming powerful, self-determining women as subject matter into a wide variety of departments and curricula. Even more particularly, many of us insisted upon our unique heritage of revolutionary teaching methods.

Final afternoon panel arrives at last with me sitting up on stage with it, though much of audience seems in a state of exhausted somnolence. When my turn comes I experience surge of clarity as I insist that we honor our consciousness-raising heritage of teaching our students to reason inductively, from experience, rather than deductively, from ideas, which I call "experiential epistemology and pedagogy" in order to get their attention. Once I have it, I tell them that all too many of us have assimilated hierarchical and professor-centered teaching methods rather than democratic and student-centered ones, and that we are in danger, however feminist our subject matter, of assimilating in the way we teach the very patriarchal norms we so deeply oppose.

Not sure how this goes down as most of audience is asleep.

It all started with those "click!" moments in our consciousness-raising groups when we realized that we weren't inferior as women, just internalizing scorn superimposed upon our otherwise authentic personalities by the patriarchy. The experiential pedagogy we developed, which was based on what went on in a student's mind in response to her personal experience, was not an entirely new teaching method, but one that John Dewey had declared as early as 1916 in his *Democracy and Education* to be the only kind of teaching appropriate for American democracy. Our use of it in colleges and universities of the 1970s and 1980s, with specific application to women's status in American society, was, nonetheless, revolutionary within a system of higher education based on an entirely different hierarchical model imported from Europe.

When I ponder the historical prototypes upon which universities are modeled I see a Calvinist divine and a European lecturer. The divine looms high up from a raised lectern that also holds an enormous Bible, funneling knowledge from the book to his people, over whom he holds the threat of damnation. The lecturer stands at a similar remove from his passive audience on an auditorium platform, expounding concepts while his students (whom he does not care to know personally) frantically scribble down every word he says in an attempt to avert academic damnation. The atmosphere in both church and lecture hall is tense with fear and anxiety.

Not only in my earlier years but consistently throughout my career, many students' initial reactions to my experiential teaching methods were incredulity and perturbation:

> I am embarrassed and disappointed by the personalizing this prof is doing: she brings in materials from her own life I'd just as soon not hear about and expects us to do the same—these issues are way too intense!
>
> I came to college to learn from profs who use their brains like my father does. I never expected to study with someone who thinks/feels (she calls it "theels"—yuck!) like my mother!

As we got into the semester, they began to see how my methods worked:

> She dangles the hook and lets us take it anywhere we want. Nor does she pull back on the line except to show us her point, which our own opinions have usually proved or concluded.
>
> She seems to absorb people's emotions and channel them into good discussions. There have been times I have been worried for

her—how, where can she go on with this discussion? And she comes out of it fine and really clarifying things.

I rarely heard any serious complaints about my methods after the first half of the course and was always pleased to receive evaluations which showed that they understood the benefits of a student-centered pedagogy:

> I liked being made to think.
> She believes in teaching how to learn rather than what to learn.

A key element in the student-centered classroom is an atmosphere in which tentative answers from the students' own thought processes are accepted and where professorial and student behaviors that limit intellection are discouraged. Professors need to differentiate between an authority that facilitates such mental growth and authoritarianism, which stifles it. When students experience verbal violence from their professor or each other their neo-cortical systems shut down and their thinking process is atrophied. To put it another way, their neo-cortical functions are overwhelmed by adrenaline surging up from the limbic or fright-and-flight region of their brains.

Combative argumentation stifles thought. Often one or two students will try to browbeat others for "incorrect" approaches and attempt to dominate the discussion. Such peer domination (considered part of a desirably conflictual interchange in academic culture) brings out the worst in louder students and silences quieter and less opinionated ones. I used my professorial authority to keep them from attacking each other verbally and to create safe spaces for intellectual growth, where trust and mutual respect foster a less terrorized atmosphere.

In my student-centered classrooms I got rid of all the podiums and platforms, replacing them with just my desk surrounded by a room full of moveable chairs. (This can be done even with classes of over one hundred, as Martin Bickman has demonstrated at the University of Colorado.) Most days I facilitated discussions based on questions handed out ahead of time. From the first day of class, I divided up the forty to forty-five students into four groups of eight or ten, which met for ten to fifteen minutes on their own, returning to the group as a whole to bring the issues that had been raised into an all-class discussion of that day's topic. I facilitated this discussion and summarized their findings on the board, devoting the last five minutes of one class and the first five minutes of the next to summarizing our findings. My only restriction on discussion was that they not pass judgment on each other or engage in any kind of verbal attack.

Students should not be discouraged by punitive grading, such as the practice of arbitrary curves, or the Calvinistic allocation into categories of blessed or damned for their first try at a paper. In my classes, all papers could be resubmitted until the last day, grades of A were given only when evidence of the student's individual thinking was present (Ds and Fs for parroting), all grades under A/B were accompanied by an explanation of how to get them higher, and faults in grammar were dealt with in a series of revisions until they got it right. Since students were perennially astonished that a professor valued their personal experiences as integral to cognition, I had to refuse grades above an A/B until they applied personal experiences.

Thus the longer I taught English and women's studies at the University of Wisconsin^Madison, the less enamored I became with lecturing as a useful teaching method. Because research universities demand huge introductory lectures, women's studies professors get infected by the professor-centered pedagogy these courses demand. I relished my professorial authority as much as anyone would, but I tried to use it for creating a classroom atmosphere of sufficient trust (between me and the students and between each other) for cognition to occur.

Affirming the value of your students' lived experiences means reasoning from their experiences rather than adjusting facts to set theories. Starting with abstract concepts also blocks student cognition, while reflecting upon their own lives promotes critical thinking and (eventual) theory formation. As human beings we developed our neocortex for pragmatic purposes, such as finding our way through the forest or figuring out how best to organize our days to forage well. My take on experiential teaching was to encourage students to collaborate in the formation of hypotheses, using as data both their own experiences and writers' depictions of women's lives.

After I had taught this way for many years, I discovered that stage theory, arrived at through inductive observation of student attitudes at different phases of development, grew out of an experiential approach similar to mine. It had an interesting early incarnation in W. E. Cross's "Negro to Black Conversion Experience" published in 1971, which was adapted for "From Passive Acceptance to Active Commitment: A Model of Feminist Identity Development" in 1985 by Nancy E. Downing and Kristin L. Roush. Women's studies teachers trying to figure out how their students' minds work can enhance their classroom teaching by examining the chart "Parallels Between the

Identity Development Stages for Women and Blacks," compiled by Downing and Rousch in "From Passive Acceptance to Active Commitment" (see Table 1).

Table 1: Parallels Between the Identity Development Stages for Women and Blacks

Stages for Women

Passive Acceptance	Revelation	Embeddedness-Emanation	Synthesis	Active Commitment
Passive acceptance of traditional sex roles and discrimination; belief that traditional roles are advantageous; men are considered superior.	Catalyzed by a series of crises, resulting in open questioning and feelings of anger; and guilt dualistic thinking; men are perceived as negative.	Characterized by connectedness with other select women, affirmation and strengthening of new identity. Eventually more relativistic thinking and cautious interaction with men.	Development of an authentic and positive feminist identity; sex-role transcendence; "flexible truce" with the world; evaluate men on individual basis.	Consolidation of feminist identity; commitment to meaningful action, to a non-sexist world. Actions are personalized and rational. Men are considered equal but not the same as women.

Stages for Blacks

Pre-encounter	Encounter	Immersion-Emersion	Internalization	Internalization-Commitment
The unaware person; acceptance of oppression as justified; values assimilation into majority culture; negative self-concept.	Catalyzed by profound event(s) resulting in increased awareness, rejection of oppression, and feelings of guilt and anger.	Initially characterized by withdrawal from dominant culture, immersion in one's own heritage and hostility toward whites. Eventually greater cognitive flexibility and pride emerge.	Development of an integrated, more positive self-image; adoption of a pluralistic, nonracist perspective.	Commitment of the new self to meaningful action for the benefit of the minority community.

Note: The data on the stages for Black women were adapted from Cross.
Source: Downing and Roush 699. Reprinted by permission of Sage Publications, Inc.

"Passive acceptance," the first stage for women, describes the attitude of many University of Wisconsin students in their early twenties, when the temptation to conform to patriarchal norms is at its highest in their lives. Many introductory women's studies syllabi of the 1980s were almost entirely devoted to "revelation," describing women's oppression. Twenty-somethings who hoped that these classes would make them feel better about being women were pummeled with patriarchal perspectives on themselves as "objects of men's gaze" in art,

advertising, film, and pornography. Their women's studies professors
thought stirring up student reactions to these materials fostered critical thinking, which they considered the final goal of intellectual
development. It seemed to me that many of these professors were
stuck themselves at the "revelation" stage of intellectual development,
characterized by "feelings of anger" and "rejection of oppression."
Many where influenced by a deconstructionist distaste for the idea
that women should "embed" themselves in womanpower, which they
termed a cop out or, more sophistically, a lapse into "gynocentric
essentialism." They brought their students from thesis ("passive acceptance") to its antithesis, critical thinking about patriarchy, but were
unable to move to the synthesis of active commitment by embedding
them in a feminist identity grounded in their power as women.

When I protested these syllabi to the lecturers, they reassured me
that only such a ferocious initiation would "blast these sorority girls in
their pink sweaters out of their complacency!" Their idea was that the
more violent the examples, the greater students' anger against patriarchy and, thus, their motivation to think critically would be. Although
critical thinking was one of my own pedagogical goals, it seemed to me
that both professors and students in these courses spent so much time
focusing on the brutalities of sexism that they might succumb to either
bitterness or hopelessness.

In my courses, in contrast, I provided maps with alternative paths for
young women who, I was convinced, had been imbued with gender
inferiority for far too long already. What they needed from a women's
studies course, I felt, was not more "revelation" but "embeddedness."
In order to bring positive materials to their attention, I developed syllabi out of women's thousands of years of power and effectiveness, sexuality and acumen, both before and during patriarchy.

The women's studies course I taught most frequently was Women
in Literature, cross-listed between the English Department and
Women's Studies. I selected women's short stories, poems, plays, and
novels from the nineteenth and twentieth centuries most likely to
empower women students. While analyzing literary technique, we
explored themes like autonomy and dependence, self and solitude,
courtship and heterosexual love, lesbian loving, and negritude.

I posited women's literature as a dialectic between what a woman
author depicts her hero desiring and the patriarchal forces thwarting
the hero's needs, and insisted that my students compare their own
experiences to what women heroes go through. Nobody could get a
grade above an A/B without writing about her life (or women's lives
around him as witnessed by a male student) in relationship to the

obstacles women heroes encounter and the qualities of character they draw upon from within themselves to survive and transcend patriarchy.

My syllabi began with short stories (better for the first weeks of a course than full-length novels or poetry, which perennially intimidated Wisconsin students). Women straight off of Wisconsin farms adored Mary Wilkins Freeman's "The Revolt of Mother," in which a farm wife, irritated for years and years by her husband's spending all their money building better cow barns while neglecting their tumbledown house, moves the cows into the house and her family into the well-equipped, sunny new barn. They also enjoyed Sarah Orne Jewett's "A White Heron," in which a young girl decides to put her love of nature ahead of her infatuation with a handsome young ornithologist who shoots birds. The same "refusal to marry the prince charming" led to intense discussions of Freeman's "A New England Nun," who prefers catering to herself to settling down with her long-time suitor and his messy habits.

Having started out in the 1960s as a professor at a predominantly Black school for women, Spelman College, where I had witnessed the effect that getting in touch with their African American heritage had on my students, I developed my teaching methods at the University of Wisconsin to help women become similarly empowered by our heritage as women. One of the ways that I did this was by focusing on myths and symbols as a way of digging into the deep background of women's lives through history. My archetypal pedagogy corresponded to Cross's and Roush and Downing's third stage of engaging students in "embeddedness-emanation," when they affirm and strengthen their identity as Blacks and/or women.

In the early years of the women's movement a kind of urban myth had gone around about a cadre of feminists who broke into the offices of the Grove Press (which published pornography, among other things) and threw a statuette of the Venus of Willendorf out the window, apparently because they considered this large-breasted, wide-hipped 25,000-year-old divinity some kind of masculine insult. This Venus of Willendorf always led off a slide show I gave during a unit on "Discovering a History of Power" early on in my Women and Mythology and Women's Spirituality courses, a choice based on my conviction that throwing goddesses out the window along with their stereotype would deprive my students of images that could transform their sense of themselves. (See the course syllabus following this article.) Once their bodily and cognitive experiences were valorized in this way, they were able to form coalitions with like-minded allies from other genders and races to achieve community goals of committed activism. To point them in the direction of this fifth and final stage of identity development, I asked final exam questions about how students planned to work from their newly empowered positions to commit their values in action.

This was the transformational process upon which I structured my intense, participatory classes on women's spirituality. Most teachers who experiment with innovative pedagogy are never quite sure how it is coming off, whether the kinds of changes they intend for their students are really happening to them. In the spring semester of 1985 I was fortunate to have Jean Saul Rannells, a graduate student in Continuing and Vocational Education, write her dissertation on changes taking place in women students enrolled in my women's studies course on Women and Mythology, which included Diane Wolkstein and Samuel Kramer's stunning translation of the Sumerian Inanna story.

Enrolling my women's studies students as "human subjects," Rannells's findings were codified from interviews with most of the students in the class and from four in-depth case studies. These case studies traced students' attitudes from the beginning to the end of the course, and I was astonished to discover that what I had envisioned for my classes was working just as I had wanted it to: "I feel the stirrings of inner reasons to study mythology. I feel enlivened by the goddesses. They give me energy! There is an ancient tradition of women's power that validates my right to have social and economic goals" (qtd. in Rannells 111). "Kris," writes Rannells, "has felt very negatively about herself at times because of learned expectations that she now fears are destructive for her life. During the semester she realized that other women feel similarly and, most importantly, she saw those women redefining those so-called negative qualities ascribed to women into positive qualities and strengths of women" (119). "Cathy," Rannells notes, "made this statement in response to a slide presentation of goddess statues and artifacts: 'I realized that (my) image has changed just by seeing these slides. Women's breasts and my own are something that's beautiful, something that nurtures life. . . . I certainly have a much better feeling about my body now since the class'" (126).

Nor did Rannells see these responses as idiosyncratic: She was able to codify them in a developmental progression that she outlined on the following chart in which she allocated the results of my experiential teaching to seven stages:

Discovery of Newness: Sudden discovery about oneself like (imitating Medusa): "Taking Action as a result of anger is sometimes good for me, rather than being bad as I had been taught."

Empowerment: An increased sense of autonomy, power and self worth (imitating Inanna): "It is empowering to know that women have done important things—like discovering writing."

Turmoil: Being stirred up, upset: "I leave this class so stirred up that I have to be very active for an hour or so before I can study again."

Self Responsibility: Making decisions demonstrating a new interest in oneself and one's future: "My stance of wait until the boss acted was not helpful."

Integration: Experiencing togetherness (where there was none before) with oneself and one's world. "I got in touch with the angry and the beautiful parts of myself." "All of us in the class were able to relate together—80, 33, 22 year olds."

Interiority: Deepening of the relationship to one's inner self, often through meditation, sometimes return to religion, or listening to hear one's inner voice: "I have developed an awareness of my inner self. My Judaism is something I've denied for a long time. . . . This has allowed me to just begin to think well, maybe that's something I want to have become part of me again."

Bond: The coming together of an aspect of mythology and the student's personal experience: "I liked Diana—her connection with nature, her at-home-ness with plants and nature. She wasn't domineering; she was herself. She reminds me of my childhood experiences. I was shy and would enjoy going into the woods and fields." (188–203) (Used by permission of Jean Saul Rannells.)

Rannells's dissertation about what happened when my students were exposed to goddess images validated my discovery that goddess archetypes are not mere patriarchal constructs but contain elements of psychological power of great value in women's lives. My pedagogical conviction is that students cannot achieve discovery of newness, self responsibility, and interiority—this last the happy occupation of one's own space as a woman—when we offer them nothing but critiques of or rebellions against patriarchy. In offering my pedagogical bequest to the Now generation of women's studies professors, I am not, however, suggesting that they need to be as quirky as I was in their choice of subject matter. I do hope that they devise teaching techniques to empower women students so that they can create alternative spaces which are in, but not of, the patriarchy, and from which they can work in sisterhood to transform their communities.

WORKS CITED

Bickman, Martin. "Active Learning in the University: An Inquiry into Inquiry." On Teaching, Ed. Mary Ann Shea. Boulder: U of Colorado Teaching Excellence Program, 1987. 31–66.

Cross, W. E. "Negro to Black Conversion Experience." *Black World* 20.9 (1971): 13–27.

Dewey, John. *Democracy and Education.* 1916. New York: Macmillan, 1937.

Downing, Nancy E., and Roush, Kristin L. "From Passive Acceptance to Active Commitment: A Model of Feminist Identity Development for Women." *The Counseling Psychologist* 13.4 (1985):695–709.

Freeman, Mary Wilkins. "A New England Nun" and "The Revolt of Mother." *Short Fiction of Sarah Orne Jewett and Mary Wilkins Freeman.* Ed. Barbara H. Soloman. New York: New American Library, 1979. 349–60, 418–32.

Howe, Florence. *The Politics of Women's Studies: Testimony from Thirty Founding Mothers.* New York: Feminist, 2000.

Jewett, Sarah Orne. "A White Heron." *By Women: An Anthology of Literature.* Ed. Linda Heinlein Kirschner and Marcia McClintock Folson. Boston: Houghton, 1976. 106–14.

Perry, William A. "Different Worlds in the Same Classroom: Students' Evolution in Their Vision of Knowledge and Their Expectations of Teachers." *On Teaching and Learning.* Ed. Margaret Morganroth Gullette. Cambridge: Harvard-Danforth Center, 1985: 1–17.

Rannells, Jean Saul. "The Individuation of Women Through the Study of Deity Images: Learning from a Jungian Perspective." Diss. U of Wisconsin–Madison, 1986.

Sidhu, Gretchen. "Academy Blues." *Ms.* August–September 2001: 38.

Spretnak, Charlene, ed. *The Politics of Women's Spirituality: Essays on the Rise of Spiritual Power Within the Feminist Movement.* Garden City, NY: Anchor, 1983.

Valian, Virginia. *Why So Slow: The Advancement of Women.* Cambridge: MIT, 1998.

Wolkstein, Diane, and Samuel Noah Kramer, trans. *Inanna Queen of Heaven and Earth: Her Stories and Hymns from Sumer.* New York: Harper, 1983.

WOMEN'S STUDIES 310: WOMEN'S SPIRITUALITY

Course Description

We will study the impact of the archetypes of Greek goddesses on literature and on women's psychological experiences. Our goal is to assess the degree of empowerment women may gain from a study of powerful female divinities and to apply our findings about this empowerment to feminist theology, ecology, and art.

Course Texts

Bolen, Jean Shinoda. *Goddesses in Everywoman: A New Psychology of Women*. New York: Harper , 1984.

Broner, E. M. *A Weave of Women*. New York: Bantam, 1978.

Cameron, Anne. *Daughters of Copper Woman*. Vancouver: Press Gang, 1981.

Shange, Ntozake. *Sassafras, Cypress and Indigo*. New York: Picador, 1996.

Units

Inanna, Queen of Heaven and Earth: Her Stories and Hymns from Sumer
Discovering a History of Power (slide show)
Greek Gods and Goddesses: Jean Shinoda Bolen, *Goddesses in Everywoman*
Artemis and Aphrodite as Psychological Experiences and Symbols in Literature: Bolen, Artemis and Aphrodite Poetry Packet.
Empowerment in Black Fiction: Ntozake Shange, *Sassafras, Cypress and Indigo*
Empowerment in Jewish Fiction: E. M. Broner, *A Weave of Women*
Empowerment in Native American Fiction: Anne Cameron, *Daughters of Copper Women*
Goddesses, Women, and Nature: Starhawk (packet); visit from local witch
Goddesses, Women, and Art: Talks from local woman artist; local woman art and myth critic; slide show on women and needlework arts (including Judy Chicago's "Dinner Party" and Birth Projects)

Recommended Reading

Charlene Spretnak, ed. *The Politics of Women's Spirituality*

Assignments

Ungraded journal handed in three times during semester
Ten-page paper on outside reading in women's spirituality and myth
Quiz on novels
Final projects: creative writing, art work, needlework or performance, all using archetypes, to be presented during last week of class
Final exam on values

Annis Vilas Pratt *is a retired professor of English from the Unviersity of Wisconsin–Madison. During the ten years since her retirement, she has been active in community issues in the Detroit Metropolitan area and has written and ecofeminist trilogy,* The Marshlanders, *as well as a humorous autobiography,* The Peripatetic Papers: The Travel Diaries of a Commuting Professor.

Still Changing Academe after All These Years

Florence Howe

In the mid-1980s, the Feminist Press began to prepare a series of original memoirs of women who had come to consciousness before and/or in the midst of the women's movement of the 1960s and 1970s. The series, we thought, responded to the need for a feminist history of those decades. Because we understood that movements change the consciousness of people who then cross cultural divides to become agents of change themselves, we called the series the Cross Cultural Memoir Series. Its first volumes, in the early 1990s, were by Arlene Avakian, Toni McNaron, and Meena Alexander. By 1993, several other authors were under contract or in discussion with me, including Jean Walton, the "mother" of women's studies for the Claremont Colleges in California.

Over Thanksgiving weekend in 1993, Jean Walton invited me to lunch to tell me some bad news. A heart attack had slowed her down, and she felt certain that she couldn't write the memoir for the series. "But who, then, will ever write the story of how women's studies came to the Claremont Colleges?" I asked.

Jean said she thought she could write an essay-length account of how, at age sixty-five, she began a cross-country trip in the early 1970s to see what information she could gather about women's studies. And then, I thought, one essay does not a volume make. I needed a lot of essays. I wrote to twenty-five people in my personal address book who had begun women's studies on their campuses, asking them to name others and asking also for key questions that the writers of these essays ought to be considering. As these suggestions came in—usually with enthusiasm about writing one of these essays—I wrote again, asking these new candidates for other suggestions. At one point I had nearly one hundred people on the list, most of whom said they were interested in writing, and the questions filled two pages.

Those who actually did write essays for the volume that came to be *The Politics of Women's Studies* represent a segment of the national community, and there is more room for others to be heard. We have called this volume the first in the Women's Studies History Series, for which I will remain general editor, along with Mariam

Chamberlain. Perhaps others will join us as we consider subsequent volumes. Remember, there are over six hundred women's studies programs, and each has a founder with a story to tell.

What has this volume taught us? I see three aspects that cross through all the differences in institutional settings and conditions, even in age, race, and status of pioneer "mothers." First, in account after account, we read about the power of women organized into collective action by the urgency of their new vision. Each of us, in our own territory, under varying conditions, saw the connections between gender and power. We were unafraid to be called "political." Indeed, we knew that all education was political: The omission of women from the curriculum for hundreds of years had been a political decision based on patriarchy, but it relied on faulty intellectual information, not only biological and psychological but historical and aesthetic. Intellectual insights drove this movement from the first and continue to drive it still.

Further, the resistances, mainly of men, to these same ideas have continuously fueled the movement over these thirty years—and fuel it still. If you have any doubts about this, listen to Annette Kolodny reminding us of a new battleground that we are losing, the virtual university:

> For the time being, women's studies programs are safe. They have firm funding lines on brick and mortar campuses, and while they have helped to change the curriculum on those brick and mortar campuses, they have failed to change the decision-making structures and the larger culture. Where women's studies is not safe is in the new online virtual universities offering degree credit. With rare exceptions, all of the faculty members engaged in developing the online universities are men. The emphasis is on vocational and practical courses or, if they want to develop high profile, high prestige humanities, teachers are reproducing the great white male curriculum. None of the online universities have women's studies courses now, and none are seeking to integrate research on women done by women's studies scholars over the last thirty years. The only exception is a course on Greek mythology taught by Mary Lefkowitz for the Global Education Network. There are some fifteen online virtual universities in the United States, some collaborating with British universities. My concern is that this education is being exported around the world, which means that women are not going to get the advantage of the past thirty years of women's studies scholarship and teaching. (Kolodny)

But of course this is not the only place to look for women's studies battlegrounds. You can find them also in the continuing debates about heredity and environment, in revisionist and antirevisionist histories, in reconstructed and new traditional literary anthologies, and elsewhere. Even in some fields, where we seem to have won significant battles, I see very real dangers.

Let me provide one specific example. In the Feminist Press office, one of our brightest staff members is also a graduate student in the women's studies program. She complained one day to me about the size of her Virginia Woolf reading assignment in nonfiction. "How lucky you are," I said, "to be reading her at all. At your age, I had never heard her spoken of as a 'feminist,' nor had I heard of *A Room of One's Own,* much less *Three Guineas,* though I had seen *To the Lighthouse* on a recommended, not required reading list." "Wasn't she popular then?" this bright, young woman asked. Surprised, I told her what bookstores were like in 1970 and handed her a short history of the Feminist Press I had written in 1985 for our fifteenth anniversary.

Here, then, is my concern and my second point. Yes, we changed academe, but very unevenly, and with different difficulties for those teaching and learning today. While we built women's studies programs and feminist scholarship on the shock of recognizing sexism and patriarchy, and on the conviction that we could change at least the curriculum, if not the world, young students today living and learning in the world we helped to construct cannot replicate our experience. Some of them will take for granted the presence of women's studies literature courses entirely filled with women writers. They will assume that the curriculum has always allowed women's studies. They may be jolted a bit if they wander from that program into a course in philosophy, for example, or eighteenth-century literature, or even modern literature that contains not a single woman writer. But what will they do about it? And what about the students who still go through four years of college never touched by a single women's studies course or section of a course? In short, students—and some younger faculty as well—may have two different kinds of experiences today: A majority may still be where we were thirty years ago, unknowingly in a male-centered curriculum; a minority may think that women have always been part of the curriculum.

But didn't we want this to happen? Didn't we want our daughters and granddaughters, our sons and grandsons, to enjoy a curriculum in which women are present? Yes, of course. But we wanted them to value this curriculum sufficiently to continue to fight for this presence should it begin to disappear, and to add to its influence through research and teaching. For this to happen, those of us teaching must tell our students of the years of struggle for this curriculum and scholarship and help them to see the backlash that represents continued resistance to our gains. How do we do this?

And here is my third and final point. Since teaching today is entirely different from what it was in the 1970s or even the early 1980s when both we and our students could see ourselves part of and mirrored in a women's movement that was increasingly worldwide, we need another strategy. For me and for the writers in this volume, the strategy has to be history. The writers in *The Politics of Women's Studies* often wrote—through all the trials of editing their essays—about how much they cared about being part of this volume, about recording this history. In several cases, they wrote that there were no records of the history they were writing down—for various reasons, records, notes, leaflets, and diaries had all been tossed out or lost. Their accounts in the volume, therefore, chart the histories of those particular times and places. Others wrote from voluminous records that, while accessible, had not been consulted before. All who wrote were urgent about being part of a volume that would capture the achievements of their groups on their campuses, and that might give not only heart but also strategy and direction to others still engaged in similar struggles on other campuses.

Unlike women's movements of the past, we have institutionalized ourselves not only in the writing of women's history but more particularly in the teaching of women's history. We are the first generation of women's movements to do so. Remember, for example, that after women gained the right to vote in 1920, most women's groups and women's units inside of national and local organizations dissolved, assuming the struggle was over. Through the 1930s and into the middle of the 1940s Mary Ritter Beard wrote about the importance of women's history but was anyone listening? Students should read her, and they should read the histories of the recent women's movements coming out, not only *The Politics of Women's Studies*, but older volumes: *Academic Women on the Move* (Rossi and Calderwood 1973); *Women in Academe* (Chamberlain 1985); and my own *Myths of Coeducation* (Howe 1984), now out of print. More recent titles include Marilyn Boxer's groundbreaking history of the women's studies movement, *When Women Ask the Questions* (1998); Jane Gould's memoir *Juggling* (1997); and Robin Morgan's *Saturday's Child* (2001). I am cheered by the prospect of more memoirs from women's studies pioneers and perhaps more anthologies.

As we celebrate thirty years, let us consider how to strengthen and build the movement that once called itself the "academic arm of the women's movement" and that was never embarrassed to be called "political." We owe it to our students who are now not only those in our classrooms but, potentially, those in front of computers around the world.

WORKS CITED

Boxer, Marilyn J. *When Women Ask the Questions: Creating Women's Studies in America.* Baltimore: Johns Hopkins UP, 1998.

Chamberlain, Mariam, ed. *Women in Academe.* New York: Russell Sage, 1988.

Gould, Jane S. *Juggling: A Memoir of Work, Family, and Feminism.* New York: Feminist, 1997.

Howe, Florence. *Myths of Coeducation: Selected Essays, 1964–1983.* Bloomington: Indiana UP, 1984.

Howe, Florence, ed. *The Politics of Women's Studies: Testimony from Thirty Founding Mothers.* New York: Feminist, 2000.

Kolodny, Annette. Telephone interview. 27 November 2000.

Morgan, Robin. *Saturday's Child: A Memoir.* New York: Norton, 2001.

Rossi, Alice S., and Ann Calderwood, eds. *Academic Women on the Move.* New York: Russell Sage, 1973.

Woolf, Virginia. *A Room of One's Own.* New York: Harcourt, 1981.

———. *Three Guineas.* New York: Harcourt, 1938.

———. *To the Lighthouse.* New York: Harcourt, 1981.

Florence Howe is emerita publisher of the Feminist Press and emerita professor of English at the City University of New York. She co-directs and is text editor of Women Writing Africa, *a project of the Feminist Press.*

Legacy

Inez Martinez

When I first composed this piece, which I delivered as a talk at the conference "Then and Now: The Politics of Women's Studies," held at the City University of New York's Graduate Center in December 2000, the World Trade Center still stood and the Pentagon seemed unassailable. While xenophobia since the dissolution of the Soviet Empire had caused convulsions ranging from hate-killings of individuals to massacres to genocides in countries around the world, the horror of differences erupting into war had not yet touched American soil. As I convert my talk into this article, mayhem grips Israel and Palestine, drawing humanity into divisions whose only unifying characteristic threatens to be the ability to die. Now that Americans have joined the suffering of those subject to the attacks of enemies in their homeland, learning how to deal with difference so as to live in peace with one another, to enrich human culture, and to proliferate the realization of individual human talents has finally become a worldwide imperative.

The Heritage of Women's Studies

Part of the heritage of women's studies has been our struggle with the challenges posed by differences. As we examined our heritage during the conference on the politics of women's studies, we saw that in other areas we have been successful beyond our first imaginings. Various speakers made clear that women's studies has had unforeseen success in knowledge production, knowledge conveyance, institutionalization, and faculty hirings. The book *The Politics of Women's Studies* establishes that, from the beginning, the heritage of women's studies was rooted in a desire to transform society and promote social justice for all (Howe). This purpose was illustrated by the academic histories of the speakers with whom I shared a panel at the "Then and Now" conference, Annis Pratt, Elizabeth Kennedy, and Margaret Strobel. We all in our respective institutional settings in the late 1960s and early 1970s worked to address issues of concern to women of color.

At Kingsborough, for example, one of six community colleges in the City University of New York (CUNY), hundreds of women of color took advantage of the new policy of open admissions to register for a curriculum in nursing. As I narrate in *The Politics of Women's Studies*, faculty resistant to helping those who had suffered years of educational deprivation obtain the skills necessary for college work ushered them out of a "revolving door." In fall 1971, three feminist faculty advised the students to organize to obtain the academic help they needed. Three hundred of them did and before the dust had settled, greater coherence between class and laboratory work in their biology courses had been established, the prerequisite nursing course they needed was offered twice instead of once a year, and a special course in biology was created specifically for them. For me, this incident represents the *sine qua non* of women's studies. Yes, we must create curricula that include questions concerning gender, race, ethnicity, sexual orientation, and class, but curricula make no difference to women excluded from higher education by arbitrary institutional policies and practices. Helping the nursing students obtain the changes in policy so they could receive the education enabling them to become financially independent was testimony to what has been perhaps the best part of the heritage of women's studies. From the beginning, however imperfectly conceived, however imperfectly understood, the goal of social justice for all has informed our vision.

This goal clearly has not been realized—nor is it to be expected that it would have been. So lofty a vision is not likely to be fulfilled in any one generation. One change that has struck me over the last three years has been that the minority of students who still see transforming society as a goal focus on the inclusive goal of social justice and have less interest in gender justice—at least at the beginning. After students have studied the situations of women, I find they often grant gender issues a higher place in their vision of social justice. Yet, since 11 September 2001, now that the United States has been successfully attacked, concern for social justice has ironically fallen even further from social consciousness as nostalgic longing for a sense of invulnerability grips Americans. I believe that no greater source of security could be conjured or imposed than the extension to all humans on this earth of the rights and privileges we Americans claim for ourselves, including access to education. Women's studies faculty and students, because of our heritage, are advantageously positioned to communicate this vision to our nation.

Allying with Other Fields Seeking Social Justice

We of course are not alone. Other area studies, such as black studies, which Sheila Tobias reminds us preceded and stood as a model for us, also strive to communicate the need for and ways to pursue social justice for all.[1] The proliferation of area studies in terms of various identities challenges women's studies to establish working connections with them as part of our commitment to working creatively with difference. On the practical level, I would like to suggest that, at least for community colleges, the creation of interdisciplinary departments is a possible way for these connections to occur and become institutionally powerful. Since community colleges typically offer specializations only in career areas, it is almost impossible for women's studies to become departments in them. The same can be said for other interdisciplinary studies dedicated to progressive social change. Women's studies and they could gain institutional strength by joining together and forming a Department of Interdisciplinary Studies. Not only would these programs then be in a position to participate in decisions concerning hires, tenure, and promotion; they could also model concretely how to find common ground so as to work out policies among people with differing priorities.

The Dynamic of Centripetal and Centrifugal Forces

On the theoretical level, I would like to suggest that this proliferation and the need for connections is but one manifestation of what I consider a defining dynamic through which we are living: We live in a maelstrom of centripetal and centrifugal forces. We have become familiar with some centripetal forces that relentlessly intertwine our fates. We have discovered, for example, that environmentally we cannot keep ourselves safe while endangering others. The pesticides America exports to Latin America, for example, return to us in our fruits and vegetables. Nor can we keep dangerous diseases trapped within national, even continental boundaries; killer viruses released by roads created by international developers in continents oceans away arrive on our shores and threaten our lives. Culturally, America has penetrated most of the planet, exporting images of western luxury to people all over the world, including the half living in utter poverty. Most recently, we have discovered that our international policies, made effective because of our wealth and power, can no longer be pursued without ill consequence to us. They have instigated some people to seek to destroy us, making us as vulnerable to violence on our land as the people in the twenty countries we have bombed since World War II.[2]

Centripetal forces are *erasing the defining power of our differences.* These erasures have different valences. The loss of the sense of invulnerability was stupefying and, whether one's politics are left or right, requires a re-evaluation of America's policies and place in the world. The return of the toxins to those exporting them seems a just come-uppance. The threat of the diminishment of spiritual depth in cultures being infiltrated by materialistic consumerism marks the loss of some-thing precious. In other words, the loss of defining differences is not inherently good or bad. In the case of women's studies, I fear the loss would render our field irrelevant.

Simultaneously centrifugal forces drive us farther and farther from one another, as in the ever widening gap between the rich and poor, the educated and the uneducated, the technologically endowed and the technologically deprived. Witness the refuge oppressed peoples take in group identities that separate them into antagonistic rela-tionships with all who are not of their group—group identifications that have led to vicious and lethal civil wars and to acts of interna-tional terrorism including the terrorist attacks on the Pentagon and the World Trade Center. As we watched, again and again, the tapes of the towers being struck, burning, collapsing, taking with them all the defenseless people inside, we suddenly understood ourselves both as more coherent as a people and as "other" to determined enemies. American nationalism immediately surged, and President George W. Bush divided the world into those with us and those against us. As many countries allied themselves with America and many Islamic peo-ple aligned themselves with the "holy warriors of the jihad against America," the centripetal forces strengthened and the centrifugal ones deepened.

Centripetal and Centrifugal Forces in Women's Studies

How do these opposing sets of forces relate to women's studies? The centripetal forces manifest in what Annis Pratt in her talk called the process of assimilation of women's studies into patriarchal university structures. This assimilation threatens our defining difference—our commitment to the intellectual honesty of being overtly political—in our best political form, of overtly trying to create, convey, and use knowledge in order to obtain equal access to justice and opportunity for all people. The centrifugal forces can be seen in the proliferation of the claims of difference on the basis of race, ethnicity, class, sexual-ity, nation, culture, subculture, religion, age, abledness, and the multi-ple ideological positions within each of these groupings. These threaten to separate us into interest groups unable to make common cause.

Women's studies, then, currently is a microcosm of a dynamic with which the world is trying to cope. To the degree that we negotiate it well—to the degree that we do not give up our defining difference of using knowledge to seek social justice, to the degree that we find ways to establish connections among identity groups claiming defining differences—we will be achieving on a local scale what needs to be accomplished on a global one. I believe that such efforts are what people in our everyday contexts can offer to the psychological work that needs to be done.

The Challenge of Difference

I do not surprise anyone by saying that many human beings continue to deal with difference badly. We kill one another for religious, ethnic, sexual, economic, and gender reasons, to name just a few; we chop off each other's hands and feet or private parts; we claim to be entitled to each other's labor, each other's obedience; we establish systems of domination for some and deprivation for others, call these systems natural, and create religious and governmental laws to enforce them. Differences in religion, political power, wealth, rights, and opportunities threaten humanity with worldwide war.

Reclaiming the Concept of Humanity

To begin to nudge this human history in the direction we want, we must, I believe, commit to a premise of the interconnectedness of separate beings—human to human, human to other creatures, human to the planet. Oppressing others, including making war against them, depends upon dehumanizing, frequently demonizing, them. I implore us to resuscitate the idea of humanity and to take control of the definition of the humanities. As is common knowledge, these terms came under attack because upon examination, humanity was usually equated with western white males primarily of the middle and upper classes, and the humanities usually consisted of answers to questions based upon their experiences and values. Attacking these terms we unintentionally drove underground vital concepts and values in working for socially just societies. It is on the ground of common humanity that I at all understand the suffering and unfair treatment of another, that I can claim equal access with another to life's possibilities, given our respective individual limitations. It is on the ground that we are all equally of the stuff of the universe and equally dependent on this earth that I can claim that we share basic rights. It is with the belief that people different from myself and/or from different cultures are as human as I that I can think that justice is served by my glimpsing the world as it appears through their eyes and their glimpsing it as it appears through mine, that I can commit to the fruition of their creative possibilities and those of their cultures for the enrichment of us all.

But we must distinguish between differences—and the unrealized goal with which we started, social justice for all, can be our guide. We need to monitor and resist those forces in cultures such as fundamentalism, in economies such as market control of social policies, and in persons such as greed, that work to create systems of domination and deprivation. The claims of cultures, for example, that their religions or customs justify subordinating some for the benefit of others cannot be justified on grounds of respecting differences; nor can metaphysical appeals to market forces as inevitable sources of the ever-expanding gap between rich and poor; nor can naked desire for personal gratification, privilege, and power. The differences that we must learn to harvest are those that promote the most complete realization of the full variety of individuals striving to be responsible to themselves and to their communities in the richest and most varied expressions of human cultures striving to be just.

Reclaiming the Humanities

In addition to rescuing the concept of humanity, we must continue to take control of the definition of the humanities. It is in studying the humanities that we encounter the ways people have imagined, formulated, and lived out their lives, that we can connect our own endeavors for good lives and a good society to theirs.

Frankly, on the community college level, it is primarily through the study of liberal arts that students have any opportunity to learn to ask questions that enable them to analyze and evaluate the ways that power is structured and operates in societies, and the kinds of lives that are consequently possible in various organizations of power. At Kingsborough, students taking women's studies courses do so under the aegis of liberal arts study. Students receiving the A.A. degree are able to obtain a certificate in women's studies. In their women's studies courses they can address social justice issues including racism and class and global economic inequities. In the interdisciplinary social sciences course required for a certificate in women's studies, for example, students, through texts such as Virginia Sapiro's *An Introduction to Women's Studies*, do comparative studies of how various constructions of gender influence the conditions of women throughout the world. Since Kingsborough's student body comes from many nations, students from Asia, Africa, the Middle East, Europe, the Caribbean, and Latin

America bring firsthand testimony about the ways gender and race have been used culturally, politically, and economically in their homelands. In addition, through reading works of authors such as Cynthia Enloe, students learn how their lifestyles—clothes, travel, gender conformities of various sorts—can help support (or not) policies of international capitalism and various governments inimical to women.

The conservative agenda that has been reshaping CUNY during the tenure of New York's Mayor Rudolph Guiliani threatens to make liberal arts study at the community college level an endangered species. It envisions community colleges as resources for the business community and as providers of occupational certifications. The drive to convert CUNY's community colleges into factories producing workers for the economy is part of a conservative national effort. John E. Roueche, director of the Ph.D. Program in Community College Leadership at Texas University, the best-funded and arguably most influential such program in the country, states this goal succinctly: "We contend that in the future there will be little difference, if any, between an educated person and a person educated to make significant contributions to the workforce" (Roueche and Roueche 10).

Career programs depend on preparing their students to serve the status quo and can only at great risk to themselves encourage socially critical thinking. Liberal arts courses, on the contrary, are charged with teaching students to question, to learn to gather and evaluate evidence, to clarify their criteria, and to make judgments. It is not an exaggeration to claim that the survival of women's studies at community colleges, not to mention the survival of meaningful education as opposed to training, depends on the preservation of liberal arts study.

An Effort to Harvest Differences

I think it is by now apparent that I see not only a future for women's studies, but a significant one, for we are in a position to attempt on a local scale the kind of negotiation of differences that peoples of the world face on an international scale. Before I close, let me offer one example of the prosaic kind of effort I mean.

The National Women's Studies Association (NWSA) has a scarred history of trying to create a professional academic organization that transforms the racist relationships marring American society. In spite of many well-intentioned efforts, moments of horrible failure mark its record, including conflicts over racism at the 1990 national conference held in Akron, Ohio, during which many women's studies faculty, women of color and white women, gave up on the organization and left in protest. But women of color and white women also remained and worked not only to save the organization but to address problems of racism through NWSA's actual structures and practices. When the women's studies administrators, for example, in 1998, decided to form themselves into a permanent part of NWSA's structure, they sought representation from the Women of Color Caucus. This collaboration worked so well that it was institutionalized in the Program Administration and Development Committee (PAD) policies, which require that a representative of the Women of Color Caucus always be a member of the Advisory Council, the group responsible for executing the policies decided upon by the PAD membership.

An early result of this representation was the development of a Women of Color Leadership Program sponsored by PAD and approved by the NWSA Governing Council. Realizing that special care had to be taken to include the perspectives of women of color, given the few women of color administering women's studies programs and departments, PAD made seeking women of color to become women's studies administrators a priority. They invited all current women's studies administrators to invite women of color colleagues interested in becoming chairs and directors of women's studies departments and programs to the national conference and to the administrators' preconference. NWSA subsidized their conference fees, a year's membership in NWSA, and a year's subscription to the *NWSA Journal.* This initiative addresses both structural and interpersonal racism. The guests attending were subsequently asked for their responses and suggestions, thus creating a venue allowing for further exchanges concerning racism, encounters necessary for transforming racist relations. NWSA has voted to continue this program. It is too early to gauge any increase in the proportion of women's studies administrators who are women of color, but the women involved in this project are examples of feminists trying neither to negate nor to reify difference but rather to transform debilitating relations into liberatory ones ("Women of Color Leadership Project" 9).

The Work of Harvesting Differences

We in women's studies are in a position to counter centrifugal forces turning differences into power relations. We can do so by consciously engaging our differences with the purpose of trying to realize the psychological and cultural wealth latent in them. To do so we will have to resist the centripetal forces erasing the differences that make us what we are. We will have to continue to pursue within the academy our political vision of a world in which differences can coexist without oppression, can in fact cross-pollinate self-realization and cultural flowering. We thereby not only can preserve the integrity of our academic enterprise but can contribute to humanity's efforts to harvest rather than exploit or crush difference. This work is not and will not be easy. We will have to endure conflict and live with tension. We will have always to develop self-knowledge. We will have to re-imagine our personal and social relationships. We will have to seek, articulate, and use knowledge to create more just societies. We will have to persevere. Doing that work is a lifelong challenge and a legacy I, for one, am proud to pass on to the next generation.

NOTES

1. In her address during the conference "Then and Now: The Politics of Women's Studies," held at the Graduate Center of the City University of New York in December 2000, Sheila Tobias reminded her audience that women's studies was the beneficiary of the pioneering efforts of black studies programs, which African American scholars had integrated into colleges and universities throughout the United States.

2. The privilege held as most precious is that of believing a privilege is a right exclusive to one's group, such as the American sense of invulnerability to experiencing war on our land. That belief rests on our being willing for others to experience war on theirs. The Indian author Arundhati Roy in October 2001 listed all the countries America has bombed since the end of World War II. They include China (1945–46), Korea (1950–53), Guatemala (1954 and 1967–69), Indonesia (1958), Cuba (1959–60), the Belgian Congo (1964), Peru (1965), Laos (1964–73), Vietnam (1961–73), Cambodia (1969–70), Grenada (1983), Libya (1986), El Salvador (1980s), Nicaragua (1980s), Panama (1989), Iraq (1991–99), Bosnia (1995), Sudan (1998), Yugoslavia (1999), and now Afghanistan (2002) (Roy).

WORKS CITED

Howe, Florence, ed. *The Politics of Women's Studies: Testimony from Thirty Founding Mothers.* New York: Feminist, 2000.

Roueche, John E., and Susanne D. Roueche. "Facing the New Millenium: Making Friends with the Future." *Community College Journal* (April–May 2000): 16–21.

Roy, Arundhati. "Brutality Smeared in Peanut Butter: Why American Must Stop the War Now." *Guardian Unlimited* 23 October 2001.

Sapiro, Virginia. *Women in American Society: An Introduction to Women's Studies.* Mountain View, CA: Mayfield, 1994.

"Women of Color Leadership Project." *NWSAction 13* (spring 2002): 9.

Inez Martinez is codirector of women's studies at Kingsborough Community College in Brooklyn, New York. She is completing a book on psychological literary criticism, "Reading for Psyche."

Women's Studies as Women's History

Marilyn J. Boxer

Thirty years after it was institutionalized in the U.S. academy, women's history now has a secure place in American higher education. The history of women's studies, however, remains mostly lost amid the politics that deny it legitimacy, both within and outside academic feminism. Philosopher Jane Roland Martin in her recent memoir declared, "Had women in the 1970s been aware of the gendered underpinnings of the academy, let alone known how powerful and persistent our education-gender system is, the women's studies movement might never have been launched" (109). How was it possible? What mixture of hope, energy, courage, and perhaps naïveté can explain the success of the scattered and motley contingent of feminist activists, students, faculty, staff, and community supporters who launched and sustained the women's studies movement through its founding years? What conjuncture of developments in the history of higher education in the United States can account for its initial acceptance and rapid growth across the country in institutions of all kinds, defying predictions that it was "just a fad"? Where does women's studies fit into the larger story of American women's history? Does this tale offer any insight into possible futures for women's studies as an academic field? What can we learn from the history of women's studies? Is Martin right?

I think not, for the generation of women who founded women's studies acted out of intellectual and emotional needs too powerful to repress, whatever the nature of the institutional "beast" we faced. (An early women's studies publication at San Diego State University bore the imprint "Inside the Beast.") Women's studies developed at a particular period in the history of the United States, of American higher education, of feminism, and in the lives of women brought up to believe in the reality of the opportunities we were promised. To contextualize the beginnings of the academic feminist movement, it is useful to follow the scheme laid out by Florence Howe, Barbara Miller Solomon, and others, according to which women's studies can be viewed as a third phase in American women's struggle for equal access to higher education (Howe, *Myths of Coeducation;* Solomon). In the pre–Civil War era, women such as Lucy Stone demanded and sometimes won admission to institutions of higher learning, but generally they had to settle for special programs of study deemed suitable for their sex. In a second phase, in the later decades of the nineteenth century, women such as M. Carey Thomas called for admission to the "men's curriculum," both in new colleges for women that aimed to equal the private Ivy League institutions that educated men of the elite, and in state-supported, land-grant universities that promised "coeducation." Thomas wanted to set to rest allegations regarding the inferiority of the female mind by requiring of women a curriculum as rigorous and challenging as any offered at the men's colleges. Beginning in the mid-1960s, enterprising women with feminist consciousness launched a third phase. Declaring coeducation a myth, they challenged the content of higher education as well as academic structures and procedures that taught a hidden curriculum of women's second-class status. In this view, courses that ignored women's experiences and perspectives subtly reinforced old ideas about female intellectual deficiencies while also perpetuating women's social, economic, and political marginality.

This third phase originated in broad historical developments including the postwar expansion of higher education through the G.I. bill; the proliferation of institutions needed to serve the children of the G.I. generation (the "baby-boomers"); governmental assumption of a central role in expanding access to higher education through funding bricks and mortar, awarding research grants to faculty, providing financial aid to students; and so forth. Across the country, as statewide systems were established to accommodate new constituencies, teachers' colleges were transformed into state universities and student populations mushroomed. Unlike the governments of other countries (such as France, for example) where national ministries of education set educational policies, establish professorial chairs, and sometimes determine curricular decisions, for the most part legislative bodies in the United States exerted minimal influence on the content of university curricula—a fact of major salience in the expansion of women's studies. Spared powerful external forces governing academic content, many local faculties and administrators readily agreed, frequently under pressure from activist students, to add the new coursework on women.

Sociopolitical currents of the 1960s—the civil rights, antiwar, free speech, and student power movements, and the New Left—constituted an equally powerful influence on the history of women's studies. As revolts against tradition and authority, they laid the basis for wholesale rejection of standard academic requirements such as western civilization courses, and for a concomitant demand by students for coursework they deemed "relevant" to their lives. For feminists this meant seeking a useable heritage and a useful ideology. The first new courses on women in history, literature, and society, taught in cities around the country in community settings as well as colleges and universities, fulfilled these needs. The first new "programs" augured a future in which women would seek a permanent place in the curriculum and in virtually all aspects of university life. Concurrent increases in the proportion of female students at all levels, and of women faculty and administrators, facilitated by affirmative action, all encouraged support for women's studies programs (Chamberlain; Pearson et al.).

The early history of women's studies reveals rapid expansion from one integrated program in 1970 to 150 in 1975, 300 in 1980, 450 in 1985, and 600 in 1990. (A recent list of programs, departments, and research centers that maintain Web sites extends the number to more than 650.) This growth attests to the passion and intellectual energy brought by feminists to the academy (Boxer, "For and About Women"; "Women's Studies: A World View"). It is worth emphasizing how critical a role students played in this history. They demanded classes at a time when student voices carried major influence in university forums, and they enrolled in massive numbers in the new courses, especially in enrollment-budgeted state institutions such as the California State University system where many "firsts" in feminist education took place.[1] As graduate students they also initiated and taught many of the early courses, for minimal cost to dollar-strapped institutions. To university administrators struggling to meet both activist student challenges and legislative demands for "productivity" measured in enrollment numbers, women's studies offered a bargain.[2] It also served at times as a proxy for affirmative action. By adding women's studies to the curriculum, universities might meet the spirit if not the letter of government mandates, as well as some academicians' desires to include women more fully in institutional life.

The role played by women's studies in the economics of higher education became clear in the 1980s. During the Ronald Reagan era, students flocked toward business and professionally or vocationally oriented programs. Attracted by career opportunities newly opened to women, often thanks to successful feminist-inspired lawsuits, female students comprised a large component of the increased enrollment in both undergraduate and graduate degree programs in accounting, finance, marketing, and related fields. A president of the American Academy of Collegiate Schools of Business (AACSB) once remarked in my presence that the explosive growth in his field in the 1980s could be attributed to women students; male enrollment had remained steady while female numbers soared. The new careers, of course, paid much more than the traditional "women's" professions of teaching, nursing, and social work.

As students deserted fields of study long favored by women such as history and literature for newer pastures, and universities eliminated graduation requirements that formerly sustained enrollments in the social sciences and humanities, the pressure of reduced demand in those fields helped boost support for women's studies. Students who declined to take History 101 or Literature 101 often signed up for Women's Studies 101 or disciplinary courses focused on women. In addition, in the curriculum revisions that many universities undertook to adjust to new campus and student priorities, women's studies faculty began to win approval for their courses in the new and generally less prescriptive general education programs that faculties adopted. Undergraduate minors and majors, masters' degrees, and Ph.D. concentrations gradually enriched traditional curricula. As more women faculty, including many interested in women's studies, attained tenured positions, they could exert greater influence in academic affairs. Women's studies was well placed by the 1990s both to survive the adverse environment that came with pervasive fiscal retrenchment and to respond to an increasing emphasis, sometimes economically motivated, on crossing disciplinary borders within universities and between universities and local communities. Newly established endowments provided program support and professorial chairs at the University of Cincinnati, Indiana University, Stanford University, the University of South Carolina, and the University of Southern California, among others. The label "department" attached to women's studies began to appear across the educational landscape, increasing rapidly in recent years from about twenty in 1997 to thirty-six or more by 2001.[3]

How can we account for the success of the women's studies movement, in personal as well as institutional terms? From my perspective, generational analysis offers a useful interpretive framework. The founders of women's studies belonged to the post-1950s generation of mothers and daughters. The older contingent had experienced, albeit as children or youth, a war fought for the "American way"; then they struggled against the hypocrisies and fallacies of the culture of "togetherness" that, in the 1950s and early 1960s, sought to limit their roles outside the family. Wives of "men in gray flannel suits" and "organization men," some of us were also daughters of Philip Wylie's smothering "moms," targets of Freudian-imbued misogyny, cruelly caricatured in popular postwar novels, diagnosed as sick, neurotic, destructive. Thanks to the new historians of women, we came to understand the 1950s as the worst decade in American history for women who aspired to personal achievement outside familial roles.[4]

The daughters of these 1950s mothers grew up along with the new ideas of the mid- and late 1960s. Like the "ideas of the 1860s" that sparked the rebellion of privileged young people in Russia a century earlier, new currents of thought about the social condition of other oppressed groups—serfs in 1850–1860s' Russia, Blacks in the 1950s–1960s' United States—elicited awareness among many women of the need for political action to liberate themselves from constricted societal roles.[5] Some of us resisted our parents, even (or especially) our mothers, as agents of repression, and set out to work actively with men in liberation movements, until we began to see the latter—at least some of them—as also the source of our problems. We needed feminist awareness to see ourselves as primary agents and to recognize that women matter. We began to ask new questions about our foremothers and ourselves. We wanted to study about women.

It is useful to recall just how audacious it was circa 1970 to proclaim that women should be the central focus of a college course. Is there enough material for a whole course, we were asked. Perhaps the most remarkable aspect of the curriculum initiated at San Diego State College (now University) in the fall term 1970 and publicized in *Female Studies I* was that it included *ten* whole courses, plus supervised field experience in the women's community (Tobias).

That was then. Now we have that many free-standing, multidisciplinary Ph.D. programs in women's studies, a development scarcely imaginable thirty years ago ("Established and Proposed Women's Studies Ph.D. Programs"). It is a history not likely to be repeated, for the context has utterly changed. Today a rapidly growing frontier for women's studies lies abroad where women's studies also serves to produce women leaders and to spur development of gender equity more generally (Howe, "Women's Education"). Instructional programs and research centers abound around the world and their numbers are growing ("Women's Studies: A World View"). According to a 1993 "international handbook" of women's studies, more than one hundred countries house educational programs, research centers, or training institutes focused on women, including many founded in the 1990s following the collapse of the Soviet Union (Brown et al.). A 1997 "international list-in-progress" encompasses more than five hundred such centers ("Centers for Research and Teaching on Women"). Feminist scholars, many thousands of whom have produced dissertations focused on women, now debate such issues as the relative merits of departmentalization, integration into gender studies, infusion into general education programs, and free-standing doctoral degrees. Some praise while others deplore shifting terminology in program and department rubrics (Boxer, "Remapping the University"). Definitions of women's experiences continue to expand as scholars with "transnational" feminist perspectives undertake new research, create new courses, and produce new instructional materials, enriching women's studies and drawing in ever more diverse students and faculty (Grewal and Kaplan).

Some things never change: Witness recent, lengthy discussions in meetings and online about student resistance to feminism and faculty vulnerability to burnout.[6] Some scholars of note continue to ignore women's studies altogether or to deplore feminist scholarship, often without ever bothering to read any of it.[7] The content of women's studies scholarship remains marginal to some disciplines where it has much to offer. In some places, instruction and administration in women's studies still depend on volunteer labor, and faculty contributions of time and talent go unrecognized and unrewarded.

But the cup is, I think, more than half full. Women's studies grew out of the needs and experiences of women and reflected the spirit of a certain time in history. Times have changed but the justification for feminist scholarship remains as valid now as then. Asserting newly developed "intellectual confidence," feminist scholars still find in abundance unanswered, important questions to research. Many errors remain to be corrected; many lacunae to be filled; new thinking to be encouraged. Each generation finds new questions to ask and pressing issues to pursue. Today, economic globalization profoundly affects the content of research and teaching, conferences and publications in all areas of women's studies. Social consciousness and behavior will be altered on the basis of the new knowledge thus produced. If some students still come to class resisting feminist awareness, they do come. Others enter with new knowledge, for insights inspired by women's studies have spread into mainstream vocabularies. A girl today may learn at two, three, or four to name parts of her body that went unrecognized by some us of until, at twenty, thirty, or forty, we read of them in *Our Bodies, Ourselves*.[8] In the aggregate, institutional support for women's studies is strong in the United States and elsewhere, and it continues to spread into new fields. For example, the Ford Foundation, long a mainstay of academic feminism, recently provided a six-figure grant to a group of Chinese scholars for the purpose of developing women's studies curricula, training faculty, and translating women's studies materials, largely from English, into their language.[9]

One task today is to pursue cultural authority commensurate with our expertise on topics related to women and human relationships (Boxer, *When Women Ask the Questions* 242–45). Women's studies has fared badly with the media. Like feminists in society, proponents of women's studies in academia have yet to convince our opponents that we represent more than a special interest, that our work is grounded in both ethical and intellectual imperatives. We have often, alas, failed even to engage the resistance in debate; we must seek dialogue with the opposition. Today we can claim as feminist few "public intellectuals." More of us might follow the example of Ruth Rosen, professor of American women's history, who for years has contributed to the press op-ed pieces that translate feminist scholarship into lively and accessible prose. Like Professor of English bell hooks, we might voice our views in strongly provocative, personal essays that elicit variously admiration, agreement, and opposition—but are heard by a large public. We should join her in "talking back" in forums and media outside the academy.[10]

Whatever the forces of resistance, another vital task is to assure the continuing survival of women's studies in U.S. higher education in the absence of a strong feminist movement. The way to do that, even while countering dominant intellectual trends, is to integrate as fully as possible into academic structures. The trend toward departmentalization is, in my view, a good thing, as are doctoral programs. The more institutionalization, the better. We must highlight the scholarly mission of women's studies. Excellence in research and teaching are the keys to maintaining and increasing the value of the feminist educational enterprise launched a generation ago. That teaching should include the various histories of women, of feminisms around the world, and of women's studies as an educational movement.

Today we have occasion to celebrate. Rather than lament our shortcomings, we must continue to work as long, as hard, and as smartly as we can. We must demonstrate that women's studies is not only an important chapter in women's history but also, thanks to the knowledge it creates, an essential part of women's future, inside the classroom and beyond, everywhere in the world. Just as women's rights constitute human rights, so women's studies forms an integral and transformative part of the history of humanity.

Notes

Earlier versions of this paper were presented at the Berkshire Conference in Women's History, University of Rochester, 4–7 June 1999, and at the conference on "Then and Now: The Politics of Women's Studies," at the Graduate Center of the City University of New York, 1 December 2000.

1. In addition to the first program at San Diego State and a program at Humboldt State that dates from 1972, pioneering programs in the California State University system soon appeared at San Francisco State (which incorporated racial diversity from the start), San Jose State (which developed one of the first women's studies master's degrees in the country), Sonoma State (where the celebration of a national women's history day was launched in a women's studies class), and Sacramento State (which in 1973 hosted the first national conference on women's studies). The founding meeting of the National Women's Studies Association in 1977 was sponsored by women's studies at San Jose State.

2. My success as department chair in building faculty lines from 2.4 to 8.1 at San Diego State between 1974 and 1980 reflects a male feminist dean's need to satisfy his superiors by increasing enrollment. Typically, during the first week of classes he would call and ask whether we could fill another class or two if given additional salary funds. We never failed to do so.

3. On endowments, information on the University of Southern California is from former director Lois Banner, personal communication, 29 April 1997; on Stanford, from former director Iris Litt, personal communication, 30 April 1997. On the University of Cincinnati, see Strumingher; on Indiana University, see Allen; on the University of South Carolina, see Rosser and Mille. In 1997 I counted twenty departments; by 2001, thirty-six; my count was based on authors' affiliations listed in journal articles and books as well as messages contributed by e-mail to WMST-L, a women's studies e-mail discussion list.

4. "Togetherness" was a slogan promoted by *McCall's* magazine to romanticize family life. Terms are borrowed from Sloan Wilson, *Man in the Gray Flannel Suit* (1956); William H. Whyte, *Organization Man* (1956); and Philip Wylie, *Generation of Vipers* (1955). Representative novels include Philip Roth, *Goodbye Columbus* (1959), and Herman Wouk, *Marjorie Morningstar* (1955), as well as anything by Norman Mailer. For depiction of Wollstonecraft and feminists as neurotic, see Lundberg and Farnham. Flexner's pathbreaking 1959 history, *Century of Struggle*, began the revisionist project in American women's history; it was reprinted six times between January 1968 and April 1971.

5. On Russia, see Turgenev and Engel and Rosenthal.

6. In an extended thread on "women's studies burnout" that appeared on WMST-L during October and November 2001, many correspondents repeated old laments, often attributing to current events attitudes that seem to be endemic in women's studies.

7. See, for example, the journal of the American Academy of Arts and Sciences, which purported to review "transformation" in the fields of economics, literary studies, philosophy, and political science for the period 1945 to 1995, with scarcely a mention of women's studies: *Daedalus* 106.1 (winter 1997).

8. Personal observation of my granddaughter, born 1996.
9. Personal communication from Wang Zheng, formerly of Stanford University's Institute for Research on Women and Gender, now at the University of Michigan, Ann Arbor, 2000. The grant is providing for translation into Chinese of my book *When Women Ask the Questions*, among many others.
10. A list of one hundred "public intellectuals" that appeared in the *New York Times* on 20 January 2002 included second-wave feminists Betty Friedan and Gloria Steinem, along with Camille Paglia and Christina Hoff Sommers, both authors of widely cited attacks on women's studies. Rosen recently left her professorship to become a full-time journalist with the *San Francisco Chronicle*. Her columns have been reprinted in the *Los Angeles Times* and elsewhere. For bell hooks's call for black women "to change the nature and direction of our speech, to make a speech that compels listeners, one that is heard," see hooks, especially 6–9.

WORKS CITED

Allen, Judith. "Fund Raising for Women's Studies." Paper presented at "The Next Twenty-Five Years," Women's Studies Program Administrators Conference, Arizona State University, February 1997.

Boxer, Marilyn J. "For and About Women: The Theory and Practice of Women's Studies in the United States." *Signs: Journal of Women in Culture and Society* 7.3 (1982): 661–95.

———. "Remapping the University: The Promise of the Women's Studies Ph.D." *Feminist Studies* 24.2 (1998): 387–402.

———. *When Women Ask the Questions: Creating Women's Studies in America.* Baltimore, MD: Johns Hopkins UP, 1998.

Brown, Loulou, Helen Collins, Pat Green, Maggie Humm, and Mel Landells, eds. *W.I.S.H.: The International Handbook of Women's Studies.* New York: Harvester Wheatsheaf, 1993.

"Centers for Research and Teaching on Women: An International List-in-Progress." *Women's Studies Quarterly* 25.3–4 (1997): 249–86.

Chamberlain, Mariam K., ed. *Women in Academe: Progress and Prospects.* New York: Russell Sage, 1988.

Engel, Barbara Alpern, and Clifford N. Rosenthal, eds. *Five Sisters: Women Against the Tsar.* 1977. New York: Schocken, 1987.

"Established and Proposed Women's Studies Ph.D. Programs in North America: A Current Listing." *Feminist Studies* 24.2 (1998): 326.

Flexner, Elanor. *Century of Struggle: The Woman's Rights Movement in the United States.* 1959. New York: Atheneum, 1971.

Grewal, Inderpal, and Caren Kaplan, eds. *Scattered Hegemonies: Postmodernity and Transnational Feminist Practices.* Minneapolis: U of Minnesota P, 1994.

hooks, bell. *Talking Back: Thinking Feminist, Thinking Black.* Boston: South End, 1989.

Howe, Florence. *Myths of Coeducation: Selected Essays, 1964–1983.* Bloomington: Indiana UP, 1987.

————. "Women's Education: Policy Implications for the New Century." *Women's Studies Quarterly* 27.3–4 (1999): 169–84.

Lundberg, Ferdinand, and Marynia F. Farnham, M.D. *Modern Women: The Lost Sex.* New York: Grosset and Dunlap, 1947.

Martin, Jane Roland. *Coming of Age in Academe: Rekindling Women's Hopes and Reforming the Academy.* New York: Routledge, 2000.

Pearson, Carol S., Donna L. Shavlik, and Judith G. Touchton, eds. *Educating the Majority: Women Challenge Tradition in Higher Education.* New York: AAC/Macmillan, 1989.

Rosser, Sue V., and Katherine W. Mille. "A Grass-roots Approach to Funding Women's Studies." *NWSAction* 1.4 (1988): 1–3.

Solomon, Barbara Miller. *In the Company of Educated Women: A History of Women and Higher Education in America.* New Haven: Yale UP, 1985.

Strumingher, Laura S. "The Birth and Growth of 'Friends of Women's Studies' at the University of Cincinnati." *Frontiers* 8.3 (1986): 83–86.

Tobias, Sheila, ed. *Female Studies I.* Pittsburgh: KNOW, 1970.

Turgenev, Ivan. *Fathers and Sons.* 1862. New York: Norton, 1966.

"Women's Studies: A World View." Special issue of *Women's Studies Quarterly* 22.3–4 (1994).

Marilyn J. Boxer is professor of history at San Francisco State University and affiliated scholar at Stanford University's Institute for Research on Women and Gender. She is the author of When Women Ask the Questions: Creating Women's Studies in America.

Hull-House and Women's Studies

Parallel Approaches for First- and Second-Wave Feminists

Margaret Strobel

Women's studies arose out of the movement of second-wave feminism in the 1960s. Its passion drew on activism, its research questions emerged out of that activist engagement, and many of its practitioners saw women's studies as the academic arm of the women's movement. As a participant in the founding of women's studies who now runs the Jane Addams Hull-House Museum, I am struck by parallels between the work of first-wave feminists at Hull-House, an internationally famous settlement house founded in 1889 in Chicago, and second-wave feminists in women's studies. Key principles for both efforts involved lessening the distance (and power difference) between the researcher and the researched, creating new knowledge out of one's own experiences and observations, and linking theory and practice in the application of new knowledge to promote social change.

Jane Addams (1860–1935) and Ellen Gates Starr (1859–1940) founded Hull-House on the near west side of Chicago, a neighborhood teeming with new immigrants and all the concomitant urban problems: congestion, crowded and unsafe tenement housing, poverty, infectious disease and malnutrition, and exploitative labor conditions. Under Addams's leadership, Hull-House attracted many talented women, some of whom went on to national and international fame.[1] For example, Alice Hamilton (1869–1970), a pioneer in the field of industrial toxicology, became the first female professor at Harvard University with an appointment at the Harvard Medical School. Julia Lathrop (1858–1932), who as a Hull-House resident assessed the effectiveness of local charitable institutions, went on to head the Children's Bureau in Washington. Hull-House residents supported striking workers; created the first Chicago public playground and public baths; started Chicago's first women's basketball team; offered classes in citizenship, English, music, drama, art, and literature; provided information on birth control and venereal disease; challenged the local ward boss; and counseled immigrants with legal problems.[2] How did they go about this work?

They sought in some ways to minimize differences between themselves and their neighbors. According to the settlement house philosophy, those wishing to help solve the neighborhood's problems were to settle—reside—in the neighborhood and share its congestion, bad odors, and exposure to disease. Upwards of seventy "residents" lived and worked in what grew to be the thirteen-building complex of Hull-House; others, nonresidents, also offered programs. Addams was adamant that Hull-House activities were not philanthropy, with the word's connotations of the rich conveying goodies to the poor, but rather "the duties of good citizenship" (Addams, "Objective Value" 45). Hull-House residents paid room and board for the privilege of living at Hull-House and initiating and running programs. Some, like Addams herself, had an inheritance. Others earned a living elsewhere and administered Hull-House activities in their spare time. Enella Benedict (1858–1942), for example, taught at the School of the Art Institute of Chicago in the morning and ran the Hull-House art program in the afternoon. Florence Kelley's (1859–1932) employment in the early 1890s as a special agent to the Illinois Bureau of Labor Statistics gave her close contact with garment workers and enabled her to observe exploitative industrial working conditions.[3]

Jane Addams articulated a notion of the reciprocity of individuals across social classes. In *Twenty Years at Hull-House,* she notes that the settlement "was soberly opened on the theory that the dependence of classes on each other is reciprocal; and that as the social expression is essentially a reciprocal relation, it gives a form of expression that has peculiar value" (80). Moreover, she saw herself and young women like her—first-generation female college graduates—as rescued from stifled lives by the opportunity to live and work at the settlement, to engage their talents and intellects in meaningful activity. In a chapter entitled "The Snare of Preparation," she reports that she "gradually reached a conviction that the first generation of college women had taken their learning too quickly, had departed too suddenly from the active emotional life led by their grandmothers; . . . had developed too exclusively the power of acquiring knowledge and of merely receiving impressions" (71). When she and Starr conceived their plan to found a settlement house; Addams expressed relief that "I had at last finished with the everlasting 'preparation for life,' however ill-prepared I might be [for settlement work]" (78). In "The Subjective Necessity for Social Settlements" (1892), she again identifies "this apparent waste of [a young woman], this elaborate preparation, if no work is provided for her. . . . The desire for action, the wish to right wrong and alleviate suffering, haunts [young people] daily" (20).

Hull-House residents attended to issues of who speaks for whom, a question of critical importance to second-wave feminists. Three of the ten essays in the social survey discussed below, *Hull-House Maps and Papers*, are written by persons from the ethnic communities described. Addams herself indicates that "I never address a Chicago audience on the subject of the Settlement and its vicinity without inviting a neighbor to go with me, that I might curb any hasty generalizations by the consciousness that I had an auditor who knew the conditions more intimately that I could hope to do" (*Twenty Years* 82).

Although they strove for reciprocity, the relationship of Hull-House residents to their neighbors was not one of economic equality. Apart from the single working women who lived in the Jane Club residence, many Hull-House residents came from backgrounds considerably better off than their working-class neighbors on the near west side. Residents often spent the summer months traveling in Europe, as did Benedict, or at vacation homes such as Mary Rozet Smith's (1868–1934) and Addams's retreat in Bar Harbor, Maine. Moreover, residents took their meals apart from their neighbors in the Residents' Dining Hall, not in the cafeteria or coffee house where their neighbors could eat.[4] Wealthy donors funded Hull-House; thus the ability of Addams and others to function in upper-class society was critical to its success. In addition, Hull-House residents did not typically adopt the present-day community organizing approach of training local leadership nor did they involve neighbors in planning and developing programs (Bryan and Davis xi). Nonetheless, Addams and others stressed reciprocity. They were not merely serving; they were benefiting.

As important to the settlement-house philosophy as residing in the neighborhood was the principle of listening to and learning from neighbors. Rather than approaching the near west side's urban problems with a template of solutions, Addams and Starr opened their "home," the former country home of real-estate developer Charles Hull, to their neighbors. Hearing from local women of their need for child care, Addams and Starr began by babysitting and ended up with a kindergarten and the Mary Crane Nursery. They sometimes tried to impose their notion of what was good, for example, a community kitchen that served food scientifically designed to be nutritious and that the neighbors boycotted because the food was unfamiliar. But Hull-House residents generally developed programs out of the needs their neighbors articulated (Adams, *Twenty Years* chs. 5 and 7; Jackson chs. 2 and 3).

Out of this environment—a mixture of urban industrial problems and enormously talented residents—came new knowledge about urban immigrant life. The social science fields that second-wave feminist women's studies scholars criticized for their bias against or tendency to ignore women were developing at the time of the establishment of Hull-House. Indeed, there was a close relationship between Hull-House residents and both the founders of the Chicago school of sociology and the Chicago school of pragmatism (Deegan; Jackson 14–16; Seigfried).

In 1895 Hull-House residents published the landmark *Hull-House Maps and Papers,* identified by historian Kathryn Kish Sklar as "the single most important work by American women social scientists before 1900" (*Hull-House Maps and Papers* 111). This study utilized the emerging social science methodologies to collect systematically information about the neighborhood. Conducting social surveys between 6 April and 15 July 1893, residents included two sets of maps, one documenting "nationalities" (what we now would call ethnicity), the other wages. Uncommon until the 1860s, color coding of maps had previously been used to illustrate public-health issues but not urban poverty. Accompanying the maps were interpretive essays that outlined the challenges facing the neighborhood. Sklar identifies five of these ten essays as "focus[ing] on what might be called female-specific issues: sweatshop labor, Cook County charities, child labor, labor organizations for working women, and the work of Hull-House residents" (*"Hull-House Maps and Papers"* 113).

In *Hull-House Maps and Papers,* Hull-House residents sought to mobilize new knowledge for social change. While employed by the Illinois Bureau of Labor Statistics, Florence Kelley directed the research for the project. In contrast to Charles Booth's *Life and Labour of the People in London* (1891) to which it is sometimes compared for their similarly path-breaking use of maps, *Hull-House Maps and Papers* was the product of Kelley's passionate commitment to social change. Working with the women's reform network in Chicago and a sympathetic governor, John P. Altgeld, Kelley and Hull-House activist Alzina Stevens (1849–1900) used the information from their research about sweatshops and child labor to achieve the passage in 1893 of the Factory and Workshop Inspection Act. The act authorized such inspectors as Kelley and Stevens to monitor sweatshop conditions as well as limitations on child labor and women workers' hours. In addition to pushing this protective legislation, Stevens used the information collected

on children's lives to support the creation in 1899 of the first juvenile
court in the world, across the street from Hull-House, to keep children
out of the adult criminal justice system.[5]

In the activities of Hull-House women we see that, long before the
emergence of second-wave feminism and the field of women's studies, there existed not only a women's movement but also ways of working that are broadly comparable to how we in women's studies
conceived our work. We sought to create new knowledge out of our
experiences and observations. Male bias had resulted in the near
invisibility of women, hence early second-wave feminist academic
books sported such titles as *Becoming Visible: Women in European History*
(Bridenthal et al.). As pro-choice activists held speak-outs on the previously hidden experience of abortion, scholars—some of whom had
received abortions—studied it. Because new knowledge often did not
fit existing disciplinary structures, women's studies developed as an
interdisciplinary field.[6]

In addition, we sought to lessen the distance (and the power difference) between the researcher and the researched. Discovering
women as a social group that lacked power, women's studies scholars
eschewed replicating the power relations of earlier researchers that
posited an all-knowing investigator studying unsophisticated communities or individuals. In her sympathetic critique "Can There Be a
Feminist Ethnography?" Judith Stacey recalls how "discussions of [sec-
ond-wave] feminist methodology generally assaulted the hierarchical,
exploitative relations of conventional research, urging feminist
researchers to seek instead an egalitarian research process characterized by authenticity, reciprocity, and intersubjectivity between the
researcher and her 'subjects'" (112).

Finally, we sought to promote social change by applying the new
knowledge we created, linking theory and practice. Through this new
knowledge generated by new research relationships, we tried to understand the oppression of women and other oppressed groups in order
to dismantle it. Research was to be *for* women, not just *about* women
(DuBois chs. 2 and 4; Harding 8).

Similarly drawing upon a women's reform movement and a community at Hull-House that supported women's intellects and
activism, Hull-House residents created new knowledge about the
neighboring community, focusing on issues of particular interest to
female reformers—child labor and working conditions for women
in sweatshops. Linked to the reform movement, Hull-House activists
used this new knowledge to buttress their campaigns for the eight-
hour day and limitations on child labor. Much like women's studies

scholars who operated on the margins of their disciplines and institutions in the 1960s and 1970s, Hull-House activists were acutely
aware of their lack of formal citizenship, although Illinois women
were allowed to vote in local elections in 1913 before the ratification
of the woman suffrage amendment to the U.S. Constitution in 1920.
Operating out of a position that was marginal in terms of gender but
privileged in terms of economic class and ethnicity/nationality, Hull-
House activists created new knowledge and programs out of their
observations of their neighbors and their own experiences in the
neighborhood. And in some ways they sought, within the limitations
of that same economic and national/ethnic position, reciprocal
rather than hierarchical relationships.

Formed out of the social and political communities that were
embedded in the first- and second-wave feminist movements, these
principles of operation are integral, not incidental, to the success of
both Hull-House and women's studies. In both instances, linking theory and practice required testing theories against real-world experience and modifying them accordingly. Since the point of knowledge
was to promote concrete and positive social change, not to describe
some abstract ideal without immediate consequences, knowledge had
to be as accurate as possible. Gaining a thorough and accurate understanding of issues and conditions necessitated attention to matters of
power, distance, and difference. Although neither Hull-House reformers nor women's studies practitioners achieved all their goals, their
application of these principles transformed, respectively, the urban
reform landscape and the university with resulting benefits for women
and men alike.

NOTES
1. Men also lived and worked at Hull-House but it is best known as a women's
    community. See Sklar, "Hull House in the 1890s."
2. The best single source on Hull-House is Mary Lynn McCree Bryan and
    Allen F. Davis, eds., *100 Years at Hull-House*, which traces, through docu-
    ments with introductions, the activities of Hull-House from its inception
    through the 1960s when the Hull-House Association dispersed its social
    service activities to other parts of the city and vacated the complex. The
    early activities are also described in Jane Addams's *Twenty Years at Hull-
    House*, edited with an introduction by Victoria Bissell Brown.

    For more information on public baths and playgrounds, see Addams,
    Twenty Years 163–64, 156; Bryan and Davis 46. For women's gymnastics and
    basketball, see Bryan and Davis 73–74. For classes in citizenship and
    English and for the Immigrants Protective League's helping immigrants
    with legal problems, see Addams, *Twenty Years* 199–200; Bryan and Davis

124–26. For music, literature, theater, and the arts, see Addams, *Twenty Years* 180–90; Bryan and Davis 39–42, 92–95, 101–3, 119–20. For struggles with the ward boss, see Addams, *Twenty Years* 155, 164–66; Bryan and Davis 55–57.

For additional information about these activities, see also the following biographies of key Hull-House residents in Rima Lunin Schultz and Adele Hast, eds., *Women Building Chicago 1790–1990: A Biographical Dictionary*: labor support—Florence Kelley, Ellen Gates Starr, and Alzina Stevens; women's gymnastics and basketball—Rose Marie Gyles; immigrant support—Grace Abbott; art, dance, theater, and music—Enella Benedict, Mary Hinman, Edith de Nancrede, Laura Dainty Pelham, and Eleanor Smith; health and birth control—Rachelle Yarros.

3. See Enella Benedict and Florence Kelley entries in Schultz and Hast.
4. Some of these class issues are explored in Jackson ch. 4.
5. See the Kelley and Stevens entries in Schultz and Hast.
6. See Ellen Carol DuBois et al., *Feminist Scholarship: Kindling in the Groves of Academe,* for an exploration of the origins of women's studies. Chapters 1 and 2 in particular address the generation of new knowledge. Editor Sandra Harding discusses women's experience as a source of empirical and theoretical insights in *Feminism and Methodology* 6–7. Addams promoted interdisciplinarity as well, encouraging the theater, music, art, and dance programs all to collaborate on annual Christmas programs; see Jackson 20–21.

WORKS CITED

Addams, Jane. "The Objective Value of a Social Settlement." *The Jane Addams Reader.* Ed. Jean Bethke Elshtain. New York: Basic, 2002. 29–45.

———. "The Subjective Necessity for Social Settlements." *The Jane Addams Reader.* Ed. Jean Bethke Elshtain. New York: Basic, 2002. 14–28.

———. *Twenty Years at Hull-House.* 1910. Ed. and introd. Victoria Bissell Brown. Boston: Bedford/St. Martin's, 1999.

Bridenthal, Renate, et al. *Becoming Visible.* 1975. Boston: Houghton, 1998.

Bryan, Mary Lynn McCree, and Allen F. Davis, eds. *100 Years at Hull-House.* 1969. Bloomington: Indiana UP, 1990.

Deegan, Mary Jo. *Jane Addams and the Men of the Chicago School.* New Brunswick, NJ: Transaction, 1988.

DuBois, Ellen Carol, et al. *Feminist Scholarship: Kindling in the Groves of Academe.* Urbana: U of Illinois P, 1987.

Harding, Sandra. *Feminism and Methodology.* Bloomington: Indiana UP, 1987.

Jackson, Shannon. *Lines of Activity: Performance, Historiography, and Hull-House Domesticity.* Ann Arbor: U of Michigan P, 2000.

Schultz, Rima Lunin, and Adele Hast, eds. *Women Building Chicago 1790–1990: A Biographical Dictionary.* Bloomington: Indiana UP, 2001.

Seigfried, Charlene Haddock. *Pragmatism and Feminism: Reweaving the Social Fabric.* Chicago: U of Chicago P, 1996.

Sklar, Kathryn Kish. "Hull House in the 1890s: A Community of Women Reformers." *Signs: Journal of Women in Culture and Society* 10 (1985): 658–77.

————. "*Hull-House Maps and Papers*: Social Science as Women's Work in the1890s." *The Social Survey in Historical Perspective 1880–1940*. Ed. Martin Bulmer, Kevin Bales, and Kathryn Kish Sklar. Cambridge: Cambridge UP, 1991. 111–47.

Stacey, Judith. "Can There Be a Feminist Ethnography?" *Women's Words: The Feminist Practice of Oral History*. Ed. Sherna Berger Gluck and Daphne Patai. New York: Routledge, 1991.

Margaret Strobel *serves as interim director of the Jane Addams Hull-House Museum and professor of gender and women's studies and history at the University of Illinois at Chicago. She has written about African women; gender, race, and empire; and the Chicago Women's Liberation Union.*

Berkeley, 1969

A Memoir

Lisa Gerrard

In my memory, the early feminists I studied in school are caricatures: Strident and histrionic, bustling about in prim hats and flounces of skirts, they fuss about women's rights until they eventually get the vote and stop complaining. The image, planted by history textbooks of the 1950s and early 1960s, is rife with stereotyping. Dainty bodies, tiny waists and feet, shrill voices, high-pitched emotions. Identified with the prohibition movement (which was likewise oversimplified and dismissed), the suffragists are shown as overreacting to trivial problems and, by undertaking political activism, venturing beyond their rightful domestic sphere. Something never seemed quite right with this image—despite their patronizing depictions of these women, the textbooks never questioned the women's right to vote—but as a child, I had neither the vocabulary nor understanding to challenge it. That was before I heard about the personal being political and vice versa.

In my photo album is a picture our neighbor Bernie took of my father circa 1945, hanging diapers on a clothesline erected in our tiny garden in Mount Vernon, New York. Bernie, a strict believer in segregated gender roles, found the sight of a man doing laundry outrageous, even hilarious—so much so that he commemorated it with his camera. When it came to defining male and female work, my family was traditional in some ways, less so in others. We understood that my father, an accomplished violinist, would be the primary support for the family, but my mother worked, too; given the instability of the theater/recording world, we needed her income. More than that, my mother sought jobs that offered intellectual stimulation. Although she had not trained for a career (her formal education stopped at high school), she found work where she could develop her interests—in an art museum, a medical research laboratory, a social work agency, a hospital. And though on one level we accepted the 1950s dictum that primary responsibility for housework and cooking resided with women, we resisted it in other ways. My mother was a meticulous housekeeper who worried about what visitors might think if they found dirt in her home, but she also resented the ethic of the time, particularly as it played out in middle-class suburbia, that a woman's value could be measured in the cleanliness of her home. She promoted what must have been a revolutionary idea in our neighborhood: that a household should be run like a kibbutz with each member contributing to its upkeep. And for the most part it was. Although I understood that my mother, sister, and I were responsible for the housework, in reality, my father did quite a lot of it; when he was home he unquestioningly cooked, vacuumed, ironed, and got groceries. Hard working and responsible, he never played king of the castle.

Discovering Feminism

When I went to college in 1964, discrimination against women was all around me but I didn't perceive it as such. They were personal difficulties rather than political injustices. Abortion was illegal, so women I knew would scrounge up money for a trip to the back streets of Mexico. In my sophomore year at the University of California, Berkeley, my roommate got pregnant, went to Tijuana, and returned from her abortion with a serious infection. A doctor at the Student Health Service saved her life but treated her with undisguised hostility. The whole experience was cloaked in fear and secrecy. It wasn't just that she had committed an illegal act. Many of the doctors saw unmarried sexually active women as sluts and made sure we knew it. One in particular gave notoriously painful pelvic exams and was rumored to be especially rough on women with sexually transmitted diseases.

But nothing developed my feminism quite like dating. It was my male peers, not my women friends, who opened my mind. Berkeley seemed to have attracted a large share of the world's sexual predators. The ones who fancied themselves hippies or radicals (or a bit of both) also cast themselves as foes of capitalism. As such, they felt philosophically and politically proscribed not only from paying for their dates' movies, but also from keeping cash on hand, thus ensuring that their dates would pay for both of them. The joke making the rounds at that time did not exaggerate: A date is when he comes for dinner and stays for the weekend. But the saying omits the coercion that dominated much of this experience. For while it was possible to go on dates that cost little or nothing, there was no avoiding the battle over sex. If you didn't sleep with the guy, more often than not, he'd deliver a harangue, always on the same theme: You were "uptight," one of the most deprecating things you could call a person in that supposedly freewheeling, self-expressive time and place.

This language enforced a form of sexual tyranny. Ironically, these free-spirited flower children (hippies) or warriors for the downtrodden (radicals) were autocrats, in love with their self-entitlement. Today much of their behavior would be labeled sexual harassment or date rape. At the very least, it contradicted their ideology. These radical men—self-righteous about the moral superiority of their politics, their opposition to an undeclared war in Southeast Asia, and to the oppression of people of color at home and abroad, quick to label a conservative professor or senator a fascist—thought nothing of forcing their will, not to mention their muscle, on the women they wanted to bed. The pressure ranged from hectoring to outright rape. Some men would refuse to leave my apartment. Others issued threats. A few were violent. Calling the police was not an option in those days; the prevailing attitude was that if you invited a man into your life, you invited what ensued. Few women reported rapes committed by strangers and if they did, the legal system was more likely to treat them as criminals than victims. As for acquaintance or date rape— legally, it didn't exist.

Dating at Berkeley in the 1960s showed me how unprepared I was for deflecting sexism or even just for standing up for myself. I'd get mad at myself for caving in to the pressure when I felt afraid—or, I'm sorry to say, merely worn down—and mad at myself again for feeling uncomfortable when, overcoming my training to "please everyone," kicked the guy out. In either case, this was not dating as my childhood mentor—*Seventeen* magazine—had described it. The disrespect was so personal, raw, and persistent, it put all the more subtle—and far more damaging—habits of a sexist society into focus. Although many of the men I met in those years were gentle souls quite sincere in their politics, it is the boorish ones, and my own difficulty fending them off, that unexpectedly taught me about feminism.

The Women's Caucus

In 1968, I graduated college. After a stint in Paris hoping to improve my French (which I did) and eventually become a French-English interpreter (which I didn't), I returned to Berkeley. In need of an immediate income, I worked as a teller for the Bank of America. On my lunch breaks, I walked up to the Berkeley campus and, in my incongruous little dress and imitation Mary Quant shoes, joined the picket lines campaigning for Third World studies. On one of these lunch breaks, I read a handwritten note card on a bulletin board inviting women to participate in a women and literature discussion group, my first acquaintance with women's studies. Six months later, in the fall of 1969, I entered graduate school at Berkeley in comparative literature and joined a consciousness-raising group made up of female graduate students in the Comparative Literature Department. Like so many feminists of the 1960s and 1970s, many of us had participated in the civil rights and antiwar movements of the 1960s and saw extending basic human rights to women as a logical extension of that effort. As in similar groups forming in other parts of the country, we discussed our personal experiences as women, generalized them, and resituated them in a political context. It wasn't long before we began to look to our immediate political situation—our graduate program—for redress of sexist practices, and the consciousness-raising group evolved into the Graduate Women's Caucus in Comparative Literature.

The caucus created a much-needed community within a graduate department that had a large number of students and faculty. And because comparative literature was interdisciplinary and all faculty members held joint appointments in two departments, the faculty were widely dispersed. The situation was similar for the graduate students. Each person in the doctoral program specialized in three national literatures, studied in their original languages, and thus took courses in different departments. As a result, the Graduate Women's Caucus in Comparative Literature served both a social and political function: It created a community among a group of graduate students who might not otherwise have met and it agitated for feminist goals.

The Women and Literature Courses

We were all white, middle-class women, privileged in many ways—particularly in our education and ambitions for an interesting career. We were the first generation of women to attend college in substantial numbers, and, in the spirit of political change that dominated the period, we challenged the male-centered curriculum in our field. The department was receptive to our initial request to institute two courses (one upper- and one lower-division) on women and literature, which it allowed us to develop and teach. In keeping with the consciousness-raising focus of early 1970s feminism, the first versions of these courses were informal and student-centered rather than governed by lecture; often we sat on the floor in a circle, using a carpeted conference room rather than a traditional classroom. We encouraged our students to weave their personal experiences into class discussion and writing assignments and asked them to write autobiographical, expressive, or self-discovery pieces in addition to literary exposition. We were eager to give them charge of their education; students often led class discussions and even taught class on specified days. While much of this pedagogy is now standard in many kinds of college courses, at the time it represented a significant departure from the lecture-centered educational practices with which we were familiar.

Our first lower division Women and Literature course was taught in the spring quarter of 1972 by Melanie Kaye Persoff, one of our caucus members. Anyone could submit a course proposal to the caucus, which would then vote on whether to accept it. (Well, probably not anyone; I doubt the caucus would have been receptive to a male teacher. In any case, only women chose to participate.) As different graduate students taught these courses, the themes varied widely, including Fairy Tales Chinese and European, Tragedies of Women's Individualism, Third World Women, The Devil's Handmaiden: Demonic Women in Literature, and Self-Image and Alternatives. Some courses emphasized self-discovery through the study of women in literature; Centering and Coping: Short Prose by Women about Women described its goals this way:

—intellectual objective: self-knowledge
—experiential objective: self-discovery
—personal objective: self-introspection.

In this version of the course, each class meeting began with an "experiential/personal phase" in which students learned different "centering" techniques and then spent "some moments of self-contemplation in which we might record our insights in our diaries or share our reactions with each other." The rest of the class time was the "academic phase" in which students made presentations about the "centering or coping" devices used by the characters in the works studied or by the authors of these works in their own lives (Carstanjen).

Other versions of the course were more traditional, devoted to literary themes (Women and Romantic Love), literary tradition (Women in Enlightenment vs. Sturm und Drang Theater), or genre (my own course, The Female Bildungsroman). Twentieth-Century Women's Poetry: Themes and Images explored the ways in which female poets spoke "for humane values in poems of wide stylistic and thematic range." Although clearly drawing on the department's traditional literary training in its emphasis on the theme and structure of the works, it departed from convention by focusing exclusively on female poets, giving equal attention to lesser-known poets "who *deserve* a wider public" as to celebrated ones, and incorporating the local poetry scene into the curriculum (via trips to women's presses and bookstores and readings by local poets) (Earnshaw).[1]

The most controversial issue was whether to admit male students into these courses, a problem that persists in women's studies classes today. We wanted to provide a forum where women's opinions, usually silenced in the presence of more vocal and assertive male students, could be heard and valued, but, legally, we could not exclude men. As it played out in our classrooms, this was less a philosophical or legal conflict than a pedagogical one. How could we effect consciousness-raising unless our students felt safe to speak openly? Our female students felt this problem acutely: Eager to connect their personal and academic lives, they argued passionately that they could not talk about their personal lives in coed classrooms. While men rarely ventured into our courses, in a few classes, verbal warfare broke out between the men (or more often, man) and women, and I do remember hearing about one sensitive male student driven in tears from the room, while in other courses, a lone man, hostile and defensive, fired off a few rounds of sexist hate speech. Fortunately these eruptions were rare. Most of our courses attracted enthusiastic students, thrilled by the subject matter and the new approach to teaching. I was a fairly inexperienced teacher when I taught my Women and Literature course, and often awkward and nervous, but my students acted as if I could do no wrong. Bless their hearts.

The Political Context

Although I was not privy to the faculty's deliberations as they approved these courses and shepherded them through university committees and into the catalog, the lack of resistance probably had to do with the increased awareness of women's issues on campus and the pressure being placed on the university, a research institution that relied heavily on government grants, to comply with federal antidiscrimination legislation. In May 1969, Berkeley's academic senate found it "surprising that so few women—only 15 at the present time—achieve the rank of full professor at Berkeley" (qtd. in Kadish 1), and appointed a committee to investigate the status of women on its campus. The committee polled department chairs, faculty members, researchers, graduate students, and former graduate students who had dropped out of school and concluded in May 1970 that women faced "a large number of obstacles in obtaining recognition as members of the academic community" (2). The committee's seventy-eight-page report cataloged a broad range of discriminatory practices, among them antinepotism rules, which prevented wives with Ph.D.s from being hired at the same campus where their husbands worked; reluctance to tenure qualified women or promote them through academic ranks; preference awarded to men in graduate admissions, and, after admission, in financial and intellectual support; crediting male colleagues for research and research reports written by women and rewarding or failing to reward them accordingly; and substantial psychological abuse at all levels of the academic hierarchy:

> There are departments in which women students are told in seminars that women are unable to think objectively or analytically. There are departments where suggestions that women might be dissatisfied are met with wit and jibes or with scornful comments about aggressive women. . . . In some instances . . . [women] are told . . . that they ought to marry and drop out. (7–9)

The university was feeling pressure from other sources as well. Less than two weeks after the academic senate published its report on the status of women, a national organization, the Women's Equity Action League, filed a complaint against the university for violating federal law, specifically Executive Orders 11246 and 11375, which forbid discrimination on the basis of sex. In December 1970, the Political Science Department's women's caucus filed a complaint with the Department of Health, Education, and Welfare (HEW) for violating these orders. In April 1971, the university's League of Academic Women and the National Organization of Women filed a class action complaint against the university for the same reason. In June 1971, the federal Office of Civil Rights initiated a review of university practice and policies, and the following month, HEW began a "contract compliance" review.

This latter review led to considerable tension between the university and HEW; a few weeks after beginning its work, HEW cut off new funding to the university for twenty-four hours for denying them access to personnel records. Throughout the investigation, the university used delaying tactics, and HEW repeatedly threatened to suspend funding of new federal contracts and grants. In February 1972, Berkeley's League of Academic Women and a dozen female academic and nonacademic employees filed a class action suit in San Francisco Federal Court, charging the University of California, Berkeley, and the president of the university system with widespread discrimination in employment and promotion. In March, the judge who heard the case gave the university 120 days to propose a plan to remedy discrimination in employment (League of Academic Women).

While the university resisted HEW's investigation throughout the early 1970s, it also made efforts to support affirmative action. In 1970, President Charles Hitch announced a policy to initiate affirmative action programs and, a few months later, named an affirmative action coordinator. At the same time, the university required departments to show that they were considering qualified women before making faculty appointments, and several departments undertook reports on the status of women. This was the climate in which our caucus activity took place.

Our work in the Comparative Literature Department was thus part of a larger political and consciousness-raising context in which women at all levels of the university were reconsidering their status and making demands on the institution. In 1970, the Comparative Literature Caucus helped form a Women's Caucus in Language and Literature Departments, and similar groups emerged in other fields and departments. In December 1971, female library employees filed a report with the university making recommendations for affirmative action. In April 1972, female union members throughout campus formed the Interunion Women's Caucus (coordinated by the American Federation of State, County, and Municipal Employees [AFSCME]) to represent their common interests. In the same month, women in the School of Education organized their caucus. A winter quarter 1973 list of women's studies courses shows, too, that academic departments besides ours—Anthropology, Asian Studies, Criminology, English, and Sociology—had begun to bring women's issues into the curriculum.

Political Efforts

In 1971, the Modern Language Association (MLA) Commission on the Status of Women in the Profession reported widespread inequities in the profession and requested that modern language departments submit a plan for internal policy changes. The commission specifically recommended that graduate students "be asked to sit with the department" throughout the planning process (Commission 3). Shortly thereafter, the Comparative Literature Women's Caucus wrote a letter to the chair and vice-chair of graduate studies in the Department of Comparative Literature, reminding them of the commission's recommendations and—"since we have already devoted considerable energy and thought to the situation of women in the university"—offering "our services and expertise" in helping the department prepare its affirmative action plan (du Bois et al. 1). The faculty, however, did not share our confidence in our "expertise" and failed to embrace this offer. Nor did they respond to a letter we wrote in December 1973 to which we appended an article from the *MLA Newsletter* on sexism in letters of recommendation. The *Newsletter* had cataloged the kinds of damaging comments professors included in letters of recommendation for academic jobs: praising the candidate's husband's achievements; focusing on the candidate's physical appearance ("her mousiness belies a sharp mind"); overt prejudice against feminists ("[she] is no fem lib type, but a real gentlewoman"); and language such as "sweet" and "shy" that suggested the candidate was ill suited to the "dignified role of college professor" (Hoffman 5).

Despite these supportive documents from the MLA and the affirmative action work taking place across campus, as graduate students in a traditional department we had little power. While the department had given us generous latitude in designing and teaching the Women and Literature courses, it was less enthusiastic about inviting us to uncover sexist attitudes in its midst. In 1976, however, we were invited to speak out by Berkeley's vice chancellor. Federal law—specifically Title IX of the Education Amendments of 1972—required the university to undertake a self-evaluation to identify and correct possible sexist practices. This time, the principal concern of affirmative action was not faculty and staff but the treatment of students; each academic department was advised by the vice chancellor to include "student input" in its self-evaluation (Heyman 1). So it was that the Comparative Literature Women's Caucus met, discussed its concerns, and presented them in a letter to the vice chancellor. We noted that while most of the undergraduate (73 percent) and graduate (67 percent) students were women, an equal number (three men, three women) received doctorates in the year under review, a shift in proportion that suggested subtle and not so subtle sex discrimination. We argued that some of the department's practices discouraged women from completing the doctoral program:

- It offered few female faculty mentors. In 1976, only two of the twenty-four tenured faculty members were women. The ratio of male to female faculty members overall was three to one, and the department was continuing to hire more men than women.
- It failed to take women's studies and literature seriously as a discipline. Students working in this area reported that their professors did not regard women's studies as a legitimate academic field nor did the department attempt to recruit faculty members specializing in this area. (Women's Caucus 1–2)

In addition to recommending that the department correct these problems (and that it offer the required graduate introductory course during the day rather than at night, so that female students could get to it safely), the letter faulted the department for tolerating "ritualized . . . . undermining of the female student's self-confidence . . . through sexist jokes and comments" and recounted experiences like these:

- During her Ph.D. exams, a student was told by one committee member that she "thought like a woman" and by another that she "thought like a man." Both comments were intended as criticisms, the first meaning that the woman was insufficiently rational, the second meaning the opposite, but implying that she was not "womanly" enough.
- Another woman was greeted by the chairman of her M.A. oral exam with the comment, "Would you like to sit in that empty chair there or in Mr. ———'s lap?"
- A third graduate student was greeted by her male advisor with this comment: "I'd kiss you, but I have a cold." He then repeated this witticism to a passing colleague. (Women's Caucus 2–3)

While we recognized that comments like these were meant to be innocuously funny, we also saw what few of us would have noticed before the feminist movement: that underneath the stance of counseling or banter was the belittling message that despite eight to ten years of graduate study, a woman could never be a scholar.

If the letter made a difference in professors' relationships to their female students, I couldn't tell. In fact, I'm not sure that we accomplished much more than irritating the department chair. As chair of the Women's Caucus that year, I had the responsibility of delivering the letter to the department chair, and though I no longer remember the conversation we had, I clearly remember the letter's icy reception. Not surprisingly the department chair did not appreciate seeing her department maligned, and though the letter made its way to the vice chancellor, it's hard to know if it had an impact. The Women's Caucus continued to meet, but the letter was our last political effort in the department. Many of us directed our feminist activism elsewhere, while in our graduate department we existed largely for the Women and Literature course and as a social group, offering one another support and mentoring.

Reading and Learning

If our political efforts were limited, our intellectual ones were expansive. Together we discovered the feminist texts just being published.[2] We were also reading literature in a new way. We were a generation of literary critics trained in the "new" criticism of the 1930s, which had downplayed social context in favor of the structure and language of literary works. I had learned to explore a text as an artifact but the historical background had always interested me, and now I could indulge that interest, analyzing male and female characters as products of patriarchal societies, both those described and those lived by their authors. And we were discovering that the literary canon we had devoted so much of our lives to exploring was not just male. As dutiful students, most of us had simply accepted the assumption underlying academic study in literature: Every course syllabus, reading list, anthology of literature, by ignoring women's work, implied that all the great thinkers and writers in the world were men. It was a revelation to read wonderful female authors we had never even heard of before—Sylvia Plath, Gwendolyn Brooks, Muriel Rukeyser, Doris Lessing, Zora Neale Hurston, Tillie Olsen—and to learn to value the uniquely female experiences they described.

What made this enterprise so engaging is that it was not only intellectually rich but it also touched us personally. As women, we identified powerfully with much of what we discovered in these works, literary and nonliterary: They spoke to our lives. Many of us were inspired to write feminist dissertations, exploring female writers or characters. Mine, a feminist study of "The Romantic Woman in Nineteenth-Century Fiction," like those of my colleagues, was very much a product of 1960s and early 1970s feminism, with its emphasis on female identity and social roles, especially those of middle-class white women.

In Sisterhood

This early women's studies effort had multiple functions. It generated some of the university's earliest feminist courses; it focused attention on the discrimination in academia; and it created a community that offered women in our graduate program emotional and intellectual support as we read drafts of one another's dissertations and shared reading lists, department lore, and advice on the sequences of exams. We weren't a perfect sisterhood, if there is such a thing; sometimes confidences meant to stay within the group spilled outside it—one woman's abortion, another's fling with a professor—but for the most part, we provided sisterly support in our enclave of the world. In doing so, we built a little piece of the feminist movement that was developing rapidly across the country and helped extend the work the women's rights activists had begun a century and a half earlier. Far from fussy ladies in fussy clothes, these were courageous, powerful foremothers.

NOTES

1. Among the writers studied in this course were Ruth Pitter, Charlotte Mew, Leonora Speyer, Elizabeth Bishop, Sylvia Plath, Denise Levertov, and the local poets Alta, Susan Griffin, and Mary Norbert Korte.
2. These included such works as the inaugural (1973) issue of *Ms.* magazine, Phyllis Chesler's *Women and Madness*, Eva Figes's *Patriarchal Attitudes*, Robin Morgan's *Sisterhood Is Powerful*, Germaine Greer's *The Female Eunuch*, and Vivian Gornick and Barbara K. Moran's *Woman in a Sexist Society*.

WORKS CITED

Carstanjen, Sonra. Course proposal for Comparative Literature 40, "Centering and Coping." Unpublished manuscript, in possession of author.

Chesler, Phyllis. *Women and Madness*. New York: Doubleday, 1972.

Commission on the Status of Women in the Profession. "Report to the Business Meeting, December, 1970." *MLA Newsletter* 3.1 (February 1971): 1–4.

Du Bois, Page, Lisa Gerrard, Marsha Hudson, Shelley Parlante, Melanie Kaye Persoff, Susan Sterling, and Judith L. Wells. Letter to Chairman Robert Alter and Vice Chairman for Graduate Studies Janette Richardson, University of California, Berkeley. 1971. In possession of author.

Earnshaw, Doris. Course proposal for Comparative Literature 40D, "Twentieth-Century Women's Poetry: Themes and Images." Unpublished manuscript, in possession of author.

Figes, Eva. *Patriarchal Attitudes*. New York: Fawcett, 1970.

Gornick, Vivian, and Barbara K. Moran. *Woman in Sexist Society: Studies in Power and Powerlessness*. New York: Basic Books, 1971.

Greer, Germaine. *The Female Eunuch*. London: Paladin, 1970.

Heyman, Ira Michael. Letter from the Vice Chancellor, "Suggestions for Departmental Self-Evaluation," University of California, Berkeley. 30 April 1976.

Hoffman, Nancy Jo. "Sexism in Letters of Recommendation: A Case for Consciousness Raising." *MLA Newsletter* 4.3 (1972): 5–6.

Kadish, Sanford, and Committee on Senate Policy. *Report of the Committee on Senate Policy*. Berkeley: U of California, Berkeley, 1970.

League of Academic Women. *Chronicle of League of Academic Women*. Berkeley: U of California, Berkeley, 1971, amended 1972.

Morgan, Robin. *Sisterhood Is Powerful: An Anthology of Writings form the Women's Liberation Movement*. New York: Vintage Books, 1970.

Women's Caucus. Letter to Vice Chancellor Ira Michael Heyman, Department of Comparative Literature, University of California, Berkeley. 18 May 1976. In possession of the author.

Lisa Gerrard holds a Ph.D. in comparative literature from the University of California, Berkeley. She teaches in the writing programs at the University of California, Los Angeles, and has published in women's studies, literature, rhetoric, and computers and composition. Her most recent work is "Beyond 'Scribbling Women': Women Writing (on) the Web," in Sibylle Gruber, editor, Power and the World Wide Web, *special issue of* Computers and Composition *19.3 (2002).*

Women's Studies on the Border

University of Texas at El Paso

Scarlet Bowen and Emma Pérez

The women's studies faculty at the University of Texas at El Paso (UTEP) continues to benefit from the feminist battles won in the 1970s and 1980s. Because of the early efforts of Mimi Gladstein, Lois Marchino, Kathy Staudt, Gaye Young, and Eleanor Duke, women faculty have legal precedents in place to challenge sex discrimination in salaries, tenure, and promotion;[1] we have witnessed the tremendous achievement of the university's first female president; we have tracked a steady increase in hires of women faculty; in the year 2000, we obtained a full-time, tenure-track appointment in women's studies and the university's first lesbian spousal hire; and we have an established women's studies program that offers students a minor in women's studies as well as educational programs and events that highlight women's and gender issues.

UTEP is located directly on the U.S.–Mexico border; El Paso is one of a series of "twin cities" along the border, with Juárez, Mexico, as its binational neighbor. UTEP's student population became majority Latina/o in 1986, five years following the establishment of the Women's Studies Program in 1981. Today, with a student population of fifteen thousand, 69 percent of those students are Latina/o and 10 percent are Mexican nationals. Female students comprise about 55 percent of the student population. Latinas are 73 percent and Mexican women are 7 percent of the female student population (Center for Institutional Evaluation 3). Female students from the United States are predominantly working class and often from the first generations of their families to attend a university. The students from Juárez, on the other hand, are mostly middle class.

Like other women's studies programs around the nation, UTEP's program continues to share the challenge with peer institutions of making women's studies vital to the students at the university. Today, while all of our women's studies courses have adequate enrollment, the number of students who minor in women's studies is surprisingly low: only twelve in spring semester 2002. It is feasible that the 1980s backlash and 1990s postfeminist milieu may be the cause of such attrition, but we have chosen to take a more self-reflexive look at this phenomenon. The women's studies faculty must look closely at our student population, assess their needs, and offer them a program that helps them make sense of their lives. We ask: How does the Women's Studies Program meet the needs of today's students living on the U.S.–Mexico border?

The most productive assumption of any women's studies program is that understanding the roots of oppression empowers students to release internalized notions of inferiority and fight for structural change. As we all know, women are affected by a constellation of oppressions related to race, nationality, abled-ness, economic class, and sexuality, among others. Along the U.S.–Mexico border, the constellation of oppressions that our students face is particularly visible. We believe that the interdisciplinary nature of women's studies, as well as ethnic studies, provides us with the analytical tools to begin addressing these issues in all their complexities.

We emphasize *begin* because the enormity of the issues here demand our utmost humility and social responsibility, both in academic and activist arenas. One example of the gravity of these issues is the decade-long epidemic of violence against Mexican women in Ciudad Juárez. The national and local media document that since 1993 over three hundred Mexican women have been murdered, most of whom were sexually assaulted and mutilated before they were killed (Valdez 2). Activist groups from Juárez report that up to 450 additional women are missing and unaccounted for. There is no particular pattern to the murders, except that most women who are abducted are young, attractive, and poor. Some are abducted in broad daylight; others are kidnapped on their way home from late-night work shifts at the *maquiladoras,* or factories along the border that have multiplied since passage of the North American Free Trade Agreement (NAFTA). After ten years, this binational community is still no closer to knowing who the perpetrators are (and there are probably several from both sides of the border), why the murders persist, or why the governments of both countries are so slow to respond to the need for women's safety and for binational cooperation in investigating the crimes.

This essay will not discuss these horrific crimes at length. In our minds, there has been enough writing about the issue but not enough action. We rely on the analytical tools of feminist studies to guide us through responsible activism and hope that the actions we take and the lessons we learn from them provide productive models for students who are beginning their own journeys into feminist study and activism.

We participate in asking a multitude of questions in university and community forums: How can we assert U.S. responsibility in this matter without perpetuating U.S. dominance in relation to Mexico? How can we address the layers of discrimination at work, from sexism to elitism? How can we be critical of U.S. companies' negligence toward female workers without jeopardizing those female workers or taking away their agency? Recognizing that coalition-building is the best way to address such complexities, many of the women's studies faculty and students have joined the Coalition Against Violence Toward Women and Families on the Border, an El Paso group composed of labor organizers, religious groups, women's nonprofit organizations, various community activists, politicians, and students. The coalition is actively pursuing the following demands:

1. A federal binational task force to investigate and bring justice to the murdered women's families,
2. The sharing by U.S. forensic scientists of all necessary resources and laboratories with Mexican investigators to identify and prosecute the criminals in these cases,
3. The creation of a fund to reward those informants who provide information leading to the arrest of the criminals in this case, and
4. Safe working conditions and transportation to and from work for the women working in the (primarily U.S.–owned) factories along the border.

What follows in this essay is a brief description of other actions various women's studies faculty at UTEP are taking to meet the needs of its unique student population and to address women's issues in this region.

Institutional Change

Our work to improve the academic institution and increase representation of female faculty is far from over. Women as a whole make up only 30 percent of tenured and tenure-track faculty at UTEP; Latinas comprise only 7 percent of tenured and tenure-track faculty. To meet student needs, we must continue to advocate with the university administration for the hiring of more Latinas. The position of director of women's studies has yet in its twenty-one-year history to be held by a scholar of color. The university administration is, however, making strides in the recruitment of Latina faculty. Last year, the History Department hired its second Chicana historian, making UTEP the only university in the nation to have two Chicana

historians on its faculty. Given that there are only twenty-four
Chicanas in the United States with Ph.D.s in history, having two
Chicanas (females) and one Chicano (male) in a department of seventeen faculty is quite an accomplishment. At a university with 69
percent Latina/o students, the representation of Latinas/os in the
faculty is nonetheless inadequate and creates an imbalanced work-
load for scholars of color.

In the fall of 2000, the university inaugurated a mentoring program for newly hired women faculty in which each mentee was
paired by professional and personal interest with two senior faculty
members, one in and one outside of her college. Senior faculty meet
regularly with junior women faculty to discuss research and publication, teaching, strategies for balancing work and family, and orientation to the university and region. While it is too early to judge the
effectiveness of the program, the feedback from junior women at this
stage is positive.

Curriculum Development

As an interdisciplinary program, Women's Studies is particularly well
equipped to address the complexities faced by UTEP students. Their
nationalities and ethnicities as well as class backgrounds bring to the
foreground the many identities that Latinas at UTEP must negotiate.
To have a majority of working-class students in the classroom means
that as professors we must be aware of the demands placed upon them.
Many of these female students come to class after, or before, eight-
hour work days; many come to class during lunch breaks from forty-
hour-a-week jobs; many are caretakers for elderly parents; and many
have children. As professors we must also acknowledge the middle-
class Mexican women from Juárez who bring different experiences to
the classroom. Socio-economic class hostilities between Chicanas from
the United States and Mexican women from Mexico present opportunities for unique pedagogical interventions. The experience they
have in common, however, is that of challenging the assumption by
many white feminist students and faculty that Chicanas and Mexican
women possess a limited feminist consciousness since "machismo" is
endemic only to Latino/a culture—a false notion, of course. It's exciting to watch cultural feminisms take hold in these classrooms among
Chicana, Mexican, Anglo American, African American, and Native
American women.

Gradually, we are transforming the Women's Studies curriculum to
be more representative of Latina and Mexicana students' experiences

and histories. The Introduction to Women's Studies course now includes segments on the history of Mexicana feminism, Chicana feminism, the suffrage movement in El Paso, the Women's Studies Program at UTEP, and contemporary women's issues on the border. Students have, for example, conducted research on the exploitation of women workers in the *maquiladoras*, where women have been made to take pregnancy tests before they were hired, and where once hired, the companies provide virtually no security assistance to help them get home late at night.

In a Gay, Lesbian/Queer Literature course, we have included a special emphasis on queer border writers. The class shows students that there are nationally known gay and lesbian writers from the region like John Rechy, Arturo Islas, and Alicia Gaspar de Alba. The course also addresses homophobia and does its own consciousness-raising on a topic that is still volatile in American society. Unfortunately, students who have attempted to revitalize a lesbian, gay, bisexual, and transgender (LGBT) organization have encountered harassment. More than once, students in the group, as well as the faculty advisor, have had their car tires slashed. The queer literature course provides a space for LGBT students to meet intellectually as well as socially since there are no other forums on campus that address queer issues.

Similarly, the History Department offered for the first time a graduate seminar on Gender and Sexuality on the Border, which explored queer history. Offering a Ph.D. in borderlands history, UTEP has the only program in the United States to emphasize border studies of the United States and Mexico. In the course, graduate students conducted research on El Paso/Juárez tracking gay, lesbian, and queer histories through the centuries. This was a daunting task; however, the students were creative as they challenged white, heteronormative sexualities in studies that explored, for example, Juárez transvestites in their workplaces, prostitution in the late nineteenth and early twentieth centuries, lesbian oral histories of the El Paso community, gay and lesbian activists of El Paso, and Mexican American women's agency in the *colonias* of El Paso County, where an estimated 72,000 people live without proper sanitation, water, or housing (Crowder 2A). Some of these studies are ongoing. The Ph.D. in borderlands history is regionally specific to the United States and Mexico and therefore draws a majority of students of color, mostly Chicano/a and Mexican nationals. A core of faculty in the department is training students whose research interests include gender, sexuality, race, and ethnicity in the borderlands; the Mexican Revolution; histories of colonial Mexico, the Southwest, Latin America, and Spain; as well as comparative world borders, to name a few.

In January 2002, the Women's Studies Program received a generous grant from the National Endowment for the Humanities to raise awareness and enrich course curriculum on the issues of gender and sexuality on the U.S.–Mexico border. Susan Rippberger of Educational Leadership and Scarlet Bowen of Women's Studies were co–primary investigators on the grant, and they brought four nationally known consultants in April 2002 to give both public talks or performances and to conduct workshops with faculty on their areas of expertise, which range from theater, literature, and history to legal and social science. Adelina Anthony, founding director of Lives United Through Community, History and Art (LUCHA) in Los Angeles, performed her original solo performance, "Mastering Sex and Tortillas." Anthony's work depicts Latina lesbian sexuality as multifaceted, joyful, and fun. Sandra Soto, assistant professor of women's studies at the University of Arizona, presented her research on racialized sexuality in film, art, and literary representations of the U.S.–Mexico border. Antonia Castañeda, associate professor and O'Conner Chair in Borderlands History at St. Mary's University, discussed the influence of Tejana migration on the making of regional history. Both Soto's and Castañeda's work evaluated critically the colonized notions of Chicana and Native American women's identity, gender, and sexuality, a topic so crucial to this region.

The speaker/workshop series concluded with a screening of Lourdes Portillo's award-winning documentary about the murders of women in Juárez, *Senorita Extraviada,* and a panel discussion of this crisis, including Elvia Arriola, associate professor of law at Northwestern University and director of the Research and Advocacy Center for Women on the Border; Patricia Ravelo, visiting professor from Mexico City; and Julia Monárrez, professor from the Colegia de la Frontera in Juárez. In addressing this topic, we took precautions not to replicate political, economic, and discursive dominance perpetuated by the United States in relation to Mexico. Speakers delivered talks in either Spanish or English, and we provided translation services for those who needed it. The speakers assessed the United States's as well as Mexico's governmental responsibility in protecting women from further harm and prosecuting the criminals, and they presented papers that promote the humanity, power, and agency of Mexicana activists, *maquila* workers, victims' rights advocates, and the families who have lost women to these horrible crimes.

In an effort to help more women in the region enhance their expertise in women's issues on the border, we expanded the scope of the Women's Studies Program by implementing a graduate certificate in women's and gender studies and developing the program's first graduate course: Interdisciplinary Feminist Theory and Methodology. We began admitting students to the program in fall 2002, and we are recruiting students from the increasing number of graduate students on campus and from the many local organizations and businesses that serve women and girls.

Connecting Theory and Practice

With these efforts to improve the institutional responsiveness and effectiveness of the Women's Studies Program, we seek to effect wider change in the area to improve nonstudents' lives, as well. Manuela Romero, assistant professor of sociology, has teamed with Tracey Yellen, a coordinator at the El Paso Young Women's Christian Association (YWCA), to conduct a research study of the needs of El Paso women and girls. The two researchers, along with many other faculty, graduate students, and community organizers, began planning and implementing the research study in February 2001. They have designed an extensive, ninety-four-question survey that covers topics like health care, education, family composition, income, well-being, and work and family balance. The questionnaire, which is written in both Spanish and English, is being given to women in El Paso of various age groups, from young adult to senior women. They are also conducting focus groups with women in different neighborhoods of El Paso, including the *colonias*. The final related study will survey resources in the area to help address the needs of local women. Once the data is collected, it will be published in a booklet and made available to nonprofit organizations, future researchers, and people who are applying for grants to benefit women and girls in this region.[2]

The projects we have undertaken at the university are beginning to stir the activist commitments of UTEP students. In fall 2001, Rocio Meza, a UTEP psychology student and women's studies minor, decided to take action by starting a campus branch of the national organization Feminist Majority Foundation. She and Marissa Chavez led the student organization. What followed were public demonstrations and protests to alert the university community to governments who refuse to take action against the violence toward women in Mexico.

Georgina Hernández and Adriana Domínguez, both UTEP theater majors, decided to organize a student production of Eve Ensler's *Vagina Monologues* in February in order to raise money for two local women's organizations, one in El Paso and another in Juárez, both of which work to protect women from physical and sexual violence. During a three-hour-long pre-show, they scheduled several university and community women to perform their songs, music, writing, and artwork, all to highlight the creative talents of women in this area.

Conclusion

At UTEP, the priorities for women's studies faculty have shifted since the 1970s and 1980s. We do not worry as much about sex discrimination in the university workplace; our focus now is to recruit and act affirmatively in terms of faculty hires and to situate women's studies both regionally and globally. There is no question in our minds that women's studies is still relevant to people's lives. The activism, curriculum revision, and public education have the potential to create a binational consciousness-raising campaign to respect and empower women and girls along the U.S.–Mexico border. We want only the support, time, and resources to accomplish all there is to do. But certainly this is nothing new in the history of women's studies.

NOTES
1. See Gladstein.
2. This study was inspired by a similar one conducted by a research group in Birmingham, Alabama. After collecting and publishing the information on women and girls in Birmingham, the research team raised money for a "Women's Fund" that helped to finance projects that addressed the women's needs discovered in the study.

WORKS CITED

Center for Institutional Evaluation. *UTEP Factbook 2001–2002.* University of Texas at El Paso, 2002.

Crowder, David. "President's Budget Includes $16 Million to Help Colonias." *El Paso Times* 8 Feb. 2002: 2A.

Gladstein, Mimi. "Deodorant of Success." *The Politics of Women's Studies: Testimony from Thirty Founding Mothers.* Ed. Florence Howe. New York: Feminist, 2000. 119–29

Valdez, Diana Washington. "Death Stalks the Border: Special Report." *El Paso Times* 23 June 2002: 1–8.

Scarlet Bowen *is director and assistant professor of women's studies at the University of El Paso. She teaches courses in feminist theory; British literature; gay, lesbian, and queer literature; and working-class women's literature. She is currently working on a manuscript entitled "Empire's Labor Lost: Working*

Women in Eighteenth-Century British Literature." **Emma Pérez** is chair and associate professor of history at the University of Texas at El Paso. She is the author of several articles on Chicana history and feminist and queer theory, as well as Gulf Dreams, a novel, and The Decolonial Imaginary: Writing Chicanas into History. She is currently completing a historical novel, "Forgetting the Alamo, or Bloody Memory," and a primary-source book of documents relationg to gender and sexuality on the U.S./Mexico border.

Doing Women's Studies on the Sly at LaGuardia Community College

J. Elizabeth Clark and Katie Hogan

You see, they had had no wars. They had had no kings, and no priests, and no aristocracies. They were sisters, and as they grew, they grew together—not by competition, but by united action.

—Charlotte Perkins Gilman, *Herland* (51)

Many feminist writers, such as Charlotte Perkins Gilman in *Herland*, Marge Piercy in *Woman on the Edge of Time*, and Suniti Namjoshi in *The Mothers of Maya Diip*, have sought to present readers with utopian visions of societies created by and for women. This work, primarily labeled science fiction because of the disjunction between everyday life and the fantasy (or a sometimes dystopic critique), seems impossible to bridge.

Contrast this fictional desire for a woman-centered world with a campus where women's studies is not "quarantined" (in the patriarchy's perspective) to a women's center or a particular space or program labeled "women's studies." Instead, the practice of women's studies is infused into the curriculum, into extracurricular activities, into the very practice of each student-faculty-staff interaction. On the very best days, this is our practice and experience of women's studies. On the more average, or the very worst days, our practice and experience of women's studies is more dystopic, like Margaret Atwood's *The Handmaid's Tale*. We are two progressive, feminist English professors committed to student-centered learning, collaborative teaching methods, and feminist pedagogy. Our two-year campus of the City University of New York, LaGuardia Community College, does not have a women's studies program but historically serves a large body of women students: 63.2 percent of the student body is female; 67 percent is non–native born; and 86 percent want to pursue their education beyond the associate's degree our institution offers.

We recognize the paradox inherent in our gendered student body and the lack of a women's studies program. However, our campus has a clear focus on general education, transfer, and job preparation.

Within the particular context of our work, we do women's studies all of the time, regardless of institutional labels. It is our firm belief that by introducing women's studies at a grassroots level, we will begin to build an institutional need for a women's studies program that cannot be ignored. Books like Paula Caplan's now-canonical *Lifting a Ton of Feathers* and Jan Zlotnik Schmidt's *Women/Writing/Teaching* have documented the male-centered climate of colleges and universities and the difficult working environment created for female faculty members.[1] A re-reading of these texts, however, provides room for arguing that the very same climate that often proves oppressive for women academics can be equally oppressive for women students pursuing their degrees amid immensely unsupportive family obligations and often challenging financial circumstances. Many of our students are single parents juggling child care, work, and school obligations with tenuous success. Others confront patriarchal attitudes in their families and communities and have been socialized in traditional gender, racial, and sexual roles. The experience of one of our students, Erica, embodies some of these obstacles.[2] A student in Clark's Composition I class, Erica entered the term timid and reluctant to participate in the discussion section of the course. During the semester, however, as she gained more self-confidence, Erica developed into a classroom leader for our research project. This transformation, not unusual to many teachers, is interesting in light of Erica's position in her family.

Erica—Living as 'The Only Daughter': Clark's Encounter

One evening, going home on the crowded subway, Clark was literally pushed into Erica. At our busy school, faculty and students sometimes have meaningful, productive experiences with one another and then, as the unrelenting course of the year wears on, we never run into one another again. The chance meeting on the subway gave Clark and Erica the opportunity to catch up. During the conversation, however, Erica was thoroughly preoccupied with the time. "It's after dark," she commented. Clark thought Erica was perhaps nervous about walking down a dark street, but Erica quickly reminded Clark that her father, a fairly recent immigrant to the United States from Pakistan, required her to come home directly after school to cook and clean. He was opposed to his daughter's educational goals of earning a B.A. and working in the business world, but the economic circumstances of the family and the fact that Erica was an only child had created some room for her to pursue a path that otherwise would have been closed to her.

On that particular evening, she was running late because she had stopped at the library to finish a research paper. She asked Clark if she remembered the time she had to write a note to Erica's father because Erica's uncle had seen her talking with a boy on the street. ("Please sign the note Dr. Clark without your first name," she had asked, thinking her father would assume the professor was a man.) The young man was a member of our class and we were on a field trip, so Clark was able to certify that Erica was appropriately "chaperoned."

"I don't think my father will ever be like Sandra Cisneros' dad," she joked as she got off the train. Her brief reference to Cisneros's "Only Daughter"—a story in which Cisneros relates her difficulties pursuing a career in writing because of her father's disapproval and the turn in his attitude toward her work as she gained some success—was a poignant reminder of the gaps between the classroom and the pressing familial and cultural constraints that face many of our students, particularly the women, when they go home at the end of the day.

Erica's situation demonstrates the "sly" nature of our work: She made a valuable connection between her life at home and "performance" as a daughter, her school life, and the many other women who face similar struggles. For Erica, Cisneros became a touchstone, a guide, and provided an empowering moment of realization that other futures are possible. Thus, for both the students and faculty at our school, we "do" women's studies on the sly, carving out precious space in the classroom, office visits, and chance meetings to teach women's studies.

The Nomadic Locus of Our Work

The various ways that we pursue women's studies at our institution despite not having a program include employing feminist/collaborative teaching methods in all our courses, from Basic Writing to Composition I to Creative Writing; using the college's pre-existing structure of learning communities to create women's studies liberal arts clusters; and coordinating our administrative and mentoring work—one of us is the faculty director of the Student Center for Women and the other is the mentor of the Straight and Gay Alliance (SAGA)—in such a way that it extends the themes, objectives, and methods in our courses. For example, we have been able to contribute to a sense of shared feminist/queer community by cosponsoring events that are linked to our course goals and materials. We also participate in the Women's Studies Committee of the Department of English, which has a strong commitment to the use of multicultural texts; all of the members of the committee (and most of the members of our department) base our composition and literature courses on texts that teach, complicate, and challenge traditional notions of gender, sexuality, race, and the constructions of gender and sexual identity. Through our teaching, programming, and mentoring, we have found that doing women's studies outside of a formal program is possible, but we also recognize that through a formal women's studies program, we would be able to accomplish much more.

By infusing feminist principles into groups and classes as diverse as SAGA, Basic Writing, Introduction to Sociology, and Composition I, however, students at our college are introduced to women's studies and feminism through a myriad of experiences. In the classroom, they experience feminist pedagogy: Team projects, collaborative writing projects, and in-class sharing of writing are some of the activities that fall under this rubric. Students also write about, and conduct research on, women's and diversity topics through activities and approaches that are clearly in keeping with the work of most women's studies programs. For example, in a liberal arts cluster on the modern American family, students study the impact of the U.S. women's movement on traditional gender arrangements within the heterosexual family structure.

In another venue, the Women's Center, students are exposed to talks and presentations that augment the themes and materials they are studying in the classroom. A class unit on gender, race, class, and homophobia in popular culture was linked to a panel discussion of scholars and artists, followed by a film screening of *Hip-Hop: A Culture of Influence* at the center. Through these classroom and extra-classroom experiences, students are strategically introduced to gender, race, class, and sexuality studies, even though they have not signed up for a women's studies class.

The Women's Center and SAGA also provide social and political forums for exploring issues often discussed in women's studies classes. For example, last semester the SAGA students explored and researched the issues related to biased blood donation regulations enforced by the Federal Department of Agriculture (FDA). SAGA challenged those regulations with a research-based information campaign and meeting with local blood bank representatives to arrange for a joint letter-writing campaign. While students might have researched and discussed these issues in a classroom, they instead used SAGA, which is organized through the Student Activities Division; therefore, their political action campaign reached far beyond the parameters of organized, institutionalized learning. Students in groups like SAGA and the Women's Center are able to apply what they have learned in order to effect social change.

Nothing to Fall Back On: Hogan's Story

A recent teaching experience illustrates one of the disadvantages of working without an academic institutional structure committed to women's and diversity studies. Every fall semester since 1999, Hogan has taught in a liberal arts cluster called The Sociology of the Family. This cluster is composed of Composition I, Writing the Research Paper, Introduction to Sociology, and Sociology of the Family. As a unit, these courses encourage students to think analytically and historically about the family and to explore social issues affecting families and alternative family structures. All four courses approach these themes through an analysis of race, gender, sexual orientation, and nationality, and all four courses include material on lesbian and/or gay families and identities.

This semester stands out from the others because two students from the cluster marched to the English Department to report that Hogan had been "promoting homosexuality" and showing films on "oral sex." As evidence, they brought with them one of the course texts, *Revolutionary Voices: A Multicultural Queer Youth Anthology*, and referred to one of the course films, *The Wedding Banquet*, directed by Ang Lee.

Interracial families, single-parent families, gender arrangements within families, immigrant families, families experiencing racism or domestic violence—all of these topics were acceptable, but not lesbian and gay relationships, sexuality, and families. Two brave students wrote their research papers on gay topics—the consequences of the closet and the effects of school homophobia on all children—but the student who wrote his paper on homophobia in elementary school met with some hostile comments from the class, one of which went something like this: "My mother hates gay people and no teacher is going to go against my mother."

Hogan began talking to colleagues about what had happened: the sociology professor who was teaching in the cluster with her; the faculty member assigned to her as a mentor; and her coauthor, Clark. Through these discussions, we came up with a plan to expose the students to the college's official statement on pluralism and diversity, which included the terms *sexual orientation, homophobia,* and *heterosexism* as well as *racism, sexism, classism,* and other forms of oppression. We would conduct an examination of the college's "Declaration of Pluralism" in the context of a previously scheduled Women's Center–Women's Studies Committee event entitled "Why Value Diversity?"

The event was organized to celebrate students' academic course-work on various multicultural texts, ranging from Esmeralda Santiago's novel *América's Dream* to students' research papers on homophobia. Evoking the authority of the college's "Declaration of Pluralism" and using the Women's Center event illustrate the need for formal, official, college-wide validation of diversity issues. Without the college's official statement, and without the Women's Center and Women's Studies Committee, Hogan felt she would have had nothing to fall back on.

While Hogan did not feel safe exploring her students' trip to the English Department to "report" her or their active homophobia by herself, the college's statement and these structures created a way to address the issue of homophobia with the help of supportive feminists. It also allowed all involved, from students to professors, to explore a central feminist concept, the "matrix of oppression." For example, after one student gave her presentation on homophobia and violence and another student read her final exam on the issue of domestic violence in *América's Dream*, Clark asked the audience to note the similar response of violence toward marginalized groups in each text.

What we believe this coordinated response to issues of oppression suggests is that formal statements, centers, and programs of study that validate what professors are doing in the classroom are indispensable. Without some kind of official, formal program, it is harder to build feminist community for faculty, students, and staff, especially in times of crisis. Although we were able to do this because our college has a Women's Center, a Women's Studies Committee, and an official statement on pluralism, there is no formal academic structure to encourage pedagogy and content based on women's studies. As a result, some students often question why they have to explore the intersections of gender, race, class, and sexuality in composition and literature courses.

In addition, women's studies programs on college and university campuses throughout the country often serve as symbols of acceptance and support of women's and diversity issues. In a 2000 National Women's Studies Association document, "What Programs Need: Essential Resources for Women's Studies Programs," women's studies programs report that they receive a large volume of requests for information and assistance from members of the academic and nonacademic communities and from the media on a wide range of concerns related to women's and diversity issues. Such responses suggest that women's studies programs serve an educational and supportive function that is crucial to change within academia and in the surrounding and even national community. They also lend support to faculty members in distress.

Settling for Sly?

While we can see the benefits of a women's studies program at our institution, a question that we continue to ask ourselves is this: Would a student like Erica *initially* see the value of such a program? Would she, given her father's control over many areas of her life, have even enrolled in a women's studies course? In a sense, by infusing women's and gender studies into all of our courses, programming, and mentoring, we suspect that we are able to reach students who would never sign up for a women's studies course. Many students will not enroll in a liberal arts cluster with the word "women" in the title but they might sign up for a liberal arts cluster about "family"—even though the teaching method and many of the materials in both clusters are similar. We also know that many of our students could thrive in a women's studies course, including our male students who, like the women, grapple with rigid ideas of gender, racism, homophobia, tradition, and poverty, but we are not sure if our students know this.

We are not arguing that our college should not have a women's studies program, however, nor are we suggesting that "sly" is a substitute for one. Instead, we are arguing that our college (perhaps like many others) needs both; it needs a women's studies program that offers students a consistent and coherent curriculum to explore the scholarship of gender, race, class, and sexuality in light of their college coursework and their personal experiences and history. Such a program is not in contradiction with our institution's focus on academic preparation for transfer and employment. Women's and diversity studies are central subjects for intellectual inquiry, for practical functioning in an increasingly multicultural world, and for contributing to progressive social change. In addition, our college needs what it already has: an innovative faculty and student body that explores women's studies in spaces where many may think such activity doesn't belong.

So while we have had mixed success in doing women's studies without a formal program, we have also had surprising moments of genuine connection and exchange with students and each other. Therefore we feel it is important to acknowledge what we, and our students, have been able to accomplish by doing women's studies on the sly. "Sly" becomes a trickster figure for us, someone who operates at the level of having "no program" while simultaneously sowing the seeds for a program indistinguishable from the mission of the college. We suspect that our teaching experience is similar to that of many others working in small colleges, community colleges, and colleges without a serious commitment to women's studies; we hope our experiences will inspire others whose situations are similar to ours.

NOTES

1. See also Berenice Malka Fisher's *No Angel in the Classroom* and Frances A. Maher and Mary Kay Thomson Tetreault's *The Feminist Classroom*.
2. The student's name has been changed for this article.

WORKS CITED

Atwood, Margaret. The Handmaid's Tale. Bostn: Houghton Mifflin, 1986.

Caplan, Paula. *Lifting a Ton of Feathers: A Woman's Guide for Surviving in the Academic World*. Buffalo: University of Toronto Press, 1993.

Cisneros, Sandra. "Only Daughter." *Latina: Women's Voices from the Borderlans*. Ed. Lillian Castillo Speed. New York: Simon, 1995. 157–59.

Fisher, Berenice Malka. *No Angel in the Classroom: Teaching Through Feminist Discourse*. Lanham, Md.: Rowman and Littlefield, 2001.

Gilman, Charlotte Perkins. *Herland*. 1979. New York: Dover, 1998.

Hartmann, Susan M. "What Programs Need: Essential Resources for Women's Studies Programs." Revised by Dorothy C. Miller and Magdalena Garcia-Pinto. Online, available: http://www.nwsa.org/resources.htm. June 20, 2002.

Maher, Frances A., and Mary Kat Thomson Tetreault. *The Feminist Classroom*. New York: Basic, 1994.

Namjoshi, Suniti. *The Mothers of Maya Diip*. London: Women's, 1989.

Piercy, Marge. *Woman on the Edge of Time*. New York: Knopf, 1976.

Santiago, Esmeralda, ed. *América's Dream*. New York: Harper Collins, 1996.

Schmidt, Jan Zlotnik. *Women/Writing/Teaching*. Albany: State University of New York Press, 1998.

Sonnie, Amy, ed. *Revolutionary Voices: A Multicultural Queer Youth Anthology*. Los Angeles: Alyson Books, 2000.

J. Elizabeth Clark is assistant professor of English and faculty mentor for the Straight and Gay Alliance at LaGuardia Community College of the City University of New York. She is the managing editor of Radical Teacher and is currently working on a manuscript on post-protease AIDS poetry. **Katie Hogan** *is associate professor of English and faculty director of the Student Center for Women at LaGuardia Community College of the City University of New York. She is author of* Women Take Care: Gender, Race, and the Culture of AIDS *(Cornell UP, 2001) and coeditor of* Gendered Epidemic: Representations of Women in the Age of AIDS *(Routledge, 1998).*

Using Women's Studies to Change the University for All Women

Report from University of Wisconsin–Superior

Suzanne C. Griffith

Women's studies has grown out of the political activism of the 1960s and 1970s. As we have moved into the academy, our activism and unwillingness to accept the status quo has been a source of contention, both inside and outside of women's studies. We face the question, Can we join the academy, present ourselves as a legitimate scholarly discipline, and simultaneously work to change it? From my perspective, being part of women's studies means that we must engage in teaching and scholarship and in activism for change. Indeed, our activism informs the discipline—its academic, research, and pedagogical components—keeping it vibrant and relevant.

Background

Within this framework of activism linked with academic legitimacy, I present the specific case of women's studies at the University of Wisconsin (UW)–Superior and our development of an activist format for addressing women's concerns within the university. First, to understand our situation, one needs to appreciate that UW–Superior is part of the University of Wisconsin System, which encompasses thirteen comprehensive universities, thirteen two-year colleges, and a statewide extension program that also has a chancellor and the usual entourage. The system is governed by the regents and the UW System president and staff, who are based in Madison. In 1989, the regents approved the development of a system-wide Women's Studies Consortium Office with a part-time director to support women's studies programs across all the campuses. The consortium sponsors annual conferences, an extensive library, outreach programs, and regular meetings of the women's studies coordinators from all of the programs. These meetings allow for women's studies faculty and staff to get together, compare notes, provide support and consultation, and, when needed, take action together. Such action took place in the 1998–99 academic year.

Despite ten years of accomplishments, members of the consortium sensed that the momentum behind improving conditions for women across the university had stalled. Data gathered over several months led us to the following analysis. Faculty women, while increasing in number, were not making expected inroads into leadership circles. Academic staff women (adjunct instructors and administrative personnel) were carrying increasingly heavy teaching loads under annual contracts rather than moving up into tenure-track positions or were pooled at the lower end of the positions and pay scale. Women students cited ongoing problems with unequal services and programs, a lack of female role models on campus and in the curriculum, and unsafe and hostile climates. Classified staff women (unionized employees) felt unrecognized and unheard. In summary, while the university campuses had made space for more women and for women's studies, the policies, procedures, and values that govern university campuses continued to reflect the established ways.

Consortium members moved directly to asking, How can we move ahead? How can we warm up the chilly climate for women at all levels? With the leadership of Jackie Ross, then Women's Studies Consortium director, we worked out a plan for meeting with the president of the UW System, Katherine Lyall, in the spring of 1998. We also joined forces with the United Council of UW Students' Women's Issues Group and together requested from the president an in-depth study on the status of women (students, classified, academic staff, and faculty).

President Lyall convened a system-wide Committee on the Status of Women and charged it with identifying existing challenges to women across the system and devising a number of practical and achievable recommendations that would improve current conditions. A year and a half later, the committee concluded that

> substantial progress has been made, but that very significant needs and concerns persist. Moreover, it appears that many of the most important problems will not be susceptible to piecemeal solutions, but will only *be solved when the UW System and each of its institutions have in place a comprehensive system for addressing women's concerns* and pursuing the goal of equity for women in the University. (Committee on the Status of Women in the University of Wisconsin System 20; italics added)

Five broad recommendations were made:

1. Expand educational opportunities for women students;
2. Increase the hiring, promotion, and retention of women faculty, academic staff, and classified staff;
3. Make the learning and working environment more welcoming to women, especially women of color and women who identify as lesbian, bisexual, or transgendered;
4. Provide conditions that allow for balancing work and personal life; and
5. Create an effective organizational structure for improving the status of women in the University of Wisconsin System. (iii–iv)

This last recommendation established a UW System Office on the Status of Women; supported the establishment of committees on the status of women at each UW institution; and mandated that each institution develop, by January 2001, a plan that addressed these five key areas. The report has the potential for changing the underlying traditional male structure of the university to address the needs and embody the values of its women members. But without action and follow-through, it is just a report with equal potential to gather dust.

Superior's Process and Actions

In 1997–98, I was co-chair of the UW System Women's Studies Consortium and one of the members who met with Lyall. I was also involved in women's studies on my campus, UW–Superior. In the fall of 1998, the Women's Studies Committee at UW–Superior decided to move ahead by conducting our own assessment and, beginning in January 1999, holding our own focus groups. Initially, students and staff met in two groups, but we changed the format to four groups after classified and academic staff complained that they did not feel heard in the larger arena. Meetings were held over a five-month period. Those attending the meetings never presumed that they spoke for all the women within their group, but they did represent a cross-section. While these focus groups were held with the support and encouragement of the administration, women in the groups still requested anonymity in the report.

Our campus report was written over the summer and presented to the individual groups for feedback and rewriting in the fall of 1999. A few of the issues specific to each group are presented here:

Students: lack of reasonable accommodations by professors for students who are pregnant or new parents; day care closes too early for students with evening and night classes; homophobic attitudes and jokes are condoned.

Classified Staff: opinions are not sought; physical conditions are uncomfortable and equipment is hand-me-down.

Academic Staff: women are clustered at the lower end of the ladder and pay scale on year-to-year contracts; women lack mentors and opportunities for promotion and professional development.

Faculty: spousal and partner employment are not seen as important; problems are systemic and entrenched, making equal and full participation difficult.

Through the process, we became sensitized to the difficulties in each others' roles, and when we looked at the big picture, many common issues and concerns were similar across groups:

1. Day care, maternity leave, and parenting issues need to be accommodated;
2. Traditional male-centered values and environments do not reflect the present representation of women on campus and their concerns and needs;
3. Mentoring and career guidance for women are often ignored;
4. Sexism, heterosexism, devaluing, and harassment are still experienced broadly; and
5. There is not an effective mechanism for addressing these and other grievances. (Committee on the Status of Women, University of Wisconsin–Superior 5)

We felt that the situation was not bleak in every department and area, but the fact that these concerns occurred at all, let alone so broadly, definitely hurt not just the women but *everyone.* The report said, "It poisons the climate and decreases productivity and vitality. Additionally, when people perceive broadly that there is no effective way to address these concerns, morale is further undercut" (7).

Two recommendations completed our report: that the university set up a Standing Committee on Women's Issues with representatives from all four areas to work with administration and hire a women's issues coordinator, on par with the multicultural coordinator, to

cooperate with the committee and administration on these issues and
create change.

In late September 1999, prior to the system report finalization,
UW–Superior women's studies leaders met with the UW–Superior
chancellor and provost to discuss the report. The reception to our
findings was cool and defensive; they felt that the efforts they had
already made were unrecognized and unappreciated. They asked that
we resurvey the students. When we brought that request back to the
committee, the women student leaders quickly circulated a petition
and then met with the administration. They presented over three hundred student signatures in support of the report's findings. After that,
a group representing all four constituencies continued the dialogue
with the administration on how we might proceed to improve the campus climate. We never did resurvey the campus, and subsequent meetings with administration members were productive. While women's
studies faculty had provided the original impetus and leadership, it
was the united front that moved it forward.

Our points were further strengthened by the formal presentation
of the UW System report to the regents and chancellors early in 2000.
The similarity of issues across the system, as presented by the system
report, and the recommendations made allowed us to move ahead
quickly. Shortly after, we asked for and received approval from faculty,
academic staff, and student senates to develop a Standing Committee
on Women's Issues. Each group appointed two members. Classified
women staff looked to their union for appointment. However, appointment to and involvement in committees like this are unusual for classified staff. Local leadership said that those who were interested could
work out who would serve. Still, those who did had to receive permission from their supervisors, even when formally appointed by the
chancellor.

The Coordinator of Women and Gender Issues

By late spring of 2000, the Standing Committee on Women's Issues
had advertised and hired a woman for a half-time position as coordinator for women's and gender issues.[1] Her role was clearly to be an
advocate, activist, and outreach educator and to put women's needs
and gender issues on the table as part of the campus discussions. In
the advertising and interviewing for this position, our intent was to
find someone who knew the academy, would have some legitimacy
within it, and had experience as an activist.

The job description laid out several responsibilities, primarily to coordinate the activities of the Standing Committee on Women's Issues; work with different constituencies on campus on issues of concern to them related to improving the campus climate and to promoting gender equity; increase awareness of and provide education on related issues, including lesbian, gay, bisexual, and transgender (LGBT) issues; coordinate activities with the system's coordinator for the status of women; and help to present women/gender concerns to appropriate institutional bodies and individuals and seek solutions early, before concerns multiply. To further strengthen the position, the coordinator reports directly to the provost and attends the provost's staff meetings. To show additional support for the position, the provost offered a half-time teaching appointment, creating a full-time job for the coordinator.

While the coordinator and the standing committee are not directed or overseen by the Women's Studies Committee, there is a clear two-way connection. The Women's Studies Committee is primarily academically focused around the women's studies minor and is interdisciplinary. Ninety percent of its present courses are crosslisted, and these are taught by faculty committed to women's studies. The Women's Studies Committee serves in the capacity of a departmental program committee, even while the program is "housed" in the History, Politics, and Society Department. Twenty percent of the campus faculty either teach in or actively support the program, which gives it a firm institutional grounding.

Because of their interests, the coordinator and the faculty members of the standing committee are all members of the Women's Studies Committee. Numerous issues are now discussed at Women's Studies Committee meetings that reach beyond academics and previous areas of concern. The faculty has been able to bring individual and committee support to critical issues the coordinator and standing committee have identified over the last two years. It has provided an appropriate level of involvement and a powerful partnership.

The standing committee has worked on the issues identified in 1999 by dividing them into four focus areas: day care, health services for students, affirmative action procedural clarifications, and climate issues for women and LGBT persons. Day care provides an example of how we have been able to initiate change on campus. While day care is available on campus and our current center is seen as providing good care, its hours are limited, there is a long waiting list, and financial assistance for low-income students is almost unavailable. The day care service is utilized by all constituents of the campus, male and female, and is an important factor in our recruitment and retention of students and staff. The building it is in, however, is an inappropriate site and is slated to be demolished. A recent campus presentation included plans for tearing it down and building a new one to house faculty offices and classrooms. There was no reference made to day care services. Indeed, day care is the type of service ignored by traditional long-range planning, budgeting, space allotments, financial aid, and the like. It is also exactly the type of service to which both UW System and UW–Superior Status of Women reports point as needed to make the university climate better for women.

There is a campus day care committee but it has not felt empowered to tackle the above issues. As the Standing Committee on Women's Issues, we have been able to get a task force appointed (spring 2002) that is empowered to work on long-range planning and a broader service array. It includes some members of the campus day care committee, the standing committee, staff and students with children, and other interested parties.

The other three areas have also benefited from our activism. Health services are limited, not well publicized, and inadequately housed. A new task force is being established to work on health care issues. A confusing tangle of procedures plague affirmative action, each of which offers different methods for pursuing complaints depending on the issue and plaintiff. These problems are slowly being untangled. These are just some of the problems that comprise the complex and difficult-to-address climate for women on our campus. The Standing Committee's close relationship with the Women's Studies Committee and the Affirmative Action Committee has allowed for shared support and activities on many of these concerns. In partnership, and by having a coordinator who keeps these issues in focus for us, we are making changes in areas where we previously had been stymied.

The coordinator not only attends the Women's Studies Committee meetings but is an active participant, as well as a scholar and lecturer in women's studies. She is also a member of the campus Affirmative Action Committee and its subcommittee on Retention of Diverse Staff and Faculty. Her regular access to the provost and position on the provost's staff, as well as her access to the chancellor, provides her with a source of legitimacy when she is working with other campus groups. Her broad networking activities mean that she is connected around campus and is able to bring an advocacy view to the discussion. Her perspective is not always new, nor is she usually the only member at a meeting with that view, but whether on her own or with others, she is able to continually put feminist topics on the table for discussion in a persistent and deliberate manner.

Can We Sustain the Momentum for Change?

In some respects, the two status reports (UW System and UW–Superior) show how little has changed in higher education and how hard it is to change the academy. It also becomes apparent from a historical perspective[2] that unless there is a desire for change at the top and throughout the institution, nothing much will change because, ultimately, hiring, reviews, supervision, and curriculum are all decentralized. Decisions and power come back to the departments and to those wanting change and willing to work for it at this level. Our very presence—in increasing numbers, positions, and diversity in the academy—while crucial, must also be accompanied by raising our feminist voices, questioning, and acting at all levels.

These necessities are borne out by Jane Roland Martin who, in *Coming of Age in Academe,* repeatedly shows that being let onto the field does not insure that the field is level, being invited to participate does not mean the rules change, and A + B continues to basically equal A, when what we want is A + B = C. The scorn and derision that once met women's desire to simply become students in the academy has changed its focus to feminist scholarship, to the inclusion of women's topics and issues in the curriculum, and to questions of what is considered knowledge (180). She calls for patience, persistence, and a wide range of political action. At the same time, Martin recognizes that change will only happen if women around the world decide that the ideal of gender equity is a cause worth striving for.

At UW–Superior, our history of networking and coalition building has been crucial to our efforts. Just as we have actively supported the goals of the Multicultural Affairs' staff for diversifying the campus and improving the climate for people of color, so they have stood up for us. Just as faculty has reached out to include and support classified and academic staff and students, staff and students have reciprocated. This kind of collaboration binds our efforts; progress in one area becomes progress for us all. This may not insure our staying power but it strengthens our chances.

In 1998, UW–Superior Women's Studies Committee members decided not to wait for the UW System's assessment to be completed but moved ahead and supported activities that led to the development of the Women's and Gender Office on this campus. Some women's studies faculty on other UW campuses were bypassed and left out of their campus's planning. On other campuses, women's studies faculty were included as partners or as minor players. From our perspective, our past activism has been instrumental to our present efforts at reshaping this university for all women and will remain crucial to our future successes.

NOTES

Part of this article was presented at the National Women's Studies Association 2001 Annual Conference in Minneapolis with Dianna Hunter, University of Wisconsin–Superior, and Louis Root-Robbins, University of Wisconsin System. My sincere appreciation to Hunter for her research and editing assistance with this article.

1. See http://frontpage.uwsuper.edu/wgi.
2. See Judith Glazer-Raymo's *Shattering the Myths* and Jane Roland Martin's *Coming of Age in Academe,* as well as *The Woman-Centered University,* edited by Melanie McCoy and JoAnn DiGeorgio-Lutz.

WORKS CITED

Committee on the Status of Women in the University of Wisconsin System, University of Wisconsin Initiative on the Status of Women. *Equality for Women in the University of Wisconsin System: A Focus for Action in the Year 2000.* 25 October 1999.

Committee on the Status of Women, University of Wisconsin–Superior. *Status of Women Report.* 17 September 1999.

Glazer-Raymo, Judith. "Implementing Change: Campus Commissions and Feminist Pedagogy." *Shattering the Myths: Women in Academe.* Baltimore: Johns Hopkins UP, 1991. 165–95.

Martin, Jane Roland. *Coming of Age in Academe: Rekindling Women's Hopes and Reforming the Academy.* New York: Routledge, 2000.

McCoy, Melanie, and JoAnn DiGeorgio-Lutz, eds. *The Woman-Centered University: Interdisciplinary Perspectives.* Lanham, MD: UP of America, 1999.

Suzanne C. Griffith is associate professor in the graduate Counseling and Psychological Professions Department at the University of Wisconsin– Superior. She publishes in the areas of women's issues, especially the intersection of race, gender, and class, and actively works to increase awareness of psychological violence and decrease its incidence. She chairs the Standing Committee on the Status of Women.

Women's Studies Without a Women's Studies Program

The Case of Hostos Community College

Jerilyn Fisher

Speaking to Smith College seniors in 1979, Adrienne Rich asked, "What does a woman need to know to become a self-conscious, self-defining human being?" In response, Rich passionately and cogently argued for the rationale and purpose still served by women's studies today:

> Doesn't she need a knowledge of her own history, of her much-politi-cized female body, of the creative genius of the past—the skills and crafts and techniques and visions possessed by women in other times and cultures and how they have been rendered anonymous, cen-sured, interrupted, devalued? . . . Without such education, women have lived and continue to live in ignorance of our collective con-text, vulnerable to the projections of men's fantasies about us as they appear in art, in literature, in the sciences, in the media, in the so-called humanistic studies. (1–2)

Students reap the most durable effects, such as the learning that Rich describes, after spending not just one semester exploring subject mat-ter from a feminist perspective; rather, the greatest gains come with longer term, in-depth examinations of women's historical accom-plishments, feminine socialization and cultural images, gender bias as it intersects with other forms of social prejudice, and the male-cen-teredness of traditional constructs of knowledge (Porter and Eileenchild 33; Rothenberg 18; Stimpson 35).

Readily available testimony speaks to students' personal and intel-lectual growth under the continuing tutelage of women's studies fac-ulty (Brush et al.; Butler; Castellano; Culley et al.; Hoffman; hooks; Omolade; Russell). One might well question, therefore, why commu-nity colleges in particular—where adult female students often consti-tute a significant majority—would not more commonly provide support for women's studies as a permanent academic offering that helps students supplant stereotypes and ignorance with informed, far-reaching feminist analyses and perspectives. Yet, among the eight hundred–plus programs offering concentrations or degrees in women's studies nationwide, only a handful of community colleges are represented.[1] More often than not, feminist educators working at community colleges engage students in women's studies without the backing of a visible, sequenced curriculum; without the continuity that even a modest budget line would provide; without structures for collaborating with like-minded colleagues equally committed to advancing feminist learning and empowerment.

Florence Howe's early study, *Seven Years Later*, documents what is minimally necessary for women's studies to achieve legitimacy as an academic discipline. Howe reports that it must have "some formal relationship, including a line budget, a paid administrator, and a curriculum which moves through committees into an official catalogue" (21). As one among many who teach women's studies without these foundational blocks in place, I borrow from Adrienne Rich to ask, What does a women's studies teacher and scholar—one who tries to facilitate feminist education without a women's studies program in place—need to keep in mind to sustain her efforts?

Like most of us, what I do best as an academic brings together the work that I know well and most love. Having earned my undergraduate and graduate degrees in the fields of women's studies and literary studies (B.A., 1974, from the State University of New York at Binghamton, the first granted there in women's studies), I have attempted to make contributions in these areas *sans* a women's studies program that would help nurture my passions and goals. To hold my grounding daily, I find myself referring to the following maxims, which may be useful to others in similar situations.

Start Where You Are but Look Beyond Present Limits: Use Successes in Sister-Institutions as a Guide

Where I am: At City University of New York's Hostos Community College, located in the South Bronx; our students range in age from late adolescence to retirement. They represent countries, cultures, and languages across the globe; almost in every case our students are first-generation undergraduates from families that can be described as poor, working poor, and aspiring middle class. They take their seats in class differently prepared for college-level work: Some arrive as already skilled readers and writers, open-minded, ready for critical thinking, curious; some come with apparent intellectual capacity but insufficient previous opportunity or encouragement to have tended that quality in themselves; some come with desire to earn a diploma but show extremely weak academic preparation. Over 75 percent of students at Hostos Community College are female, most between twenty-two and forty years of age. These demographics are reflected similarly at other City University of New York (CUNY) community colleges.[2]

Each of CUNY's senior colleges offers a women's studies concentration, minor, or baccalaureate degree. At a majority of these campuses, a women's studies director receives some administrative release time; faculty generally teach women's studies while also assigned to a traditional academic department. Among CUNY's six community colleges, only Kingsborough Community College boasts a full-fledged, funded concentration in women's studies with administrative release time for two directors, an office, a budget, and college assistants.[3]

The structure and breadth of Kingsborough's Women's Studies program can serve as a model for community colleges elsewhere. For instance, the program has established a Curriculum Committee to review discipline-based courses that will be crosslisted under Women's Studies; a separate advisory board, drawn from discipline-based faculty teaching in the Women's Studies program, considers advisement issues, policy, and procedure. Having two Women's Studies committees with discrete functions and different members would seem to maximize faculty participation and thus enhance faculty commitment to the concentration. At Kingsborough, as elsewhere among CUNY's community colleges, women's studies courses are taught in the disciplines; there exists no interdisciplinary introductory course.

For those of us teaching at other community colleges, the Kingsborough program seems exemplary and enviable, surely. Referring to this model, those of us "without" can imagine and advocate for new possibilities in women's studies, projecting our institutions beyond present confines. Indeed, we can draw upon sister institutions' successes nationwide as we attempt discussion, once again, with administrators who may express resistance to building a concentration or program, mistakenly considering women's studies to have little prospect for practical value at a community college.

In response to my annual campaign to advocate for women's studies on our campus, I was once asked to develop a survey to assess the impact of women's studies courses students had taken at Hostos. Overwhelmingly, respondents cited the value of making connections between ideas they were encountering for the first time and the realities of their own lives. One twenty-six-year-old student raised in Mexico expressed a sentiment echoed by others:

After studying Jane Eyre, I am more committed than ever to follow my dreams for myself, even though my family thinks my "job" should be to find a husband and "settle down." But I won't let my traditional father pressure me into what he thinks every woman needs, pushing me far from my dream career—to be a journalist. Charlotte Brontë would be proud to know how she influenced me!

A younger student wrote about her joy in getting to know others who feel as strongly as she does about women's rights. Yet another woman, age forty-two, spoke of her academic pursuits and perseverance against the odds modeling, for her two teenage daughters, women's independence and thirst for intellectual stimulation.

Comments such as these accumulate as abundant evidence in favor of teaching women's studies to nontraditional students. But this commitment, when unsupported institutionally, of necessity weakens from the pull of many built-in difficulties that characterize community college students' lives, particularly in an urban setting. For instance, our students suffer financial constraints that influence the editions and number of texts we can reasonably order for each course; students' obligations for earning money and caring for children outside the classroom cannot help but affect the amount of reading we assign. Our students typically arrive in class less familiar with theory than other undergraduates might be, which usually means proceeding quite slowly over conceptual terrain, thus delimiting the ground we can travel in a single semester. In proposing a women's studies concentration or program, one must take into account some of these "real life" factors that will shape what can be reasonably expected in both introductory level courses and electives.

Possibly the most difficult problem for fostering women's studies on a campus without a program in place is not being able to count on departments' offering courses consistently. This seriously impedes sequenced learning in the discipline. Moreover, without institutional support for faculty development in women's studies, promoting an intellectual community focused on women's studies scholarship becomes extremely difficult, as does fostering coalitions among colleagues who might also be the best-positioned to reach out to potentially interested students. Finally, there is a problem experienced by community college faculty in particular: Since we must always take on weighty teaching loads in subjects other than women's studies, we find it especially challenging to devote the time needed for keeping up with the ever-burgeoning body of feminist scholarship and theory.

As we all know, Virginia Woolf once proclaimed that for creativity to thrive women need money and rooms of their own. Certainly, Woolf's assertion applies to women's studies: Where there is a budget and office space, there is visibility and permanence. Still, a strong cadre of women's studies faculty, like myself, who teach without programmatic support, persevere for the simple reason that teaching women's studies to remarkable students such as we have at Hostos Community College provides motivation for continuing the uphill struggle.

No Matter What Else, Teach Women's Studies

As feminist educators in settings that do not offer the women's studies courses we might like (most) to teach, we should not be shy about putting gender (and other identity issues) at the center of our discipline-based courses. For example, in introductory literature classes, I introduce students to women's studies through reading and writing assignments. Moreover, I use feminist pedagogies in my classrooms: building trust for authentic exchange; engaging in cooperative learning; seeing connections between women's studies and women's everyday struggles for equality and social progress. Whatever the subject I am teaching, no matter the size of the group, the classroom becomes a place to facilitate feminist consciousness-raising, helping students bridge theory and practice, analysis and activism (Schniedewind 25).

Noting how interested students become as we examine gender bias and gender images, I recently decided to convert a traditional first-year composition course into a survey course in women's studies. Advertised by flyer and word-of-mouth, this expository writing class features studies of masculinity and femininity and thus encourages both women's and men's inclusion. Students soon learn that to study about women's history and women's lives often means speaking and reading in relation to the men we know: our (grand)fathers, brothers, lovers, friends, sons. Organized as an interdisciplinary course, this section of college composition offers me the chance to teach an introductory women's studies class where none exists in the college catalog. Since teachers of first-year writing typically assign a range of interdisciplinary essays and shape assignments based on both personal experience and research, a composition course is especially well-suited for adaptation to women's studies. I use a women's studies textbook that presents the material thematically, calling attention to the field of women's studies, discussing its social and historical origins within the women's movement(s).

Take Any Opportunity to Put Women's Studies on the Table

To jump-start discussion of women's studies by our faculty, I invited to campus Professor Dorothy O. Helly, professor emerita of history and women's studies at Hunter College, to speak about strategies for initiating a women's studies program. In attendance were both women and men representing different fields of study across the college—from nursing to business to physical education. Creative ideas flowed: Everyone seemed energized thinking about what she or he might do within their courses to shift both content and perspectives to reflect women's issues in relation to the requisite content. While this activity did not result in our housing a program, recognizing those with a common interest in women's studies has helped to identify who among us wishes to be associated with feminist education and women's issues on our campus.

Think Extracurricular

Having noted that our campus lacked academically oriented celebrations of Women's History Month, a colleague, Frances Singh, and I developed an annual essay contest to showcase our students' remarkably rich personal writing. Together we have successfully created and organized this campus-wide event, the theme of which is "Writing Women We Know into History." Students write essays focused on a crucial decision made by a woman they have actually known. We recruit colleagues across the disciplines as judges and a faculty steering committee extends our base of support. The contest culminates in an awards ceremony to which all students who participate in the contest bring parents, siblings, children, and friends. Both women and men enter; both women and men emerge as prize winners; in fact, every student who writes an essay is recognized publicly at the ceremony: Each is given a book about women's history and a framed certificate that acknowledges her or his having participated in the making of women's history by sharing the story of an "ordinary" woman's life. The contest and awards ceremony have generated vibrant student and faculty interest in giving voice to and hearing women's narratives, a notable component of a feminist curriculum that strives to recover "lost" herstories—the heretofore untold stories.

Keep Trying until Something Happens

Every year for the past four years, I have submitted to the administration an outline for a women's studies concentration. The proposal emphasizes the theme of women and work, including a required introductory women's studies course that highlights this interdisciplinary topic. Additionally, following nine elective credits in women's studies courses, students would be required to take a capstone seminar, Women and Work, designed to help them analyze structural and interpersonal workplace dynamics that they encounter in a sponsored internship that same semester. Not yet successful in my pursuit, every year I resubmit the proposal, resolutely putting women's studies on the agenda "until something happens." Every year I show the proposal to and ask for comments from a few more colleagues, hoping to engender a growing trail of support each time I approach the administration.

Build Bridges across Campus and across Other Campuses

Orphaned women's studies faculty can help themselves maintain their sanity by finding on their campuses the few or many intellectual and political allies and professional soul mates. Simply sharing titles of books that students have enjoyed becomes one way to connect; working on extracurricular activities is another. Encouraging students to take each others' classes is yet a third way to work together outside the structure of a formal program. Also important is to include each other in discussions with the administration about advancing women's studies on campus. Moving outside the bounds of our disciplinary bases, we can build restorative alliances, offering each other encouragement and commiseration.

To celebrate thirty years of women's studies as an academic discipline, Cheryl Fish and Tricia Lin of Borough of Manhattan Community College (BMCC) and coeditors of this volume, organized a CUNY-wide, day-long forum for faculty, staff, and students on 17 November 2000. Participants shared reports and strategies, and those in attendance testified to the miracle of women's studies at CUNY: that so much is accomplished despite shrinking budgets and mostly rudimentary institutional support across the campuses. Importantly, Fish and Lin, with the assistance of Web artist Béatrice Coron, developed a Web site that has been widely used by faculty, staff, and students to initiate and sustain conversations and to post information.[4] This organizational work, which began at the conference held at BMCC (Fish and Lin), allows many of us to feel that we can put our fingers on the pulse of women's studies at the university, making our campus-based work seem closer to the mainstream and, thus, more productive and rewarding.

Strive for Women's Studies Visibility

Since in a community college faculty rarely teach students in women's studies classes beyond a single semester, we must work fast to give students tools to assess, question, and challenge oppressive structures or circumstances, which ultimately may help them work toward making the world a more equitable place. We want our students to be reminded that there are other responses than despair to relational, political, and/or institutional discrimination. We want them to see feminism as a framework for understanding power relations in our society; to recognize feminism as a viable cause and social movement that they not feel inhibited about "joining." We would like students to self-consciously form personal relationships based on equality, cooperation, and affirmation of their diverse and androgynous strengths; we would like to have students speak about sexism and sex discrimination as limiting both women's and men's potential.

To accomplish these aims, women's studies must be supported with institutional visibility. We need bulletin boards announcing local and (inter)national events, positioned where students will easily see them; we need visual displays of women's accomplishments and places for posting gender-related news items that impact policy and people's lives. We need the words *women's studies* to be heard, spoken, and understood as part of everyday academic vocabulary.

In community colleges especially, women's studies is often promoted by the efforts of a few devoted faculty who will, for the sake of the "cause," go at it single-handedly, almost always against the odds. Wherever and however it exists, women's studies—then and now—in its "bonding of women" can release, as Adrienne Rich told that same Smith College graduating class, "the yet unexplored resources and transformative power of women . . . calling up the voices we need to hear within ourselves" (10). This bonding, this empowerment, these authentic voices, are just what we who teach at institutions without programs need to fortify and advance our worthy work from within the margins.

NOTES

1. See http://www.umass.edu/wost/grads.htm and www.mus.edu/˜wmstdy/wsmjr5.htm.

2. Typically, CUNY students who graduate with an A.A. or A.A.S. degree will apply for transfer to a senior college, most often another part of CUNY. Within CUNY, eleven of the seventeen campuses are senior colleges where students can minor and/or major in women's studies. Generally, women's studies credits taken at a community college may be applied to

the distribution requirements or the major at a senior college. Community college students with coursework in women's studies can also put these credits toward a B.A. or B.S. degree in women's studies through the CUNY Baccalaureate Program.
3. See www.bmcc.cuny.edu/womens_studies/Visibility.html.
4. See http://www.bmcc.cuny.edu/womens_studies/.

WORKS CITED

Brush, Lorelei R., Alice Ross Gold, and Marni Goldstein White. "The Paradox of Intention and Effect: A Women's Studies Course." *Signs: Journal of Women in Culture and Society* 3.4 (1978): 870–83.

Butler, Johnella. "Toward a Pedagogy of Everywoman's Studies." *Gendered Subjects: The Dynamics of Feminist Teaching*. Ed. Margo Culley and Catherine Portuges. Boston: Routledge, 1985. 230–39.

Castellano, Olivia. "Canto, Locura y Poesia." *Race, Class, and Gender*. 2d ed. Ed. Margaret L. Andersen and Patricia Hill Collins. Belmont, CA: Wadsworth, 1995. 304–13.

Culley, Margo. "Anger and Authority in the Introductory Feminist Classroom." *Culley and Portuges* 209–18.

Culley, Margo, Arlyn Diamond, Lee Edwards, Sara Lennox, and Catherine Portuges. "The Politics of Nurturance." Culley and Portuges 11–20.

Fish, Cheryl, and Tricia Lin. "Dynamic but Unevenly Supported: An Overview of Women's Studies at the University." *CUNY Matters* Spring 2001: 5.

Hoffman, Nancy Jo. "Breaking Silences: Life in the Feminist Classroom." Culley and Portuges 147–54.

hooks, bell. *Teaching to Transgress*. New York: Routledge, 1994. 117–18.

Howe, Florence. *Seven Years Later: Women's Studies Programs in 1976*. Old Westbury, NY: National Advisory Council on Women's Education, 1977.

Omolade, Barbara. "A Black Feminist Pedagogy." *Women's Studies Quarterly* 15.3–4 (1987): 32–40.

Porter, Nancy M., and Margaret T. Eileenchild. *The Effectiveness of Women's Studies Teaching*. Women's Studies Monograph Series. Washington, D.C.: National Institute of Education, 1980.

Rich, Adrienne. "What Does a Woman Need to Know?" *Blood, Bread, and Poetry*. New York: Norton, 1986. 1–10.

Rothenberg, Paula. "The Hand that Pushes the Rock." *The Women's Review of Books* 6.5 (1989): 18–19. (Special section featuring books for women's studies)

Russell, Michele. "Black-Eyed Blues Connection: Teaching Black Women." Culley and Portuges 155–68.

Schniedewind, Nancy. "Teaching Feminist Process in the 1990's." *Women's Studies Quarterly* 21.3–4 (1993): 17–30.

Stimpson, Catherine, with Nina Kressner Cobb. *Women's Studies in the United States*. New York: Ford Foundation, 1986.

Jerilyn Fisher, associate professor of English at CUNY's Hostos Community College in the South Bronx, most recently published articles on feminist theory and fairy tales and on the work of Buchi Emecheta. Co-editor of Analyzing the Different Voice: Feminist Psychological Theory and Literature *(Rowman and Littlefield, 1998) she is currently co-editing* Women in Literature: Reading Through the Lens of Gender *(Greenwood, forthcoming).*

Developing Women's Studies at Georgia Institute of Technology

Sue V. Rosser, Mary Frank Fox, and Carol Colatrella

Over the past thirty years, the impact and interaction between the emerging interdisciplinary field of women's studies and the proliferating technological disciplines has increased from nonexistent to minimal. In many respects, the paucity of crossover reflects the dearth of women in science, engineering, and technology, in general, and the particular identification and intertwining of technology with masculinity in U.S. culture.

Although the number of women degree-recipients at both undergraduate and graduate levels within the biological and social sciences has increased, the numbers of women degree-recipients in the physical sciences, engineering, and computer science have actually reached a plateau or decreased in recent years (American Association of University Women 2; National Science Foundation 50). Further, the number of women receiving doctoral degrees in scientific and technological fields over the past three decades has not translated into expected representation of women in faculty ranks, especially at the senior level, over time (Fox, "Gender" 448–49; Fox, "Women, Science, and Academia" 272–73). During this same thirty-year period, however, the U.S. economy has become increasingly focused on science and technology, and current and projected increases in the more lucrative portions of the workforce, in areas such as information technology, biotechnology, and engineering, reflect this focus (Fox, "Women, Men, and Engineering" 249–50).

As feminist science and technology scholars have lamented, the impact of science and technology on women's studies has been negligible (Fausto-Sterling, "Building Two-Way Streets"; Fausto-Sterling, *Sexing the Body*; Quinby; Rosser, "Balancing"; Rosser, "Editorial"; Rosser, "Impact of Feminism"; Rosser, *Re-engineering*). Since women's studies originated in the humanities, spreading secondarily to the social sciences, faculty from those disciplines continue to predominate in women's studies teaching and scholarship. Recognizing the need for women's studies critiques in science and technology and acknowledging the void in women's studies caused by the absence of scientists and engineers, some have worked to build the "two-way street" needed to connect women's studies with the scientific and technological communities as first articulated by Fausto-Sterling ("Building Two-Way Streets").

Building women's studies at a technological institution provides one model for such a "two-way street." The creation and implementation of the Center for the Study of Women, Science, and Technology (WST) at the Georgia Institute of Technology (Georgia Tech) illustrates the potential and positive influences and interactions that women, gender, and women's studies can have on scientific and technical disciplines, and suggests ways that a focus on science and technology can build curriculum and research for women's studies.[1]

Many see WST and its programs as a critical component to attracting and retaining women at Georgia Tech.[2] The WST Center grew out of a curricular minor that is still active. It currently coordinates campus programs open to all students, faculty, administrators, and guests, including research panels, lectures, and workshops. WST also underwrites undergraduate and graduate research partnerships and jointly sponsors (with the Department of Housing) an undergraduate residential learning community for female students.

The WST Curricular Minor

Like faculty at many other universities in the 1970s, professors in Georgia Tech's humanities and social science programs developed courses on gender and social inequality in response to growing student interests in women's studies and minority studies. The 1990 founding of the Ivan Allen College (IAC), which connected the School of Management with transformed humanities and social sciences units, created the first liberal arts degree programs at Georgia Tech. In tandem with establishing interdisciplinary science and technology major courses and degrees, IAC faculty revised core curricular and elective courses, including those on gender and social inequality.

Four faculty members within two IAC units—the schools of History, Technology, and Society (HTS) and Literature, Communication, and Culture (LCC)—developed the Women, Science, and Technology (WST) minor in 1995. The first iteration of the WST minor involved packaging together already taught courses into a logical sequence of interdisciplinary requirements. The first jointly sponsored minor curriculum at Georgia Tech, the WST minor program is the nation's only women's studies curriculum focusing on the study of gender, science, and technology.

Administrators and faculty in the units contributing to the program favored the economic expediency of the WST minor: No new courses were created, no new faculty-lines were created, and no new costs were associated with creating or revising the minor. Carol Colatrella and Mary Frank Fox volunteered to serve as co-coordinators for the WST minor, supervising the curriculum and advising students without any increase in salary or other benefits.

In 1995, Fox applied for and received funding from the Georgia Tech Foundation (GTF) to underwrite WST student-faculty research partnerships. The grant enabled WST minor faculty to sponsor undergraduate and graduate students assisting with faculty research in the gender studies of science and technology. The fifteen thousand–dollar GTF grant supported twenty faculty-student partnerships over a four-year period and sponsored programs connecting students, faculty, administrators, and alumni.

Students minoring in WST—whether women or men—come from the sciences, engineering, social sciences, and humanities. In theoretical emphases, WST minor courses encourage students to think about values associated with scientific culture, to reflect upon the diverse human side of science and technology, and to deal with social factors affecting participation and performance in scientific and technical occupations and institutions.[3] Students in WST courses study the cultural, social, and historical dimensions of science and technology and find that focusing on gender and social inequality enhances their understanding of their disciplinary majors. The WST courses include Science, Technology, and Gender; Science, Technology, and Race; Sociology of Gender; Women and Gender in the United States; and Women in Science and Engineering. Students provide testimonials to the value of these classes in their course evaluations and office visits and advising with WST faculty. They particularly mention the ways in which WST classes complement their study of science and engineering and how feminist analyses relate to their experiences, recognizing gender studies as deepening "their understandings of themselves and others" (Stenecket al.)

In a practical sense, the WST program prepares students to understand factors such as current work and professional environments, to become equipped to deal with them, and to assume leadership roles toward improved participation among women and men in science and technology. Many upper-level courses at Georgia Tech require team projects. WST courses consider theoretical and practical issues associated with creating diverse teams, allowing students to develop important team-building skills to use in other courses and in their careers.

Students are also encouraged to apply for WST's research partnerships or research partnerships offered by various Georgia Tech colleges.

The Center for the Study of Women, Science, and Technology

From the onset of the minor, many WST students reported the value of research partnerships and many faculty throughout Georgia Tech were interested in expanding the network of faculty researchers to reach beyond Ivan Allen College. In addition, three particularly significant projects in the late 1990s included WST principals: an institute-wide study of gender, a study of the College of Engineering, and an ad hoc group advocating for the creation of a campus women's center. In 1995, Georgia Tech researchers began studying the campus climate as part of an NSF grant that led to a comprehensive report describing the environment for women faculty at GT from 1993 to 1998.[4] The College of Engineering created a task force to look at gender equity and related issues, producing a report in 1998 entitled "Enhancing the Environment for Success: Report from the Task Force for Opportunities for Women in Science and Engineering."[5] In 1996, a group of students, faculty, and administrators worked together to persuade the president to establish the Women's Resource Center, created in 1998, and later to fund the hiring of a full-time director in 1999 as a new staff appointment in Student Affairs.[6]

In 1999, creating an academic research center focusing on women, science, and technology became a priority for the WST minor co-coordinators (who took on new roles as center codirectors) and for the incoming dean of Ivan Allen College. The WST codirectors worked together with administrators in Ivan Allen College and the colleges of Engineering and Sciences on formulating the plans for the center. Supported by the colleges of Engineering and Sciences and endorsed by the incoming dean of IAC, WST sought and received increased funding from the Georgia Tech Foundation to support student partnerships and programmatic initiatives. It also received an award through the competitive, peer-reviewed Focused Research Program, coordinated by the vice provost for graduate studies and research.[7] These helped to launch the Georgia Tech Center for the Study of Women, Science, and Technology.

The Center for the Study of Women, Science, and Technology links issues in the study of science and technology with those of gender, culture, and society. The center brings together faculty and students, addressing issues of gender, science, and technology in research and programmatic initiatives. In key characteristics, the WST Center is interdisciplinary, collaborative across Georgia Tech colleges and in alliances with Atlanta-area colleges and universities and Georgia Tech alumnae, and cooperative in partnerships with students.

WST Programs and Initiatives

The *WST Focused Research Program* extends and coordinates research on women, science, and technology; enhances faculty connections; supports research collaborations among faculty and students; and provides critical, continuing bases for research-based practice and policy for improved participation and performance in scientific and technological education and careers. The program sponsors WST Center Focused Research Panels, held each semester, which feature faculty research on gender, science, and technology. Past programs have focused on the statistical analysis of admissions related to gender and race in engineering, the social implications of information technology, the professional career and reputation of Marie Curie, gender variations in aging and athletic performance, and international perspectives on gender, science, and technology.

Twenty-seven faculty across all six Georgia Tech colleges participate in the program. The publications of faculty in the WST Focused Research Program, limited to those on women, science, and technology for academic years 1999–2001, appear as a bibliographical resource in appendix 1. The WST Focused Research Program has taken strides to strategically mobilize research connections and build upon individual research initiatives, expanding collaboration and enhancing external support. In academic year 2000–2001, seven grant proposals were submitted by WST Center faculty to external agencies. Four proposals were funded, and the total of these externally funded projects is over four million dollars.

Building on the successful program of WST minor faculty-student partnerships, WST Center *faculty-student partnerships* are key to the program. Undergraduate student partners from a variety of programs work with individual faculty on research projects. In addition, WST graduate partners work with the WST codirectors on programs and initiatives. The WST graduate partners help coordinate and publicize the research and programmatic activities of the WST Center, including the events and informal advising for the WST Learning Community (described below). The student-faculty partnerships support students' intellectual growth, activism, leadership, and partnership in the community of Georgia Tech. The WST initiative aims to launch students for a lifetime of learning and productivity.

The *WST Reading Group* provides another structured opportunity to discuss ideas, enhance research networks, and promote collaboration and curricular innovation in gender and technology. In founding the reading group in 1999, a senior faculty member agreed to invite diverse faculty affiliated with WST to join the group. At the time of this writing, the group has thrived for two and a half years. A direct outcome from the group is a new book series with the University of Illinois Press on Women, Gender, and Technology, described in appendix 2. All three series editors come from the WST Reading Group, and the inaugural volume will contain chapters written primarily by group members.[8]

WST Center Annual Activities

Lectures: Each year, the WST Center has sponsored a lecture series with expert, outside speakers focusing on a central topic. The first WST lecture series concentrated on restructuring education for inclusiveness in science and engineering. The second year the series looked at women, computing, and information technology. In the third year, it considered international and global dimensions of women, science, and technology. To attract faculty and students from the constituent colleges of the WST initiative, speakers come from a range of disciplines and address topics that are interdisciplinary and which build bridges among disciplines and between faculty and students.

Reception: At the beginning of the academic year, WST cosponsors (with the Women's Resource Center) a reception introducing and honoring new women faculty and administrators and the students and mentors of the WST Learning Community. The program begins with welcoming remarks from the provost and the vice president for student affairs and includes remarks from the dean of students, the coordinator of the Women's Resource Center, and the WST codirectors.

Town Hall: As part of the events during Women's Awareness Month (WAM), the Georgia Tech version of Women's History Month, the WST Center sponsors a town hall on gender equity bringing together faculty, students, and administrators in a forum designed to share new information and programs available on campus and to provide the opportunity for a broad campus conversation on what is needed at Georgia Tech.

Kavita Philip, an assistant professor who has participated in the WST Center since its inception, notes the impact of the programs:

The WST Center has significantly altered my campus experience. When course readings set [students] alight with a newfound feminism, I need no longer tell them to browse the web in search of community. We have an active, energetic community of women students working on a daily basis. The WST Center has given me the chance to interact with colleagues across campus around the issue of feminism in science. Finally, an active colloquium series is essential to the vitality of any research program. (Personal communication, April 2002)

WST Learning Community

Modeled on residence halls for women in science at the University of Michigan, Rutgers University, and Purdue University, the Women, Science, and Technology Learning Community is a joint venture of the WST Center and the Georgia Tech Department of Housing. The Georgia Tech WST Learning Community enhances the academic and professional development of resident undergraduates from all majors, and it provides an academic and social network that enriches the quality of campus life for all.

Following on the successful Freshman Experience program sponsored by Georgia Tech Housing, sophomore and junior students live together in a residence hall and participate in programs for women entering scientific and technological fields that "enhance for success." These programs include workshops, informal discussions, and a pairing of each student with a faculty mentor from a discipline related to the student's major.[9] In addition, students living in the WST Learning Community create informal peer study and social groups. WST Center graduate partners have an office in the residence in which they hold afternoon office hours and work on WST Center and WST Learning Community events. WST Learning Community students and student partners also attend WST Center lectures and focused research panels, which include receptions where they can converse with faculty mentors and other interested students, faculty, and alumni.

WST Learning Community students are high achievers interested in doing well academically, living with others who are serious about their studies, and engaging informally with faculty and mentors, especially toward topics that link curriculum and careers. Christi Lurie, a sophomore bioengineering major, enthusiastically participates because the program improves the environment: "It's nice to be around others that deal with the same problems and issues as a female college student . . . especially at Tech. The encouragement and support are constant reminders that I actually can do this." Aisha Avery, a sophomore in industrial engineering, speaks to the strength in diversity: "WST is a community that encourages women from all backgrounds to come together for networking, stimulating conversation, and academic, as well as emotional, support."

The WST Learning Community was founded in 2000–2001 and expanded in its second year to include twenty-four students in residence, twenty-four faculty mentors, and twenty other undergraduates also participating in programs.[10] Plans for 2002–3 call for doubling the current number of students in the WST Learning Community and increasing the number of WST faculty mentors.

Outreach and the Future

Georgia Tech's WST program maintains many connections with related programs in the Atlanta area. These include WST faculty's connections on the advisory board for a Ford Foundation–funded project at Spelman College, participation in the National Conference on the Ph.D. in Women's Studies held at Emory University, review of the Women's Studies program at the University of Georgia, an appointment as a Rockefeller Fellow in Public Culture at Emory University, crosslisting of courses with Agnes Scott College, and participation in the meeting among Atlanta-area institutions with women's studies programs that endorsed creating a research consortium.

WST programs enhance the campus climate by eradicating barriers— among students, faculty, and students and faculty—and by providing structured research, educational, and programmatic initiatives that rest on collaboration and cross-disciplinarity, and are explicitly linked to science and technology. WST collaborates in research, education, and programmatic initiatives across all six Georgia Tech colleges (Ivan Allen College of Liberal Arts, Architecture, Computing, Engineering, Sciences, and Management). WST complements the success of Georgia Tech's Center for Education in Science, Mathematics, and Computing,[11] which focuses on K–12 education; and often partners with Student Affairs, Housing, and the Women in Engineering program to promote education and diversity.[12]

That the WST program, centered on increasing access and opportunity, can be woven throughout the fabric of Georgia Tech's institutional structure is testament to feminism's flexibility and the possibility of enhancing values and outcomes associated with science and technology on other campuses. Within a technological institution in which most students pursue a tightly structured curriculum with few electives, students' exposure to feminism through WST serves crucial, related functions. Feminism acts as a liberal art that broadens the education of students in science and engineering, providing them with analytical frameworks to critique and understand the knowledge in their technical courses. Feminist theories and pedagogies also become prime means to attract and retain men of color and women in science and technology by providing perspectives in the historical, social, and cultural contexts of the science and engineering disciplines in which they pursue their daily work.

NOTES

1. See http://www.wst.gatech.edu.
2. Thirty years ago, Georgia Tech had very few women students or faculty; in 1972–73, only 6.06 percent of the students were women. Because many concluded that the dearth of women resulted from the limited majors available in engineering, sciences, and architecture, active recruitment of women was encouraged. By 1978, the percentage of women climbed to 18.29 percent. In 2001–2, 29 percent of the students were women. Thanks go to the Georgia Tech director of institutional research for help in providing these data.
3. A WST minor must complete two required courses and four elective courses in HTS and LCC. Sample topics covered in WST minor courses include women in the history of science and technology; organizational influences affecting the participation of women in scientific and technological careers; gender issues in professions; women and the organization and management of science and technology; the gendered impact of scientific and technological policy; feminist perspectives on science and technology; and cultural analyses of gender, race, and class factors in the practice of science and technology.
4. See http://www.academicgatech.edu/study/.
5. See http://www.coe.gatech.edu/publications.
6. See http://www.womenscenter.gatech.edu.
7. Funding from the Georgia Tech Foundation was for a three year period (1999–2001); renewal in each year is based upon results from the prior year and plans and prospects for the next. Funding through the Focused Research Program was obtained in 1999, 2000, and 2001; in each year, the awards were made through a competitive, peer-reviewed process. These awards represent funding that is internal to the institution. Externally funded research projects are discussed subsequently.
8. In addition to defining the parameters for volumes in the series, writing the inaugural volume provides collaborative opportunities for junior faculty to receive some mentoring from more senior faculty.
9. The monthly dinner workshops (supported by the WST Center) and weekly lunches (underwritten by the Department of Housing) for the WST Learning Community are open to all students on campus. Topics of

the workshops vary each term and have recently included discussions of campus climate, strategies for success, work-life of an academic engineer, a history of feminist politics, women in oceanography, and possible career options in industrial engineering.

10. The 2001–2 WST Learning Community includes eleven Engineering students, five in Ivan Allen College, four in Sciences, two in Computing, and one each from Architecture and Management.

11. See http://www.ceismc.gatech.edu.

12. See http://www.coe.gatech.edu/wie/.

WORKS CITED

American Association of University Women (AAUW). *Tech-Savvy: Educating Girls in the New Computer Age*. Washington, DC: AAUW Educational Foundation, 2000.

Fausto-Sterling, Anne. "Building Two-Way Streets: The Case of Feminism and Science." *NWSA Journal* 4.3 (1992): 336–49.

———. *Sexing the Body: Gender Politics and Construction of Sexuality*. New York: Basic, 2000.

Fox, Mary Frank. "Gender, Hierarchy, and Science." *Handbook of the Sociology of Gender*. Ed. Janet Chafetz. New York: Kluwer Academic/Plenum, 1999. 441–57.

———. "Women, Men, and Engineering." *Gender Mosaics: Social Perspectives*. Ed. Dana Vannoy. Los Angeles: Roxbury, 2001. 249–57.

———. "Women, Science, and Academia: Graduate Education and Careers." *Gender and Society* 15.5 (2001): 654–66.

National Science Foundation (NSF). *Women, Minorities, and Persons with Disabilities in Science and Engineering: 1998*. Arlington: NSF, 1999. 99–338.

Philip, Kavita. Personal communication. April 2002.

Quinby, Lee. "Women Confronting the New Technologies." *Women's Studies Quarterly* 29.3–4 (2001): 5–9.

Rosser, Sue V.. "Balancing: Survey of Fiscal Year, '97, '98, '99 POWRE Awardees." *Journal of Women and Minorities in Science and Engineering* 7.4 (2001): 1–11.

———. "Editorial on Women and Science." *Women's Studies Quarterly* 23.1–2 (2000): 6–11.

———. "The Impact of Feminism on the AAAS Meetings: From Non-existent to Negligible." *Feminism Within the Science and Health Care Professions: Overcoming Resistance*. Ed. Sue V. Rosser. Elmsford, N.Y.: Pergamon, 1988. 105–16.

———. *Re-engineering Female Friendly Science*. New York: Teachers College, 1997.

Steneck, Nicholas H., Barbara M. Olds, and Kathryn A. Neeley. "Recommendations for Liberal Education in Engineering: A White Paper from the Liberal Education Division of the American Society for Engineering Education." *Proceedings of the 2002 American Society for Engineering Education Annual Conference and Exposition*. American Society for Engineering Education, forthcoming.

APPENDIX 1: WST FOCUSED RESEARCH GROUP PUBLICATIONS, 1999–2001

Note: Updates on these references to WST publications can be found at www.wst.gatech.edu.

Barnum, Carol, Kavita Philip, Alison Reynolds, Michele Shauf, and Teresa Thompson. 2001. "Globalizing Technical Communi-cation: A Field Report From China." *Technical Communication* 48, November.

Berman, Joshua, and Amy Bruckman. 2001. "The Turing Game: A Participatory Exploration of Learning in Online Environments." *Convergence.* 83–102.

Blanchard-Fields, Fredda. 1999. "Human Development: Adulthood." In D Levenson, J. J. Ponzetti, and P. F. Jorgensen, eds., *Encyclopedia of Human Emotions.* vol. I, 386–90. New York: Macmillan.

Blanchard-Fields, Fredda. 2001. "Adult Cognitive Development." In W. Kintsch, ed., *International Encyclopedia of the Social and Behavioral Sciences.* Amsterdam: Pergamon.

Blanchard-Fields, Fredda. 2001. "Social Cognition." In D. Ekerdt, ed., *Encyclopedia of Aging.* New York: Springer.

Blanchard-Fields, Fredda. 2001. "Social Cognition and Aging." In N. Eisenberg, ed., *International Encyclopedia of the Social and Behavioral Sciences.* Amsterdam: Pergamon.

Blanchard-Fields, Fredda, and C. Hertzog. 1999. "Introduction to the Special Section on Cognition in Everyday Life: Adult Developmental Aspects." *International Journal of Behavioral Development* 23: 545–52.

Blanchard-Fields, Fredda, and C. Hertzog. 2000. "Age Differences in Social Schematicity." In U. von Hecker, S. Dutke, and S. G. Sedek, eds., *Generative Thought and Psychological Adaptation.* Dordrecht: Kluwer Academic.

Blanchard-Fields, Fredda, and T. M. Hess. 1999. "The Social Cognition Perspective and the Study of Aging." In T. M. Hess and F. Blanchard-Fields, eds., *Social Cognition and Aging.* San Diego, California: Academic Press.

Blanchard-Fields, Fredda, and R. Stein. 1999. "Age Relevance and Context Effects on Attributions Across the Adult Life Span." *International Journal of Behavioral Development* 23: 665–83.

Blanchard-Fields, Fredda, C. Hertzog, R. Stein, and R. Pak. 2001. "Beyond a Stereotyped View of Older Adults' Traditional Family Values." *Psychology and Aging,* 16, no. 3.

Bruckman, Amy. 2000. "Situated Support for Learning: Storm's Weekend with Rachael." *Journal of Learning Sciences* 9: 329–72.

Bruckman, Amy, Elizabeth Edwards, and Carlos Jensen. 2000. "Uneven Achievement in A Constructivist Learning Environment." *Proceedings of ICLS.* Ann Arbor, Michigan.

Bullard, Alice. 1999. "Gendering the Theory of Civilization." *Figurations, Quarterly Publication of the Norber Elias Foundation.*

Bullard, Alice. 2001. "The Truth in Madness." *South Atlantic Review* 66, no. 2: 114–32.

Chen, Y., and Fredda Blanchard-Fields. 2000. "Unwanted Thought: Age Differences in the Connection of Social Judgment." *Psychology and Aging* 15: 475–82.

Choudhury, Mita, co-ed. 2002. *Monstrous Dreams of Reason: Body, Self, and Other in the Enlightenment.* Bucknell University Press.

Cochran, Molly. 1999. *Normative Theory in International Relations.* (Includes feminist case study.) Cambridge: Cambridge University Press.

Cochran, Molly. 2001. "A Pragmatist Perspective on Ethical Foreign Policy." (Includes case study of Women's Internationalist League for Peace and Freedom.) In K. Smith and M. L. Light, eds., *Ethics and Foreign Policy.* Cambridge: Cambridge University Press.

Colatrella, Carol. 1999. "Science Fiction in the Information Age." Review essay. *American Literary History* 11: 554–65.

Colatrella, Carol. 1999. "Representing Female-Friendly Science and Technology in Fiction and Film." *Women and Technology—Proceedings of the 1999 International Symposium on Technology and Society.* Piscataway, NJ: IEEE.

Colatrella, Carol. 2000. "Work for Women: Recuperating Charlotte Perkins Gilman's Reform Fiction." *Knowledge and Society* 12: 53–76.

Colatrella, Carol. 2001. "From Desk Set to The Net: Women and Computing in Hollywood Films." *Canadian Review of American Studies* 31: 1–14.

Fox, Mary Frank. 1999. "Gender, Hierarchy, and Science." In Janet Chafetz, ed., *Handbook of the Sociology of Gender,* 441–57. New York: Kluwer Academic/Plenum Publishers.

Fox, Mary Frank. 1999. "Gender, Knowledge, and Scientific Styles." *The Annals of the New York Academy of Sciences* 869: 89–93.

Fox, Mary Frank. 1999. "Women and Professional Careers in Engineering." In B. Bogue, P. Guthrie, S. Hadden, and B. Lazarus, eds., *Tackling the Engineering Resources Shortage: Creating New Paradigms for Developing and Retaining Women Engineers.* SPIE–The International Society for Optical Engineering vol. x44.

Fox, Mary Frank. 2000. "Organizational Environments and Doctoral Degrees Awarded to Women in Science and Engineering Departments." *Women 's Studies Quarterly* 28, no. 1–2: 47–61.

Fox, Mary Frank. 2001. "Science Studies and Feminism." In Cheris Kramarae and D. Spender, eds., *Routledge International Encyclopedia of* Women. New York: Routledge.

Fox, Mary Frank. 2001. "Women in Science and Engineering: What We Know About Education and Employment." In Daryl Chubin and Willie Pearson, eds., *Scientists and Engineers for the New Millennium: Renewing the Human Resources*, 25–8. Washington, D.C.: Commission on Professionals in Science and Technology.

Fox, Mary Frank. 2001. "Women, Men, and Engineering." In Dana Vannoy, ed., *Gender Mosaics; Social Perspectives*, 249–57. Los Angeles: Roxbury Press.

Fox, Mary Frank. 2001. "Women, Science, and Academia: Graduate Education and Careers." *Gender & Society* 15: 654–66.

Fox, Mary Frank. 2002. "Gender, Faculty, and Doctoral Education in Science and Engineering." In L. Hornig, ed., *Women in Research Universities*. New York: Kluwer Academic/ Plenum Publishers.

Fox, Mary Frank, and John M. Braxton. 1999. "Self-Regulation and Social Control of Scientific Misconduct: Roles, Patterns, and Constraints." In John M. Braxton, ed., *Perspectives on Scholarly Misconduct in the Sciences*, 315–30. Columbus, Ohio: Ohio State University Press.

Fox, Mary Frank, and Paula Stephan. 2001. "Careers of Young Scientists: Preferences, Prospects, and Realities by Gender and Field." *Social Studies of Science* 31: 109–122.

Grant, Linda, Ivy Kennelly, and Kathryn Ward. 2000. "Revisiting the Gender, Marriage, and Parenthood Puzzle in Scientific Careers." *Women's Studies Quarterly* 28: 62–85.

Harpold, Terry, and Kavita Philip. 2000. "Of Bugs and Rats: Cyber-cleanliness, Cyber-squalor, and the Fantasies of Globalization." *Postmodern Culture* 11.

Harrold, Mary Jean. 2000. "Distributed Mentor Project: Evaluation of Impact and Experiences of Participants." *Computing Research Association News* 12, September.

Johnson, Deborah, and Shirley Gorenstein. 2000. "Gender and Work: Domestic and Public Spheres." *Knowledge and Society* 12: 1–16.

Jones, Brian, Carolyn Cole, and Andrew Quay. "i-rasshai: An Immersive Cultural Learning Environment." International Cultural Heritage Informatics, Milan, Italy, 2001<www.archimuse.com/ichim2001/index.html>

Knoespel, Kenneth. 1999. "Interpretive Strategies in Newton's' Theologiae gentilis orgines philosophiae." In James Force and Richard Popkin, eds., *Newton and Religion.* Kluwer Academic Publishers.

Knoespel, Kenneth. 1999. "Model and Diagrams within the Cognitive Model." In N. Nersessian, L. Magnani, and P. Thaggaard, eds., *Foundations of Science,* Kluwer Academic Publishers.

Knoespel, Kenneth. 1999. "Russian Discourse Communities in the Information Age." In Y. P. Tretyakov, ed., *Open World of Science.* St. Petersburg: Russian Academy of Sciences.

Llewellyn, Donna, Marion Usselman, and April Brown. 2001. "Institutional Self-Assessments as Change Agents: Georgia Tech's Two Year Experience." *Proceedings of the 2001 American Society for Engineering Education Annual Conference and Exposition.*

Miller, Patricia. Sue V. Rosser, Joann Benigno, and Mireille Zieseniss. 2000. "A Desire to Help Others: Goals of High Achieving Female Science Undergraduates." *Women's Studies Quarterly* 28: 128–42.

Murray, Janet. 2000. http://ww.jwa.org. The Jewish Women's Archive website including "Women of Valour" exhibits for 2000 (executive producer).

Philip, Kavita. 2001. "Science and Technology Studies and Indigenous Knowledge." In N. J. Smelser and P. Baltes, eds., *International Encyclopedia of the Social and Behavioral Sciences.* London: Elsevier.

Philip, Kavita. 2001. "Seeds of Neo-colonialism? Reflections on Globalization and Indigenous Knowledge." *Capitalism, Nature, Socialism* 12.

Rosser, Sue V. 2000. "Controversies in Breast Cancer Research." In S. Ferguson and A. Kasper, eds., *Breast Cancer: The Social Construction of an Illness.* New York: St. Martin's Press.

Rosser, Sue V. 2000. "Editorial on Women and Science." *Women's Studies Quarterly* 28: 6–12.

Rosser, Sue V. 2000. "When Body Politics of Partial Identification Collide with Multiple Realities of Real Academics." In D. King, ed., *Body Politics.* Bloomington, Indiana: Indiana University Press.

Rosser, Sue V. 2000. *Women, Science, and Society: The Crucial Union.* New York: Teachers College Press, Columbia University.

Rosser, Sue V. 2000. "Women's Studies: A Model for a Specialty in Women's Health and Afterward." *Transformations* 11: 17–40.

Rosser, Sue V., and Patricia Miller. 2000. "Feminist Theories: Implications for Developmental Psychology." In P. Miller and E. Scholnick, eds., *Developmental Psychology Through the Lenses of Feminist Theories.* New York: Routledge.

Rosser, Sue V., and Julie Montgomery. 2000. "Gender Equity Issues in Science Careers." *Women's Educational Equity Act Digest* December: 3–7.

Rosser, Sue V., and Mireile Zieseniss. 2000. "Career Issues and Laboratory Climates: Different Challenges and Opportunities for Women Engineers and Scientists." *Journal of Women and Minorities in Science* 6: 1–20

Rosser, Sue V. 2001. "Balancing: Survey of Fiscal Year 1997, 1998, and 1999 POWRE Awardees." *Journal of Women and Minorities in Science and Engineering* 17: 1–11.

Rosser, Sue V. 2001. "Will EC 2000 Make Engineering More Female-Friendly?" *Women's Studies Quarterly* 29, no. 3–4.

Rosser, Sue V. "Themes Which Link Through Time." Forthcoming. In P. Freeman and J. Z. Schmidt, eds., *Teaching in Time: Reflections of Women at Mid-life.* New York: Routledge.

Usselman, Marion. 1999, "InGEAR: Integrating Gender Equity and Reform." Poster at NSF Program for Gender Equity PI Meeting.

Usselman, Marion, and D. Whiting. 1999. "SummerScape: Gender Equitable Science for Students and Teachers." Poster at NSF Program for Gender Equity PI Meeting.

Yaszek, Lisa. Forthcoming. "A Grim Fantasy: Remaking American History in Afro-Feminist Science Fiction." *Signs: Journal of Women in Culture and Society.*

Yaszek, Lisa. In press. *The Self-Wired: Technology and Subjectivity in Contemporary Narrative.* New York: Routledge.

APPENDIX 2: WOMEN, GENDER, AND TECHNOLOGY BOOK SERIES

Published by University of Illinois Press

Series Editors: Sue V. Rosser, Mary Frank Fox, and Deborah Johnson

Volumes in the Women, Gender, and Technology Series bring together women's studies and technology studies, focusing on women and technology, feminist perspectives on technology, and/or the gendering of technology and its impact on gender relations in society. Volumes may be written from multiple perspectives and approaches, reflecting and aimed toward audiences including women's studies, science and technology studies, ethics and technology, cultural studies of science and technology, history of technology, and public policy.

Topics include

- Cultures and societies: comparative approaches in the study of gender, science, and technology; representations of gender and technology; politics and the state as they reflect and reinforce patterns of gender, science, and technology.

• Institutions: gender in technological training; structures of education and outcomes; work and organizational contexts among women in technology; programs and interventions to support gender equity.

• Individuals: social psychology of gender, science, and technology; interactions, expectations, identities, and networks as they are embedded in institutions (e.g., education and work) and outcomes of science and technology; effects of technology on human development and life-span development between generations.

Send inquiries and proposals to:

Sue V. Rosser, Dean, Ivan Allen College, Georgia Tech, Atlanta, Georgia 30332–0525; *sue.rosser@iac.gatech.edu*

Mary Frank Fox, NSF ADVANCE Professor of Sociology, School of History, Technology, and Society, and Codirector, Center for Study of Women, Science, and Technology, Georgia Tech, Atlanta, Georgia 30332–0345; *mary.fox@hts.gatech.edu*

Deborah Johnson, Olsson Professor of Applied Ethics, Division of Technology, Culture, and Communication, School of Engineering and Applied Science, University of Virginia, P.O. Box 400744, 351 McCormick Road, Charlottesville, Virginia 22904–4744; *dgj7p@virginia.edu*

Sue V. Rosser is dean of the Ivan Allen College, the liberal arts college of Georgia Institute of Technology in Atlanta, where she is also professor of history, technology, and society. Author of eight books and editor of two special issues of Women's Studies Quarterly, she has also published more than ninety-five journal articles on the theoretical and applied aspects of feminism and women in science, technology, and health.

Mary Frank Fox is NSF ADVANCE Professor of Sociology and codirector, Center for Study of Science and Technology, Georgia Institute of Technology. Her research focuses on women, science, and academia. She is the author of two books and of publications appearing in forty scholarly journals and collections. Her current research includes a study of programs for women in science and engineering, and the ADVANCE Institutional Transformation for Women in Science and Engineering.

Carol Colatrella is associate professor of literature and cultural studies and

*codirector of the Center for the Study of Women, Science, and Technology,
Georgia Institute of Technology. Her scholarly interests focus on narratives
emphasizing moral transgression, rehabilitation, and social marginalization,
and her current project is a study of toys, tools, and cultural narratives in gender, science, and technology. Her publications include* Cohesion and Dissent
in America (1994) and Literature and Moral Reform: Melville and the
Discipline of Reading (2002).

Copyright © 2002 by Sue V. Rosser, Mary Frank Fox, and Carol Colatrella

Sustaining and Disbanding the Women's Studies Committee at Greenfield Community College

Anne M. Wiley

Women's studies is an institutional change movement that continues both to flourish and flounder in the academy with varying degrees of success for institutions, faculty, and program directors as well as students (Luebke and Reilly; Mahar and Tetreault; McTighe-Musil, *Courage to Question*). At Greenfield Community College (GCC), a small rural community college of 2,200 students located in western Massachusetts, our journey into women's studies has certainly been both joyous and perilous. GCC is the only higher educational institution in the poorest county in Massachusetts. Yet nearby to the south is the Five-College Consortium of Amherst College, Hampshire College, Mount Holyoke College, Smith College, and the University of Massachusetts–Amherst. These institutions have women's studies programs and/or minors as well as the Five-College Women's Research Center. Such an atmosphere has provided ongoing professional development opportunities and resources for the women's studies faculty and staff at GCC.

In our college, women's studies courses began with the efforts of six committed women faculty.[1] For nearly twenty years, this small group has sustained the interdisciplinary curricular offerings, strengthening them for women students by collaborating with other programs and services within the college and in the community. It also has secured outside funding to support its work.

Despite these strengths and successes, the Women's Studies Steering Committee recently disbanded itself after nearly two decades of work. Over the years, the committee worked diligently to balance its own vision for itself with the larger administrative and institutional demands. Our committee believed its primary function was to develop and promote the curriculum, teach women's studies courses, advise students, and foster women's studies and more inclusive content in the larger college curriculum. Administrators, however, often considered the committee's primary role to be coordinating the annual speaker series, arranging and hosting events to celebrate Women's

History Month in March, and serving as a liaison and resource on women's issues for the surrounding community. Given the limited financial and human resources and different expectations, tensions ensued. This past fall our efforts to reach yet one more compromise on the coordinator's job functions failed. The Women's Studies Steering Committee found itself at a crossroads and the members of the committee made the heart-wrenching decision to disband.

Nevertheless, over the nearly twenty years of its existence, the Women's Studies Steering Committee did manage to sustain the balance of coordinating the curriculum and coordinating the public role with regularly scheduled events. We accomplished this through the development of alliances with other campus groups and a simultaneous willingness of the members of our small committee to labor under a constant work overload. The collaborations promoted and strengthened the women's studies curriculum and our connections with the community. However, the constant overload and tension between our own view of our roles and the administrative view of the public events role continually stretched our personal resources.

In building and maintaining a women's studies program, each institution must consider its role in its own institutional culture and environment. Our committee found it most helpful to remain connected to various other marginalized groups, both in the college and the community, and to form alliances with them. Over the years, these have included committees or groups involved with diversity and multicultural issues; international studies and global issues; affirmative action; sexual harassment; health awareness and violence prevention; gay, lesbian, bisexual, and transgendered students; and disability groups. As difficult and time consuming as these cross-institutional alliances are, they are important for institutional change and as models of change for students. Much research suggests that a diverse, inclusive institutional culture and curriculum in conjunction with an institution that has women faculty and professional staff serving as mentors for students can have a significant impact on student learning (Hayes and Flannery). In that spirit and based on our experiences, I offer to other women's studies programs a list of suggestions that assisted our small program:

- Develop both formal and informal strategies that foster dialogues across disciplines.
- Develop and create your own college committee, yet seek eventual institutionalization within the college committee structure.
- Hold public forums, lectures, and panels.

- Secure an institutional budget, no matter how small, and work to maintain and expand it each year.
- Establish links with other services and programs on campus and form alliances and sharing resources with other marginalized groups.
- Establish a community advisory board for the women's studies curriculum.
- Develop a scholarship and give an annual award for academic excellence to a student in women's studies.
- Establish ongoing links with community agencies and/or public schools, especially regarding gender equity.
- Maintain regional and national connections and visibility through individual and panel conference presentations.
- Write short commentaries and longer articles.
- Serve on local boards.
- Secure testimonies from students and alumnae and use their quotes in publications and press releases regularly.
- Have current students speak to student groups, general education classes, and/or community groups. Students are often underutilized and are very eloquent and articulate emissaries for women's studies.
- Bring community speakers into the college and the classroom.
- Find ways to have fun by meeting off campus at least once a semester for a meal.
- Show up en masse at important institutional meetings and sit in the front row.
- Read poems or short quotes at the start of meetings.
- Share effective teaching strategies or teaching challenges and/ or set aside longer meetings each year to focus on content and pedagogy.

Additional recommendations on how to work with college administrators include the following:

- Get administrative support early and often. Develop a relationship with at least one academic administrator who can advocate for the cluster of courses or program, however small, at the institution-wide discussions and budget forums.
- Secure at least one, preferably two reassigned times (course releases) each semester for a coordinator; get a year-long administrative commitment.
- Collect data and write year-end reports every year for administrators even if it is not requested or required; collect evaluations on

public forums and events; collect informal feedback from students; include this summary information in year-end reports.
* Seek outside funds using both private foundations and governmental grants to support curricular and institutional transformation.[2]

To better understand how the committee and program evolved, a case history describes our process. The case will explain the roots of our program, our collaborations and connections with other groups, as well as the procurement of outside funding, and some of the change strategies used in our institutional culture. Finally, the case will describe the disbanding of the committee and our hopes for the future.

The Roots of Women's Studies at Greenfield Community College: Curricular Change

Similar to such programs in many colleges in the United States, women's studies at Greenfield Community College had its beginnings with a few courses. In the early 1980s, Professor Virginia Low proposed and designed two English courses, Women in Literature I (nineteenth century) and Women in Literature II (twentieth century). Both have been very successful electives in English for many years and are still part of our core women's studies courses. Shortly after these courses were instituted, a five-member faculty team attended a national curriculum transformation conference (Spanier et al.) and two additional courses were developed: Introduction to Women's Studies and the Psychology of Women. With a concerted effort by our gender project team, the College Curriculum Committee eventually approved the new courses. The psychology course was offered immediately and regularly. Yet it was another four years before college administrators supported a pilot of the introductory women's studies course. Initially, it was offered only to a small group of returning adult women students in a specialized grant-funded displaced homemakers program. Within two semesters, the introductory course was successful and popular, with other students eager to enroll.

During the mid-1980s, some of the committee members as well as other institutional allies were active in the National Women's Studies Association (NWSA) and New England Women's Studies Association (NEWSA). These activities encouraged collegiality and support across institutions. Indeed, our small college committee co-sponsored the NEWSA day-long regional conference in 1991 with over two hundred participants, which was a massive undertaking for a rural, resource-poor community college.

Such internal and external visibility provided momentum for program development and additional funding. Since the initial four courses had become regular offerings, the committee applied for and was selected as one of fourteen community colleges nationally to receive an award and participate in a Ford Foundation curriculum grant. Similar to other national curricular transformation projects, this year-long project had three foci: to develop new courses through small stipends to interested faculty, promote community understanding of women's issues through public lectures and drama presentations, and develop a liberal arts advising option in women's studies. Under this grant, the ad hoc committee finally formalized itself, naming and claiming the identity of the Women's Studies Steering Committee, with its six active members. Nearly a dozen years after the first courses were offered, the College Curriculum Committee approved the liberal arts option in women's studies, formally authorizing the program of study.

Similar to earlier efforts at four-year colleges and universities, full- and part-time faculty members continued to meet in study groups to discuss interdisciplinary content and pedagogy. We also created joint course assignments and collaborations with our students (Wiley). Additionally, our expansion of curricular transformation continued. In 1996, the American Association of Colleges and Universities (AACU) selected GCC as the only community college among ten colleges nationally to receive grant monies, originally from the National Science Foundation.[3] The purpose of the grant was to infuse science and math content into women's studies courses and women's studies content into science and math courses. The project's frequently asked questions that guide science and feminism assisted our curricular efforts to change a three-credit Women and Science course to a four-credit course that included a laboratory component (McTighe-Musil, *Gender, Science* 145–56). Furthermore, our introductory course in women's studies increased the readings and content in mathematics and science.

Our Collaborations and Connections

The connections and continued collaborations with women's groups on and off campus sustained our energy and helped us strengthen our services to women students, contributing to a more woman-friendly institutional culture. Over the decade between 1985 and 1995, several members of the Women's Studies Steering Committee were actively

involved in teaching specialized women's re-entry programs that were
prominent in community colleges across the nation. Since community
colleges often serve students who are part of the first generation in
their families to attend college, as well as nontraditional aged women
students, our women's studies courses and women's services offered
resources for students in these programs. The programs frequently
included a cluster of academic courses coupled with personal and
career support for returning adult women. Our first displaced home-
maker program and its subsequent iterations were mostly funded
through vocational grants from the state and federal government.
Occasionally, minimal institutional funds were also provided.

Currently, we have a Women-in-Transition (WIT) program that supports some returning adult women students during their first semesters in college and a professionally staffed Women's Resource Center
(WRC). Both are grant-funded from private foundations; therefore,
some uncertainty of funding exists each year.[4] Current academic services include a set of specialized advising, personal and career counseling, and a loosely configured selection of basic college courses
during "mother's hours" (9 A.M.to 3 P.M.). Such block-scheduled courses
permit adult women to begin college while their children are in school.

Initially, our Women's Resource Center was created by enclosing a
hallway approximately nine by twelve feet. The center became a small
safe space for students to gather and meet informally in a "room of their
own." Eventually, with private funds and an opportunity produced by
college renovations, a larger, more accessible space was made available.
Today, a clothing exchange, free donated food, a refrigerator and
microwave oven, computer terminals, and other women-centered
resources are available. The center continues to provide a safe, quiet
space for informal study groups and conversations. The center staff provides some special outreach, advocacy, and referrals to local community
agencies for support. In addition, periodic programming occurs, including sessions with local legislators on welfare reform, exercise and nutri-
tion demonstrations, and career-exploration workshops. Informal brown
bag lunch and bagel breakfast discussions have included topics such as
"Responding to Terrorism in Post September 11" and "Let's Talk about
Race" this year as well as "Pay Equity" and "The Superwoman Syndrome"
last year. Currently, a full-time advocate, a part-time counselor, and a
work-study student staff the center with some resource and research support from one women's studies faculty member.

More recently, another collaboration emerged to provide gender
equity services. In the late 1990s, outreach to local public schools concerning gender equity was also established. One successful project

supported by a statewide gender equity grant for four years integrated a coalition of four area community colleges and nine technical high schools; this coalition fostered the development of a Gender Equity Center. The project, coordinated by a full-time director and support staff located at a nearby urban community college, had an advisory board with faculty and staff from the participating community colleges and high schools. The project coordinated a gender equity Web site and provided regular in-service professional development opportunities on gender equity for high school teachers.[5] While today the Gender Equity Center remains only in a virtual format, area community college faculty and staff remain involved as an informal advisory focus group.

Since 1998, GCC has also provided regular gender equity in-service professional development to our local county middle- and high-school girls and their science and math teachers. These efforts began first with the small steps of a "day in the lab" with a small group of girls and their teachers. Later efforts included annual and semiannual daylong conferences for teen girls and their teachers for over 125 participants. The workshops for girls were designed to interest them in science, technology, engineering, and math (STEM) careers. The professional workshops for teachers focused on how to infuse their existing courses with content about women and minorities. These workshops also offered pedagogical strategies to examine classroom environments for inclusivity. Again, various state and private foundation grants supported these efforts. One women's studies faculty member with a course release provided technical and research resource support. The efforts continue but are subject to the availability and continuation of a combination of private, federal, and state resources.[6] Still, for our rural community, this outreach has given the college a gender equity visibility and expertise in support of girls and women in STEM careers. Our dedicated professionals in gender equity and the women's resource center continue to provide a rich, supportive network to girls and women in the college and community.[7]

Change Strategies and Institutional Culture

In an effort to change the institutional culture and policies, the early focus of GCC's Women's Studies Steering Committee was to transform the curriculum in our regular discipline courses and to create specific courses within disciplines that placed women centrally in the content. Similar to the strategies used by other curricular transformation projects, we coordinated and offered campus-wide book and article discussion groups, outreach breakfasts for adjunct faculty, and presentations and discussions on assignments and course content. These activities gave us the benefit of institutional visibility as change agents. Over the years, we formed alliances with similar on-campus and community groups. We presented at national and regional conferences including the National Women's Studies Association and local and regional teaching and learning conferences. We secured grant funding to support curriculum and public lecture efforts and held community forums and panels that dealt with women's issues and inclusivity issues, including race, class, gender, heterosexism, and homophobia.

Another successful strategy that promoted institutional change and visibility involved our committee's regular planning efforts and annual reports. Three times a year, our committee held off-campus, day-long retreats designed to build community among ourselves and to promote change. We collectively wrote our strategic plans, annual objectives, and year-end reports based on the systematic data collected over the previous year. For example, at every forum, lecture, and public event we collected evaluation feedback forms from the audience and used the data to plan and establish the goals for the following year. For instance, based on evaluations, we altered, the "by-invitation-only luncheon" often held after a public lecture. Instead, we provided lighter refreshments for all interested attendees. Such an atmosphere provided more informal opportunities for students and community audience members to meet with the speaker or panelists. Other suggestions included shorter talks and longer question-and-answer periods, which we incorporated into longer workshop delivery models.

Over the years, other strategies have enhanced our program and curricular visibility. We developed our own brochure and a women's studies Web site within the college's Web site.[8] We also fostered relationships with the local press, particularly women reporters, and encouraged press coverage on our outstanding students and graduates. Additionally, we constructed a community advisory board and an e-mail list for the board. Finally, most recently, we created and raised funds for an annual women's studies student scholarship.

Despite our many successful strategies, we were only partially successful at the development of long-range plans. Our committee made numerous efforts to develop such plans, including a three-year course schedule and a procedure for new course development. Yet we never moved beyond planning for the next semester or two. In addition, regardless of the continued efforts by our committee to focus centrally on curriculum, teaching and learning, and our students, such endeavors were often redirected by external broader college needs. These demands included holding more public events, designing outcome assessment tools, infusing our courses with technology, and writing accreditation reports and/or specific financial reports.

Amid the successes of our curricular and programmatic accomplishments, a cautionary note is warranted. Similar to the experiences of four-year colleges and universities, our experience with such visibility also had shortcomings, including the backlash and negative feedback that women's studies courses "weren't academically rigorous." Since the goal is to reshape institutions, one understands when one embarks on such curricular, pedagogical, and institutional change that there will be anger, resistance, and even personal attacks (Fischer; Palmer). Sometimes the criticism focused on an individual, but more often, it was generic and targeted the curriculum, the public forums and lectures, the issues raised, or the alliances with other groups. At our college, examples have included statements such as "that's not the business of our college," "that event is not appropriate to our college mission," "she's a ———," "don't take that course; it's the same as (another women's studies) course," "those courses are not real, they aren't academically rigorous; it's just male bashing," and " you don't want to have women's studies on your transcript, do you?"

Still, sustaining small women's studies courses and programs through backlash and criticism is not new to women's studies nor is it likely to go away. Offering ways to continue discussions and change the curriculum and the institution will also remain a priority, especially given the real need to serve the variety of our future students (McTighe-Musil, *Students at the Center*). Our committee, with its changing membership, continued over the years to discuss the challenges and issues we faced, sometimes without much administrative support. Other times a collegial administrator would support us by running interference to promote both curricular efforts *and* public events. In the end, the collective committee with its core of five to six committed individuals nurtured our curriculum, our institutional change efforts, and our larger collaborations with colleagues on campus and in the community. Ultimately, we sustained and challenged ourselves in these exciting cross-institutional and community connections.

Nevertheless, women's studies programs and curricular offerings, particularly in small colleges and community colleges, are initiated and maintained in "survival" or "thriving" mode mostly by the good will, interests, and stamina of individual faculty and professional women in these programs/colleges. It has to do partially with the interdisciplinary nature of women's studies. This is both its strength—allowing

cross-college conversations about teaching and learning—and its lia-
bility—administrations rarely know how the program fits, to whom the
program belongs, or how to distribute the limited resources of personnel, space, time, and money. Women's studies and sometimes other
interdisciplinary or marginalized programs, both in inclination and
reality, often serve the larger college and community via its public outreach—speakers, panels, public lectures, student presentations, and
other public events. Nevertheless, coordinating events or responding
to public requests is rarely credited in college structures' reward systems for the amount of time it takes. Numerous documents from the
NWSA further identify what college administrators and faculty must do
to sustain both the women's studies curricula and programs and what
must be done to be responsive to the public (Gerber; Hartmann).

Epilogue

Of course, one knows that progressive movement forward and positive institutional change do not occur without setbacks. Our story has
an ambiguous ending. Our Women's Studies Steering Committee
believed its priorities were to develop and promote the curriculum,
teach women's studies courses, advise students, foster women's studies and more inclusive content in the larger college curriculum, and
fundraise and award an annual student scholarship. However, our
administrators prioritized the primary role of the committee as community outreach and the consolidation of women's events, women's
studies, women's services, and gender equity under the title of
women's events coordinator. Unable to reach a compromise despite a
concerted effort by all, the Women's Studies Steering Committee disbanded itself at the end of fall 2001. As Parker Palmer cautions in writing about teaching and institutional change, "Movements have the
power to alter the logic of organizations, because an organization is,
at the bottom, a system of social sanctions: do this and you will be pun-
ished, do that and you will be rewarded" (180).

Our long-standing committee took this drastic step with sadness
but also with hope. As a collaborative group, we wanted to refocus
our energy on our curriculum, our classroom teaching, and sustaining our student scholarship. At the same time, with no Women's
Studies Steering Committee, some of the crucial areas in our institution are diminished: outreach, public events, gender equity, services to women students, and women's studies visibility. As with any
college-wide committee that never fully became institutionalized, we
maintained our independence. However, we were also limited by the

lack of institutional support. Indeed, it remains a fine balancing act to be part of an institution yet apart from some of its official structures. As the institution struggles with its inevitable round of budget cuts, competing priorities, mission realignments, outcomes assessments, and accountability, our women's studies faculty and staff hope to help the college refocus itself by continuing to ask questions about how to serve and educate all of our students better. We have also recommended that a college-wide task force on inclusivity be established in the near future. At this very important moment in our world and in our institutional history, we hope that our deliberative actions will help the college recommit to diversity and inclusivity with all its resources for curricular and programmatic efforts. We believe we can simultaneously reaffirm our commitment to teaching *and* institutional change and "we will discover that there is no essential conflict between loving to teach and working to reform education" (Palmer 183).

NOTES

This article is dedicated to the wisdom and spirit of Virginia Low, professor emerita, who passed away in December 2001.

1. These six women include Catherine (Kate) Finnegan, Joanne Hayes, Mary Ellen Kelly, Virginia Low, and Phyllis Nahman as well as myself. Special thanks to all of them for their generosity.
2. For editorial assistance and suggestions for this list, special appreciation goes to Steven Budd and Phyllis Nahman.
3. NSF-AACU Award #9555808: Women and Scientific Literacy: Building Two-Way Streets, with special thanks to colleagues Ana Gaillat, Beth Erviti, and Dale MacLeod.
4. Mary Stuart Rogers Foundation and Greenfield Community College Foundation.
5. See www.genderequity.org.
6. See www.tep.k14.mass.edu/perkins/gender.html.
7. These dedicated professionals in the Women's Resource Center and Gender Equity Services include Rosemarie Freeland, Erica Goleman, and Suzanne McGowan. Special thanks to all of them for their generosity.
8. See www.gcc.mass.edu/folderdeg/womenstudies.html.

WORKS CITED

Fisher, Berenice Malka. *No Angel in the Classroom: Teaching Through Feminist Discourse.* New York: Rowman and Littlefield, 2001.

Gerber, Barbara W. "An Ethics Statement for Women's Studies Practioners. " NWSA Membership Brochure. 18 Jan. 2002. http://www.inform.umd.edu/EdRes/Topic/WomensStudies/Development+Support.

Hartmann, Susan M. *What Programs Need: Essential Resources for Women's Studies Programs.* Rev. by Dorothy C. Miller and Magdalena Garcia-Pinto. Nov. 1991, rev. Jan. 2001. http://www.nwsa.org/resources.htm.

Hayes, Elizabeth, and Daniele D. Flannery, eds. *Women as Learners: The Significance of Gender in Adult Learning.* San Francisco, CA: Jossey-Bass, 2000

Luebke, Barbara F., and Mary Ellen Reilly. *Women's Studies Graduates: The First Generation.* New York: Teachers College, 1995.

Mahar, Frances, and Mary Kay Thompson Tetrault. *The Feminist Classroom: An Inside Look at How Professors and Students Are Transforming Higher Education for a Diverse Society.* New York: Basic, 1994.

McTighe-Musil, Caryn, ed. *The Courage to Question: Women's Studies and Student Learning.* Washington, DC: Association of American Colleges and Universities, 1992.

————, ed. *Gender, Science and the Undergraduate Curriculum: Building Two-Way Streets.* Washington, DC: Association of American Colleges and Universities, 2001.

————, ed. *Students at the Center: Feminist Assessment.* Washington, DC: Association of American Colleges and Universities, 1992.

Palmer, Parker J. *The Courage to Teach: Exploring the Inner Landscape of a Teacher's Life.* San Francisco, CA: Jossey-Bass, 1998.

Spanier, Bonnie, Alexander Bloom, and Darlene Boroviak. *Toward a Balanced Curriculum: A Sourcebook for Initiating Gender Integration Projects.* Cambridge, MA: Schenkman, 1994.

Wiley, Anne M. "Identity and Diversity: An Exploratory Assignment." *Women's Studies Quarterly* 24.3–4 (1996): 55–68.

Anne M. Wiley is professor of psychology and women's studies at Greenfield Community College, Greenfield, Massachusetts, and an adjunct professor in women's studies at Keene State College, Keene, New Hampshire. She currently serves as the resource support to the GCC Women's Center and gender equity efforts.

Unpacking the Mother/Daughter Baggage

Reassessing Second- and Third-Wave Tensions

Cathryn Bailey

We want to use our newfound freedoms, and talk about them, and maybe even modify them a bit, but older feminists seem more concerned with just sitting on them, sticking blindly with a single political agenda. No deviation allowed!

—Janis Cortese (1999)

[Y]oung women are celebrating pluralities, embracing their personal and political contradictions: (i.e.: choosing to wear makeup while maintaining a critical stance toward the misogyny inherent in the cosmetic industry) and refusing the feminist party line.

—Krista Jacob (2001)

Now in my mid-thirties, I am the age of many of those who, since the 1990s, have identified themselves as third-wave feminists. As a student of women's studies and philosophy through the late 1980s and early 1990s at the University of Missouri, it was feminist teachers grounded in the second wave who first inspired me. They led me through the theory and poetry of Andrea Dworkin, Adrienne Rich, Audre Lorde, Marge Piercy, and Susan Griffin, the incisive womanist writings of Angela Davis and Alice Walker, the philosophical flights of Mary Daly, and even the gritty critique of "The Scum Manifesto." This work continued to shape my thinking, even after friends steered me toward the exciting work of Judith Butler, Ani Difranco, and the third-wave Web sites and anthologies that began appearing around 1995. Perhaps it is because the contours of my own feminism have been formed by both second- and third-wave ideas and sensibilities that I have never had much patience for dismissive criticisms between second- and third-wave feminists.

I have, in fact, argued that when third wavers such as the influential Rebecca Walker accuse second wavers of such crimes as "rabid identity politics," they are writing as if the second wave were monolithic, as if there existed some agreed-upon party line that older feminists have been imposing on everyone else. Since I know that there is and always has been disagreement and flexibility among older feminists about all kinds of things, I have been inclined to brush off such younger women's critiques. What I am beginning to think, however, is that just because there is no one set of clearly articulated values emanating from feminism, there may still be some legitimacy in talking about recognizably feminist values of which younger feminists might be critical. After all, there is no one set of clearly articulated misogynistic mandates emerging from an easily identifiable site called the patriarchy, but this does not undercut the legitimacy of feminist critiques of it.

In this essay, I look at how feminism, especially the academic feminism born of the second wave, can be understood as significantly affecting younger feminists in their very constitution as emerging feminist subjects. Through an appropriation of some Foucauldian ideas, I show how a movement such as feminism must contain the very kinds of pressures that serve to produce feminist subjects who can then be expected to resist that same feminism. Specifically, I describe how some of the practices of feminism in the college classroom serve as examples of how, through various explicit and implicit cues, feminist subjects are produced. Next, I contextualize some younger women's criticisms, situating them in such a way that they can be seen as legitimate expressions of resistance, but ones that do not necessarily require the falsification of earlier feminist claims. I analyze the general question of the nature of feminist choice as an especially fruitful point of tension between younger and older feminists, one that accounts for some of the looming communication gap that sometimes appear between the waves. As I see it, the generation gap between these groups of feminists is not based so much on disagreement about particular issues as on a failure to communicate honestly in the first place. There is a disingenuousness about the nature of power and resistance on both sides, one that not only results in gross misunderstandings as reflected in the popular media, but that also will affect the nature and quality of cross-generational collaboration in the academy.

Regimes of Feminism

One of Michel Foucault's most useful insights is that power need not be located in one site or wielded by one readily identifiable authority to be effective (*Discipline and Punish* 1979). Thus, for example, Foucault could write about the effectiveness of modern educational practices to mold students even though he understood that such power did not merely trickle unidirectionally from a dictator to the masses through a clearly visible hierarchy (*Discipline and Punish* 1979). Similarly, the fact that we cannot speak of a singularly identifiable feminist power does not mean that it does not exist with the capacity to affect subjects. In the wake of the current backlash against feminism, many of us are accustomed to thinking of it as an increasingly disempowered movement, but but we need to see how it continues to be enmeshed in power relations. If not, we can never comprehend why someone who has some appreciation for feminism might, nevertheless, feel a need to resist aspects of it, as many younger women clearly do.[1]

Feminists have been remarkably thorough in their conceptualizations of how patriarchal power functions to oppress women. The insidious nature of that power has been unveiled in explanations of how patriarchy shapes women's very subjectivities. For example, feminist philosopher Sandra Bartky analyzes such practices as dieting, exercise, bodily comportment, makeup and cosmetic surgery, concluding that: "In contemporary patriarchal culture, a panoptical male connoisseur resides within the consciousness of most women: they stand perpetually before his gaze and under his judgment" (71). The patriarchal force initiates automatic self-policing actions and attitudes within the subject. No one has to stand in front of the woman and tell her she's ugly without makeup; she learns to experience herself as ugly.

Additionally, whether we are discussing patriarchal sites of power or feminist ones, we should sometimes expect to find a conflation between aspects that are empowering and those that are not. What can serve liberatory interests can also function repressively. For example, initiatives to document paternity for the collection of child support can be exploited to threaten mothers' custody. Modern science serves as a more dramatic example. Initially a movement that served to empower individuals against state and religious authority, modern science has also aided in the oppression of whole populations in the contemporary world (Harding 96). Social movements must, by their very natures, repress some possibilities while they foster others. "All order is, after all, double edged, at once prohibitive and productive" (Cocks 70).

In the conceptual meanings and practices it elaborates, a social order shapes the forms of experience that a subject may have, including a circumscription of the range of meanings that those experiences will have for the subject. For example, feminist conceptualizations of sexual harassment meant that women began to be experienced and to experience themselves as victims or, perhaps, survivors, of this insidious practice, rather than as uncomfortable individual accomplices to off-color jokes or inappropriate touches. Among the rules that have been variously embodied in feminist cultures are imperatives about gender-inclusive language, egalitarian sexual and work relations, and so forth.

The crucial point here is that feminism does not cease to exert normalizing power over subjects simply because it is an ideology associated with a genuinely liberatory movement. The particular ways of being a feminist may never be fully enumerated, but it is necessary, in order for the concept of feminism to be meaningful, that certain options be experienced by subjects as foreclosed. In addition, "it is only through the process of subjectification that we become subjects capable of resisting the institutions, discourses, and practices that constitute us as subjects" (McLaren 119). Part of what feminist teaching encourages is the recognition and respect of one's own ideas, desires, and so forth. Thus, to some extent it is a testament to the success of feminism that such teaching produces younger feminist subjects who resist, on feminist terms, the very feminism that has helped to shape them.

The Micro-Practices of Academic Feminism

As Foucault theorized it, power at the "micro level" informs relations between specific individuals or groups. It is within the context of such power relations that subjects come to be constituted. "Subjects do not first preexist and later enter into combat or harmony. . . . Subjects emerge on a field of battle" (Dreyfus and Rabinow 109). Feminists, then, as subjects, do not logically precede the exercise of feminist power; rather, it is through the influence of feminism that it becomes meaningful to speak of feminist subjects. Perhaps nowhere is the emergence of the feminist subject more explicit than in the feminist classroom.

While the modern academy hardly resembles the disciplinary power of the schools, hospitals, and factories analyzed by Foucault, we can imagine a sense in which feminist classrooms, too, exert a form of disciplinary pressure upon students. It is in the feminist college classroom that many women first come to understand what it is to be a feminist.

Many experience, for the first time, instructors and older students who identify as feminists. Here, pedagogical methods are frequently explicitly set forth as emphasizing the equality of student and teachers, avoidance of hierarchy, and the mutuality of learning. Such values may even be expressed through the aesthetics of the classroom, for example, desks set up in a circle with a teacher who sits among her students.

However, I think that much of the perception of the feminist classroom as a place of equality is an illusion, and not an effective one at that. Even if students are asked to participate as equals, for example, contributing to curriculum development or sharing in teaching responsibilities, they frequently act and speak in ways they think professors want them to, or, in a reactionary manner, perhaps what they think professors most do not want to hear. The educational system as a whole does not promote students' or professors' being the kind of subjects that egalitarian rhetoric asks them to be. It is no wonder, then, that students and teachers often find themselves behaving in scripted ways automatically, scripts that may reflect power differences based on age, race, and class as well.

In the feminist classroom, one's physical presence is likely to be a locus of attention. For example, one can expect others to notice what one is wearing in part because dress is an issue that the class itself likely politicizes. In many classrooms, women can expect others to notice the status of their leg hair, a kind of attention that can be especially disturbing for women who have already been socialized to be self-conscious about their bodies. The requirements of sisterhood demand support for one's personal experiences but the principle that the personal is political makes suspect the claim that anyone's personal choices are truly, simply personal. What one eats or does not eat may come under scrutiny, too, because food may be politicized through discussions about eating disorders. In principle, no part of one's life is off limits—the very distinction between public and private has been called into question.[2]

The discussion of one's personal experiences can become a part of the feminist classroom in a way that is reminiscent of Foucault's analysis of confession. The Foucauldian notion of confession can also be useful for analyzing the feminist classroom. Foucault emphasizes the significance that the confession has come to have for attaching individuals to particular identities. As he describes it, the confession "plays a part in justice, medicine, education, family relationships, and love relations. . . . One confesses one's crime's, one's sins, one's thoughts and desires, one's illnesses and troubles; one goes about telling, with the greatest precision, whatever is most difficult to tell" (*History of*

Sexuality 59). The constitution of the "truth" of what one confesses is completed when it is interpreted by the authority (66–67), when it comes to be seen as helpful in describing the truth of who the subject is. Thus, in the context of the feminist classroom, the woman who expresses her desire for other women, or her experience of rape or battery, comes to be understood by herself and others as saying something about who she fundamentally is, a "lesbian," or a "survivor," for example, and not simply a woman who has had certain feelings or experiences.

The confessor can be helped to see the deeper meanings of her or his experience, "but what neither he nor the authority directing the hermeneutic exegesis can see is what the exegetical situation is doing to both of them and why . . . the hidden truth is not the final truth about what is going on" (Dreyfus and Rabinow 124). The "truth" is not something extracted from the confessor, but something produced together with that authority. While many feminists do not endorse aspects of the confessional mode in the classroom, and while it may not represent the ideal mode for any feminist teacher, it has been my experience that the dynamic it describes is often present, something which may be partially explained by the implicit modeling of some classroom discussions on the confessional aspect of consciousness-raising groups. The point here is not whether the confessions are desirable or not, but simply to make explicit that the confessional mode itself may also contribute to a situation in which young feminists become constituted as feminist subjects and that it, too, may conceal something about the nature and practice of feminist power.

Contextualizing Some Younger Women's Challenges

Defining third-wave feminism has itself been a focus of many third-wave writings largely because there have been no watershed political events to mark either the death of the second wave or the birth of the third.[3] Here, I limit my discussion to works in which the editors explicitly identify as third-wave feminists, although individual contributors may not. Some may be more comfortable with the punk feminist identity of "Riot Grrl," while others simply call themselves and their peers "younger feminists" or, simply, "younger women." In general, third-wave feminists tend to position themselves by age and attitude; they see themselves as being able to take for granted some of the things for which older feminists had to fight, although there is often appreciation expressed to second wavers. Although it is really no easier to define the agenda of third-wave feminism than that of second-wave feminism, I have mostly restricted my focus to issues of sexuality and bodily aesthetics as these figure most prominently in the third-wave material I have encountered.

In her introductory essay, Rebecca Walker, editor of the seminal third-wave anthology *To Be Real: Telling the Truth and Changing the Face of Feminism*, claims that "to be a feminist in the way that we have seen or understood feminism is to conform to an identity and way of living that doesn't allow for individuality, complexity, or less than perfect personal histories" (xxxii–iii). Like Walker, many of the other contributors to the anthology focus on sexuality and bodily aesthetics. Another contributor remembers her experience with an activist, feminist mother:

> My sister, brother, and I were mortified as we ran alongside the march, giggling and pointing at the marching women chanting "Women Unite—Take Back the Night!" The throngs were letting it all hang out: Their breasts hung low, their leg hair grew wild, their thighs were wide in their faded blue jeans. Some of them donned Earth shoes and t-shirts with slogans like "A Woman Needs a Man Like a Fish Needs a Bicycle." They weren't the least bit ashamed. But I was. I remember thinking, "I will never let myself look like that." (Senna 7–8)

Another contributor also defines her young adult identity reactively, against what she perceived to be the prevailing second-wave aesthetic (or lack of it): "I felt part of a new generation of feminists. We wanted to make room for play in our lives—dying our hair, shaving our legs, dressing in ways that made us happy" (Allyn 144). More recently, aesthetic and sexual issues remain central to younger women's complaints with the insistence that one can "wear makeup, shave your legs, wear dresses, have a traditional wedding, or celebrate your femininity and still be considered a 'feminist'" (Jacob). Amy Richards, one of the authors of *Manifesta: Young Women, Feminism, and the Future*, explains in an interview, "I don't think these women are saying 'I'm going to be female, going to be objectified, going to wear sexy clothes and so on and be part of the backlash against feminism.' I think they're saying, 'I'm going to do all these things because I want to embrace my femininity" (Straus).

Despite the fact that this woman's conception of second-wave feminism is, I think, conditioned by backlash stereotypes (the "hairy, humorless, man-hater"?), clearly, for some younger women, one important perceived site of dissent is the personal experience of the body. This is not the only locus of concern. *Manifesta,* in particular, has some focus on traditional political issues, at least, liberal political issues, but here, too, issues of bodily aesthetics and sexuality are quite prominent, and not in a way that is likely to comfort older feminists. Referring to the "Third Wave revalorization of beauty, sexual power and femininity," one critic of *Manifesta* worries: "What happens to feminism when it reclaims the very sources of power the patriarchy has always been happy to grant us?" (Jensen 4). Certainly, there is a rich understanding among many second wavers about the risks of embracing traditionally feminine qualities that younger feminists ought to consider.

Nonetheless, I think that the intense focus on these kinds of issues, however misguided some of them are in the details, is a wake-up call for older feminists that what appears, from one perspective, to be conformist, may, from another perspective, have subversive potential. Since the 1970s, things may not have changed as much as any of us would have liked, but they have changed. We cannot assess the meaning of younger women's actions and attitudes without recognizing that the backdrop against which their actions are performed is, in many cases, significantly different. As one younger feminist explains: "The legacy of second wave feminism had taught me that, as a girl, I could do anything I wanted to do, but the backlash let me know that this was possible only as long as I wasn't a girl—as long as I wasn't soft and feminine and weak" (Shoemaker 115). Another younger feminist puts it this way: "We want not to get rid of the trappings of traditional femininity or sexuality so much as to pair them with demonstrations of strength or power. We are much less likely to burn our bras communally than to run down the street clad in nothing but our bras yelling 'Fuck you!'" (Klein 223). Whether such an action is usefully subversive would be a worthwhile question for discussion, but that cannot occur if older feminists simply assume that it is patriarchally conformist now simply because it would have been thirty years ago.

Feminist Choice and the Communication Gap

While I think Walker is simply incorrect in her claim that feminism typically involves "policing morality" (xxxv) or rabid "identity politics" (xxxiv), we can take seriously her kind of resistance to older feminism without invalidating or oversimplifying the message of the second wave. Here, we are at an impasse based on problematic understandings and uses of the concept of feminist choice. My analysis highlights not so much a disagreement between younger and older feminists as an inability to communicate effectively enough to even get to the point of fruitful disagreement.

The difficulty begins, I think, with feminists who attempt to hide behind the tired liberal rhetoric of individual freedom to avoid the charge that feminism advocates some values while eschewing others. It is a maneuver designed precisely to avoid been seen as "policing morality." On this view, the shift in consciousness that leads a woman to identify herself as a feminist is understood as one that helps her gain access to a more authentic self. It is not, then, the content of the choices themselves that are significant, but the fact that they emerged from an authentically feminist subjectivity.

The concept of an "authentic self," however, is too slippery to be useful in any kind of political context. Even if it were true that each of us had such a self (and I'm not at all sure that it is) we could still have no way of knowing which desires emerged from that true self and which from one's "patriarchal self." There simply is no readily available, external standard of authenticity relative to which individuals' desires can be assessed. This is one of the theoretical difficulties that underlies many historically important feminist debates. For example, is the woman who "chooses" sadomasochistic sex merely acting from her patriarchal conditioning or is it possible that her motives emanate from her true self?

Consider, for example, another of the third-wave contributors who asks, "Is it horrible to say that reading about real-world rape and torture sometimes turns me on?" (Minkowitz 79). She goes on to offer an explanation and defense of her behavior including a plausible account of its psychological genesis in her childhood abuse. In her foreword to the anthology in which Minkowitz's essay appears, Gloria Steinem writes that reading it "makes [her] as sorrowful as reading about a gay person, someone who is Jewish, or a person of color who finds homophobic, anti-Semitic, or racist violence to be a sexual turn-on." Steinem further claims that Minkowitzs' essay "is a powerful reminder of the power of socialization" (xxi).

Minkowitz implies that her desires are traceable to her own socialization, but also attempts to validate them, suggesting that her desires are at least partly a function of her nature, that is, who she is without the veneer of society (85). Steinem suggests that the content of Minkowitz's desires is itself enough to show that they are inauthentically patriarchal in their origin. According to Steinem, the fact that Minkowitz would claim to freely choose to masturbate while reading actual accounts of rape is itself enough to mark her behavior as coerced by socialization. Adopting a model that relies this way upon the concept of authentic choice, Steinem cannot help but feel sorry for Minkowitz and Minkowitz cannot help but feel patronized by the suggestion that Steinem seems to think she has better access to Minkowitzs' true self (and others like her) than has Minkowitz herself. While Walker claims to offer a new brand of feminism that emphasizes "self possession" and "self determination," Steinem responds that feminism has always encouraged such ideals. In her foreword to *To Be Real,* Steinem expresses a general resentment to charges such as Walker's: "Imagine how frustrating it is to be held responsible for some of the very divisions you've been fighting against, and you'll know how feminists of the 1980s and earlier may feel as they read some of these pages" (xxiii). However, when confronted by what women such as Minkowitz claim to be their choices, Steinem denies that they are real choices. This is a denial that, to Walker's eyes, must look a bit like denial of individual freedom itself.

As I have argued, it simply isn't plausible or useful to insist that feminism is for individual choice in the sense that feminism endorses whatever individuals affirm simply on the grounds that they have chosen it. Steinem promulgates this view, however: "If I were to choose one common lesson taught by these many feminists, it would be this: The greatest gift we can give one another is the power to make a choice. The power to choose is even more important than the choices we make" (xxvi). But skepticism about the very possibility of pure choice based on the recognition that sexism shapes the nature and range of the choices is what has always motivated feminist ambivalence about such things as women's involvement in sadomasochistic sex, pornography, prostitution, and surrogate motherhood. The knee-jerk response is to deny that any such choices, under patriarchy, truly qualify as free. This type of response, though, risks suggesting that one has, as a feminist judge, access to an objective standard against which to assess others' choices. No wonder younger feminists might feel the need to rebel. One younger woman refers specifically to Steinem, who has placed herself in public conversation with third wavers and whose name appears regularly in their essays: "A woman—sorry, an *icon*— more than twice my age, as old (older than) my mother—was going to tell *me* what I think about . . . myself?" (Leibovich 2).

Younger feminists who complain about the restrictive nature of second-wave feminism may be picking up on the sheer falsity of the claim that feminism is simply interested in increasing the number of choices available to women without regard to the content of those choices. Surely, it's more honest to describe feminism as aiming to increase the number of *feminist* choices available to women, even if we do not claim to know in advance (or, perhaps, ever) precisely what would count as such a choice. We may even need to commit to the circular claim that part of what conditions a choice as feminist is that it was chosen by a feminist, taking some of the emphasis away from the content of the choice and placing it on the nature and context of the agent's intention. Being up front about the fact that not all choices can possibly count as feminist ones is the sort of step towards honesty that might improve generational communication.

We might also be honest about the fact that women in feminist settings, too, may experience some light sanctioning for failing to adhere to certain norms. In one of my first women's studies classes as a student (which would have been in 1986 or so), I recall one teaching assistant who consistently teased a student about the heavy makeup she wore. While I have previously brushed aside this memory with the knowledge that that teaching assistant wasn't an official representative of feminism, I now remind myself that there are no official representatives of the patriarchy, either, but that doesn't mitigate the influence. Moreover, it is clear to me after nearly fifteen years of experience in women's studies settings, that this sort of "ribbing" isn't rare. In light of the emphasis placed on the political nature of the personal, we should be surprised if part of the constitution of feminist subjects did not involve sanctioning for "personal" choices, especially by other students. This may sometimes reflect a misguided application of the principle that the personal is political, but it is an understandable misapplication. It would be far more productive to honestly acknowledge that this sort of thing occurs and to take seriously some younger women's rebellion against it, than to deny it and claim to be mystified by younger women's complaints.

Forms of Younger Women's Resistance

[A]n Iraqi woman wearing a mini-skirt may be making a political statement in the expression of gender quite different from a U.S. woman wearing the same skirt. The illusion of sameness, the parallax, arises from ignoring different points of departure.

—Nancy J. Finley (4)

What counts as resistance is, to some extent, a relative matter. For example, in a traditionally heterosexually oriented club, a woman's appearance in a very short skirt, heels, and dramatic makeup might be easy to dismiss as patriarchally complicit. In the context of a lesbian bar where the prevailing aesthetic is quite different, such a woman's presence might have a different meaning. It is reasonable in the second context to consider this woman's costume to be a sign of resistance. I am not so much interested in convincing readers that this actually is the case; rather, I want to push the point that part of what makes an act count as subversive is the context in which it occurs.

For example, contextualizing third-wave feminist Eisa Davis' continued devotion to hip-hop music, which she acknowledges as sexist, may allow us to appreciate her position as resistance to racism. As she claims: "Hip hop, after all, is the chosen whipping boy for a misogyny that is fundamental to Western culture. Why should I deny myself hip hop but get a good grounding in Aristotle?" (132). Listening to hip-hop, even hip-hop that is blatantly sexist, may reasonably be understood as an act performed to counter the racist currents that may too selectively focus on the sexism of Black men. It is clear that differences in context can give one and the same act different meanings.

One of the factors that contributes to whether or not an act should be considered one of resistance is the agent's intention. On the other hand, there must be some external criteria to help define an act; otherwise, the fact that I believe myself to be waving in greeting would determine that that is what I would be doing even if my arm were actually anesthetized and hanging by my side. Similarly, acts of resistance should be defined by considerations both of intention and relevant external factors.

However, the difficulties in engaging in an enumeration of the "proper" criteria for determining what counts as genuine resistance are prohibitive. Should Minkowitz be solely responsible for accurately naming her intention or might Steinem legitimately be thought to have a voice in the matter? There must be a balance between the subject's own interpretation and that of others. But there is no practical way, beyond some vague recommendation for dialogue, to arrive at that balance of interpretations. The important point, though, is that some acknowledgment be made that in naming what counts as resistance, factors that are both internal and external to the agent must be considered. Thus, actions that may not have been subversive in the 1970s may be so today, but the simple fact that the agent thinks that this is the case is not enough to guarantee that it actually is.

It is especially important that subtler forms of resistance be recognized, especially given that some "forms of third wave activism don't always look 'activist' enough to second wave feminists" (Heywood and Drake 4). This is especially true when what an agent is resisting is the process of subjectification itself, that is, the processes through which one becomes tied to a particular identity. Many younger women see themselves as struggling against becoming the kind of feminist subjects they thought they were supposed to become. As such, they may be offering a kind of resistance that is not immediately directed at actual feminists, but rather to an internalized version of a feminist governor—a "panoptical feminist connoisseur"—to adapt Bartky's term (71). I am not arguing that there actually exist such policing figures in the world, but rather suggesting that we acknowledge how young feminists might come to internalize a judgmental feminist eye. Utilizing the "social parallax lens" in this way might permit us to understand more of what younger women say and do as gestures towards progressive resistance rather than as merely whiney and/or ignorantly complicit with the backlash.

Conclusion: Beyond the Mother/Daughter Impasse

I have been emphasizing similarities in how feminism operates as a disciplinary power and how other social forces, especially sexist ones, exert their pressures. I've done this not so much because I think that feminism is like the patriarchy, but because, as feminists, it is patriarchal forces that we've done the most thinking about. In particular, we need to uncover the "costs of our self-constitution," the price we pay for the benefits of becoming who we are (Sawicki 165). The urgency for self-criticism is made greater by the realization that many younger women are critical of feminism. We do not need to agree that feminism is fundamentally repressive in order to be concerned about those elements that may be experienced as repressive, especially by younger women.

Feminism principally exerts the kind of disciplinary power that produces subjects, agents capable of acting in various ways, rather than exerting it on women as objects. To borrow from the language of Foucault's later work, feminism exerts power, but it is not dominating. "Whereas 'domination' refers to a situation in which the subject is unable to overturn or reverse the domination relation—a situation where resistance is impossible—'power' refers to relations that are flexible, mutable, fluid, and even reversible" (Sawicki 170). Some younger feminists have incorrectly suggested that feminism is dominating, but there have always been voices within second-wave feminism crying out for diversity and individual variance. There is a level of ignorance about second-wave feminism in some third-wave critiques that is disappointing. Even worse, it is an ignorance that is rarely honestly acknowledged. It is, in part, the second wave's capacity for being so openly self-critical that has made concerns about diversity such a focal point for everyone else, including third wavers.

However, some second wavers sound as though they're denying the exercise of feminist power at all. Consider, for example, Jane Gallop's account of her experience in the self-referentially titled *Feminist Accused of Sexual Harassment.* She acknowledges that "students can experience feminist teachers as having power over them. And that makes it possible to imagine a feminist teacher as a sexual harasser," but she does not acknowledge that it is possible for a feminist to actually be a sexual harasser. There is a disingenuousness to Gallop's analysis that one reviewer summarized as follows: "Based on her own words, Jane Gallop is guilty of behaving irresponsibly and unethically toward students, who are not equal partners. She is guilty of abusing power that she will not acknowledge she wields" (Lane 9). While Gallop's denial may be extreme, I think it is not utterly different from disingenuous denials of feminist power in other contexts.

Only if we take seriously that feminist power exists, power that works to shape subjects, rather than innocently facilitating the emergence of young women's "authentic selves," can we appreciate that there might be something in these young women's experiences of their own feminist identities to be resisted. In addition, the resistance that feminism has inspired in younger women may tell us something worth reflecting upon, but not necessarily that older feminists are simply wrong. As Foucault's analysis suggests, power need not be simplistically authoritarian or totalizing in order to have great impact. Even though feminists have not, by and large, been dictatorial, we still have the responsibility to appreciate how younger women may have felt themselves to be structured and limited by second-wave values.

On the other hand, younger women have a similar responsibility, one that they, too, often fall short of meeting. Consider, for example, how the authors of *Manifesta* react to Phyllis Chesler's *Letters to a Young Feminist.* They reject it out of hand, complaining that "[y]ou're not our mothers. . . . You have to stop treating us like daughters" (Jensen 6). But as Jensen accurately observes,

> Despite its stylistic goofiness . . . Chesler's book remains one of the few Second Wave feminist "memoirs" (and there are now many) that work to instrumentalize, rather than glorify or recant, the feminist past in order to serve the feminist future. . . .[The authors of *Manifesta*] are unable to recognize how Chesler's book, like their own, attempts to build a bridge between the Waves. . . . As much as our authors say they want to connect with the Second Wave, they

clearly want the connection on their own terms. It's OK for Chesler
to participate in the Third Wave as an icon, as an inspiring bit of history, but Baumgardner and Richards would rather she quit trying to
contribute her own work. (4)

The biggest problem is not so much that second- and third-wave
feminists disagree as that they have not yet even gotten to the point of
honest disagreement. What is needed from older feminists is a more
realistic acknowledgement of feminist power that does not lead to a
brushing aside of younger women's complaints. From younger women
there must be a commitment to engage with the women and work of
the second wave in ways that are politically and academically serious,
rather than token acknowledgements of its merely "historical" importance. As the authors of *Manifesta* have put it so well, second wavers are
not third wavers' mothers. As such, older feminists should not expect
automatic and uncritical deference. But it is equally worth emphasizing that third wavers should not be indulged as rebellious daughters
whose limitations are to be explained away as mere symptoms of their
inexperience or growing pains. If we approach the table, not as mothers and daughters, but as peers with different strengths and weakness,
we might get somewhere. Maybe then, at least, honest communication
will take us to the point of productive disagreement.

NOTES

1. An ambivalence toward feminism both as a general ideology and as it is
   practiced in women's studies classrooms figures prominently in much
   third-wave work. See, for example, Findlen, and Heywood and Drake.
2. My point is not that feminist teachers actually encourage students to scru-
   tinize one another in this way, but that the kind of awareness women's
   studies students have of this important principle makes it especially likely
   in feminist classrooms.
3. This point is developed more fully in Bailey.

WORKS CITED

Allyn, Jennifer, and David Allyn. "Identity Politics." *To Be Real: Telling the Truth
and Changing the Face of Feminism.* Ed. Rebecca Walker. New York: Anchor,
1995. 143–55.

Bailey, Cathryn. "Making Waves and Drawing Lines: The Politics of Defining
the Vicissitudes of Feminism." *Hypatia* 12.3 (1997): 17–28.

Bartky, Sandra. "Foucault, Feminism, and the Modernization of Patriarchal
Power." *Feminism and Foucault: Reflections on Resistance.* Ed. Irene Diamond
and Lee Quinby. Boston: Northeastern University Press, 1988. 61–68.

Baumgardner, Jennifer, and Amy Richards. *Manifesta: Young Women, Feminism,
and the Future of Feminism.* New York: Farrar, 2000.

Chesler, Phyllis. *Letters to a Young Feminist.* New York: Four Walls, Eight Windows, 1998.

Cocks, Joan. *The Oppositional Imagination: Feminism, Critique, and Political Theory.* New York: Routledge, 1989.

Cortese, Janis. *The 3rd WWWave: Feminism for the New Millenium.* Online, available: http://www.io.com/~wwwave/. 1999.

Davis, Eisa. "Sexism and the Art of Feminist Hip-Hop Maintenance." Walker, *To Be Real.* 127–41.

Dreyfus, Hubert L. and Paul Rabinow. *Michel Foucault: Beyond Structuralism and Hermeneutics.* 2d ed. Chicago: U Chicago P, 1983.

Findlen, Barbara, ed. *Listen Up: Voices From the Next Feminist Generation.* Seattle: Seal, 1995.

Finley, Nancy J. "The Concept of Social Parallax." *Women and Language* 20.1 (1997): 5–8 (4).

Foucault, Michel. "Afterword: The Subject and Power." Dreyfus and Rabinow, *Beyond Structuralism.* 208–26.

———. *Discipline and Punish: The Birth of the Prison.* Trans., Alan Sheridan. New York: Vintage, 1979.

———. *The History of Sexuality, Volume I: An Introduction.* Trans., Robert Hurley. New York: Vintage, 1990.

———. "On the Genealogy of Ethics: An Overview of Work in Progress." Dreyfus and Rabinow, *Beyond Structuralism.* 229–52.

Gallop, Jane. *Feminist Accused of Sexual Harassment.* Durham, NC: Duke UP, 1997.

Harding, Sandra. *Whose Science? Whose Knowledge? Thinking From Women's Lives.* Ithaca, NY: Cornell UP, 1991.

Heywood, Leslie, and Jennifer Drake, eds. *Third Wave Agenda: Being Feminist, Doing Feminism.* Minneapolis: U of Minnesota P, 1997.

Hekman, Susan J. *Feminist Interpretations of Michel Foucault.* University Park: Penn State U P, 1996.

Jacob, Krista. "Engendering Change: What's Up with Third Wave?" *Sexing the Political: A Journal of Third Wave Feminists On Sexuality.* Online, available: http://www.sexingthepolitical.com/. 2001.

Jensen, Michelle. "Riding the Third Wave." Rev. of *Manifesta: Young Women, Feminism, and the Future,* by Jennifer Baumgardner and Amy Richards. *The Nation Online.* Available: http://www.thenation.com/. December 2000: 11.

Klein, Melissa. "Duality and Redefinition: Young Feminism and the Alternative Music Community." Heywood and Drake, *Third Wave Agenda.* 207–25.

Lane, Ann J. "When Power Corrupts." Rev. of *Feminist Accused of Sexual Harassment,* by Jane Gallop, *The Women's Review of Books* 14.12 (1997). 8–10.

Lee, Jee Yeun. "Beyond Bean Counting." Findlen, *Listen Up.*

Leibovich, Lori. "Hey Hey, Ho, Ho, The Matriarchy's Got to Go!" *Salon.* Online, available: http://www.salon.com/. 1998.

McLaren, Margaret A. "Foucault and the Subject of Feminism." *Social Theory and Practice.* 23.1 (1997). 109–29.

Minkowitz, Donna. "Giving it Up: Orgasm, Fear, and Femaleness." Walker, *To Be Real.* 77–85.

Sawicki, Jana. "'Subjects' of Power and Freedom." Hekman, *Feminist Interpretations.*
Senna, Danzy. "To Be Real." Walker, *To Be Real.* 5–20.
Shoemaker, Leigh. "Part Animal, Part Machine: Self-Definition, Rollins Style." Heywood and Drake, *Third Wave Agenda.* 103–21.
Steinem, Gloria. "Foreword." Walker, *To Be Real.* Xiii–xviii.
Straus, Tamara. "A Manifesto for Third Wave Feminism." *Alternet.* Online, available: http://www.alternet.org/. October 24, 2000.
Walker, Rebecca, ed. *To Be Real: Telling the Truth and Changing the Face of Feminism.* New York: Anchor, 1995.

Cathryn Bailey *is associate professor of philosophy at Minnesota State University, Mankato, and currently serving as a Mellon Fellow at Duke University. Her recent work focuses on questions in feminist theory related to body, language, and identity.*

Outsiders, Interlopers, and Ingrates

The Tenuous Position of Women of Color in Women's Studies

Patti Duncan

And if we don't fight / if we don't resist / if we don't organize and unify and / get the power to control our own lives / Then we will wear / the exaggerated look of captivity / the stylized look of submission / the bizarre look of suicide / the dehumanized look of fear / and the decomposed look of repression / forever and ever and ever / And there it is

—Jayne Cortez

These lines from the poem "There It Is," by Jayne Cortez, serve as the prelude and point of entry to the syllabus for my WS330 class, Women of Color in the U.S., a regular course offering in the Women's Studies Department at Portland State University. By introducing students in this class first and foremost to ideas about organizing, coalition-building, and resistance, I hope to convey to them the empowering aspects of studying women of color in the United States, as well as the long histories of struggle spearheaded by women of color. My objectives for students in this class are threefold: I expect them to gain some understanding of the histories, writings, and experiences of women of color. I hope that women of color students in the class will develop greater awareness of the obstacles surrounding them, in order to create coalitions with other students in the class and obtain knowledge of practical strategies to confront and resist all forms of oppression. And I hope that all students in the class will develop the skills and strategies associated with becoming good allies to people of color, and to consciously and actively challenge and resist racism and other forms of oppression in their own lives and communities.

Each time I have taught Women of Color in the U.S. and other classes focused on the experiences and writings of particular groups of women of color, however, I have found myself confronted by various forms of resistance or deflection from students within the class. While it would be tempting to chalk these tensions up simply to the sexism, racism, classism, and/or heterosexism and homophobia on the part of such students, I want to suggest here that some conflicts within classes about women of color in women's studies arise as symbols of deeper problems within the field of women's studies. In this essay, I offer a description of some of the tensions that arise in the Women of Color in the U.S. class. Then, I attempt to contextualize such tensions by pointing to the ways in which women of color have historically been marginalized within women's studies and ostensibly included in more recent years through the development of classes like Women of Color in the U.S.

Teaching WS330: Women of Color in the U.S.

In the spring of 2000, Portland State University hired me as a new assistant professor of women's studies.[1] My contract stipulated that I would be responsible for teaching core and elective courses within the department. In particular, it listed WS330 as a central part of my job criteria.[2] Upon my arrival at Portland State University, I learned that students and faculty within the department were engaged in multiple conversations regarding the place of this course and other courses about women of color, and the complex meanings, both literal and symbolic, around which such courses continue to revolve. At the same time, members of the women's studies community at this institution were also involved in complex and often painful discussions about the exclusion of women of color and allegations of racism within the Women's Studies Department. In particular, students reported a lack of attention to women of color and issues of race in some of their core classes and therefore demanded a restructuring of the curriculum. At first glance, the meanings of WS330 within the context of women's studies programs seem to offer a remedy to the long history of racism experienced by women of color in women's studies. As an antidote to decades of exclusion and oppressive practices, such a course reconfigures women of color at the center of women's studies.

At Portland State the Women of Color in the U.S. course indeed figures at the center of the department—it lies, along with other courses, at the core of women's studies.[3] As such, it is situated at the critical nexus of the department's course offerings, highlighting the experiences of women of color within women's studies. As elsewhere, however, there is here a peculiar disjuncture. Namely, while figured at the core, the course is also maintained along the periphery of women's studies. For instance, it is not a required course for women's studies majors. While the class usually fills to capacity, few women's studies majors actually take the course. In fact, a large number of students from other departments—in particular Black studies and Chicano/a / Latino/a studies[4]—enroll in this course, and it often serves as their introduction to women's studies, a process which Rachel Lee refers to as "off-shore manufacture"—the importation of "colored bodies" to women's studies from other places via courses such as this. In developing her analysis of this process of "off-shore manufacture," Lee suggests that when women of color are perceived to be too centrally located "inside" women's studies, this perpetuates a new crisis in the field, one that sometimes results in outright hostility over the belief that women of color have now "taken over" the discipline (86, 96).

Indeed, women's studies courses about women of color have recently proliferated in programs and departments across the United States. However, like WS330, such courses are often positioned both within and outside of women's studies, thus paralleling and maintaining the "outsider-within" status experienced by many women of color in women's studies. And this movement of women of color studies into the core of women's studies frequently does lead to charges that women of color have "taken over." These notions are long-standing and consistently circulated within women's studies publications, at conferences, and in classrooms. Often such sentiments are expressed by students who wonder why it is necessary to spend so much time addressing the issues of women of color in "general" women's studies classes (e.g., Introduction to Women's Studies, Feminist Theory, etc.). At other times, students may express great anxiety over finding themselves displaced from the center, even in classes that explicitly focus on women of color.

In my course, one student mentioned how angry and "hurt" she felt by the fact that the bulk of our class reading assignments focused almost exclusively on women of color. As a white woman of northern European descent, she wondered why her own experiences were not covered in the class. Another white student consistently attempted to tie the themes of our class discussions to her own experiences: When we discussed white standards of beauty and the politics of appearance, she stated, "I feel oppressed by beauty standards, too. Other people make fun of me because I'm so pale and I never tan." When we discussed women of color and reproductive politics, she refused to hear the specificities of women of color's experiences, arguing that white women face "those problems" too. And when we talked about women of color immigrant family networks, she asserted, "My [white] family is like that, too. What's so special about women of color families?"

At other times, I have found our course topics derailed by certain white students who, intentionally or not, repeatedly shifted the focus to themselves.[5] In one class period, after discussing the material effects of racism on people of color, I asked students to consider the psychological tolls exacted by racism on the psyches of women of color. A white woman raised her hand and stated, "I imagine they might feel low self esteem, sometimes even self-hatred." Another white woman jumped in to say, "Yeah, I feel a lot of self-hatred over racism—I wish I could change myself and the people in my family." A third white woman student added, "I also feel intense guilt and sadness, like that we live in a culture that's so oppressive." Other white women were nodding and raising their hands. At this point, I interrupted the conversation to ask them how we had moved from my question—about the psychological effects of racism for women of color—to a discussion about the effects of racism for white women. Much like the scenario described by Gloria Anzaldúa in her introduction to *Making Face, Making Soul / Haciendo Caras: Creative and Critical Perspectives by Women of Color*, regarding her own teaching of a similar course, white students in my class, too, "attempted to subvert the focus from women-of-color's feelings to their own feelings of confusion, helplessness, anger, guilt, fear of change and other insecurities" (xx).[6] This dynamic is repeated each time I teach classes about women of color, and it hints at larger issues surrounding the inclusion of women of color within the field of women's studies.[7]

Even while there are those who believe that women of color now dominate the field of women's studies, women of color sometimes feel otherwise. Students of color in women's studies and other disciplines often experience a great degree of discrimination and isolation. Elsewhere, I have suggested that the constant centering and recentering of white students in college classrooms functions hand in hand with the messages students of color receive about "not belonging" in higher education.[8] Such messages are conveyed by faculty, administrators, and other students in both explicit and subtle ways. For example, students of color encounter racism in the university on multiple levels—through curricular exclusions and misrepresentations, isolation, a lack of mentoring and/or intellectual and social support, and frequent tokenism, as well as blatant practices of racist exclusion, exploitation, and sabotage.[9]

For students of color in higher education who have previously received negative messages about their place in academia, it is imperative to disrupt conventional practices within women's studies. Having long been characterized as the "outsiders," "interlopers," and "ingrates" suggested by my title, women of color in women's studies find ourselves even now confronting, if no longer outright exclusion, then very specific forms of inclusion that do not always result in the much-needed transformations of the discipline. The Women of Color in the U.S course and courses like it are crucial to the development of a truly inclusive women's studies. The incorporation of such classes into existing women's studies curricula also poses significant problems, however, necessitating interrogation of some of the complex processes occurring in the proliferation of such courses.

The Need for Classes about Women of Color in Women's Studies

Since the inception in 1969 of women's studies programs in institutions of higher education in the United States, women of color have pointed out the ways in which we have been excluded and struggled for inclusivity. Writers and scholars such as Audre Lorde, Gloria Anzaldúa, Angela Davis, Cherríe Moraga, Barbara Smith, Mitsuye Yamada, Maxine Baca Zinn, Chela Sandoval, Judy Yung, and Paula Gunn Allen, among others, have all challenged women's studies to examine its own racist practices. In her 1981 essay "The Uses of Anger," Audre Lorde takes members of the women's studies community to task for responding to racism with guilt, fear, and denial. Instead, she urges us to recognize anger as an appropriate response to racism. Because all of our oppressions are linked together, Lorde suggests, women must come together to understand our racial differences in order to challenge racism effectively. Barbara Smith argues that feminism is and should be "the political theory and practice that struggles to free *all* women . . . [and that] anything less than this vision of total freedom is not feminism, but merely female self-aggrandizement" (25). Others, like Mitsuye Yamada and Paula Gunn Allen, have pointed out ways in which women of color of particular racial groups are rendered invisible within women's studies and feminist movements, arguing that the racist practices within women's studies are deeply entrenched and will need to be confronted at multiple levels.[10] Lynet Uttal argues that women of color are tokenized by "inclusion without influence." Finally, Maxine Baca Zinn, Lynn Weber Cannon, Elizabeth Higginbotham, and Bonnie Thornton Dill in their landmark essay, "The Costs of Exclusionary Practices in Women's Studies," document practices of racist exclusion in women's studies, suggesting the price we all pay when women of color are excluded from women's studies. In particular, they suggest that traditional methodologies employed in women's studies (and in other disciplines) serve to exclude women of color by divorcing feminist "theory" from the actual lived experiences of women of color, "render[ing] feminist theory incomplete and inaccurate" (33).

Women of color in the United States, facing multiple forms of oppression, have individually and collectively developed strategies for survival. In higher education, as elsewhere, we rely on a range of creative (and not always "healthy") responses to oppressive situations. Women of color faculty members, in particular, have adapted strategies including the following:

1. Sometimes women of color realize that a particular program is deeply entrenched in racist practices and not worth the personal price it would take to stay and fight, so they simply quit (either the program or women's studies altogether).
2. Some of us remain in women's studies but we disengage from the field by removing ourselves from interactions with colleagues. We proceed in isolation or with support from outside of the field.
3. Some of us become extremely professionalized, deciding that the way to gain respect is to assimilate as much as possible into traditional modes of academic interaction. Thus, we may decide to dress in certain ways, to speak in certain ways, and to interact with others only in very particular ways (very formally and business-like, for example, or perhaps in stereotypical ways that fulfill others' expectations of us). We decide that one way to maintain our coveted (often tokenized) place is to play the role of gatekeeper to other women of color, shutting out those who may threaten our false reality.
4. Some of us create coalitions with one another and with allies and attempt to transform the field of women's studies through teaching, research and writing, and political organizing. In doing so, we create spaces for reconceptualizing the field of women's studies and for empowering ourselves and other women of color.

Until recently, Shirley Geok-lin Lim argues, the field of women's studies has "elided the contributions of nonwhite women to social movements and neglected the study of these communities and their culture-specific, immigrant-history-specific struggles in the United States" (31). Until recently, women of color who spoke out against such elisions were deemed ungrateful and labeled "troublemakers." Thus, two positive results of the agitation of countless women of color in women's studies are the challenge to such stereotypical representations and the recent proliferation of courses about women of color in the United States, not only general courses but also ones focused specifically on the experiences and writings of Asian Pacific American women, African American women, Chicanas/Latinas, Native American women, and Middle Eastern American women. In such courses, students learn that even seemingly general topics within women's studies must be problematized by considering intersecting forms of oppression. Because many themes within women's studies have historically been explored from the point of view of white, heterosexual, middle-class women, they have come to be commonly understood according to such norms.

In Lim's essay, "The Center Can(not) Hold: U.S. Women's Studies and Global Feminism," she argues that our understandings of eating disorders and the politics of appearance for women must be reconceptualized to take into account the experiences of women of color and Third World women. By discussing the racial dimensions of beauty ideals and the different types of cosmetic surgeries sought by different groups of women, Lim demonstrates the need for more careful discussion of the intersections of gender, race, class, nationality, and sexuality. In fact, analyzing gender in relation to any topic, including family structures, economic systems, labor, political representation, media images, legal systems, and so on, will offer a narrow view of white women's experiences unless we can understand how women of color are affected by all of these structures. As Johnnella E. Butler argues, "Because of the imbalanced power relationship between White women and women of color, information about one group tends to make more apparent the experiences of the other group" (177). Courses like Women of Color in the U.S. offer resistant paradigms, calling into question the single-focus gender lens often used in women's studies classes. Thus, to document the history of exclusion, tokenism, marginalization, and stereotyping of women of color, and to genuinely explore experiences for all women related to social, economic, and political institutions in all their complexity, such courses are crucial to the future of women's studies.

The Women of Color in the U.S. course, now a staple course in women's studies programs all over the country, revolves around a set of complex issues, all of which complicate the objectives I mentioned in my introductory paragraph. As Lee discusses in her essay, "Notes from the (non)Field: Teaching and Theorizing Women of Color," this course has come to function as a symbol for "complex and troublesome investments on the part of women's studies' faculty [which] sustain this course and also incapacitate it deeply" (85). Having been hired to teach the course and to function primarily as a (the?) woman of color in her department at the University of California, Los Angeles, Lee comments on the peculiar conflation between the body of knowledge on women of color—a growing area of research and writing within women's studies—and the actual bodies of women of color, which become invested with particular meanings. The course itself is situated in a curious location between the desire for diversification and a demand that women of color "represent" our respective racial and cultural groups. As such, it lends itself to multiple misreadings from various constituencies, including women's studies faculty members, administrators, and students.

The Further Marginalization of Women of Color in Women's Studies

The tensions revolving around classes about women of color highlight larger, historically based problems within the field of women's studies. While there has recently been a surge of women's studies departmental course offerings centered on the history, literature, and social movements of women of color, and more and more college and university programs now offer substantial course offerings and programs about women of color, I suggest that we commit ourselves to asking, What progress and/or changes have actually been made in women's studies? How effective are such changes, and what new barriers might they introduce or represent for women of color? Whose interests guide such changes and who benefits the most?

Because women of color classes like WS330 often rely on the "offshore manufacture" described by Lee, women of color students in such classes find themselves both within and outside of women's studies. At the same time, it becomes increasingly clear that "women of color," much like the category "women," while politically useful terminology, can also function to elide differences and subsume particular experiences under generalizations. Race in the United States is frequently conceptualized in terms of binary opposition, resulting in the notion that women of color can safely be posited in opposition to white women. While women of color scholars and activists have politicized the term "women of color" and joined together across differences to challenge forms of racism and sexism, such a framework, when used for course offerings, can also serve to reinforce the place of white women at the center of women's studies, with women of color designated along the margins. Tessie Liu writes, "As women of color, we were classed together, in spite of our obvious diversity, simply because we are not white. However well-intentioned such acts of inclusion are, they raised the question: who

is doing the comparing?" (629–30). Without awareness of and attention to the different histories and experiences of women of color
both within the United States and globally, courses about women of
color risk positing women of color as a single, natural or always
already defined group, rather than multiple socially and politically
constructed groups.

The positioning of a course like WS330 within—and liminal to—
the core curriculum of a women's studies department may function as
part of an "add women of color and stir" formula. While most of us in
women's studies have come to recognize the limitations of additive
approaches to gender and race (and other social categories) within
our teaching, such frameworks are still frequently replicated in curricula on a larger scale. It is problematic to design a course like
Introduction to Women's Studies with one day, one week, or even one
unit on women of color because such an additive approach does nothing to change the underlying structure of the course. Recalling the
many attempts within her department to transform introductory
courses on western civilization, Liu writes, "For those who have been
left out of the story of Western civilization, it is perfectly possible to be
integrated and still remain marginal" (628). Moreover, as Liu points
out, the fundamental narrative underlying western civilization courses
relies on the notion of the privileged white, male subject. Thus, the
very premise of such courses must shift. Simply adding a few readings
or lectures about previously excluded groups will not result in actual
"inclusion" as much as tokenism. According to Liu,

> [The] new problem was how to de-center the privileged white male
> (and sometimes female) subject—the *I*—in the story of Western civ-
> ilization, which, not coincidentally, corresponds closely to the sub-
> jectivity students have been socialized to develop in relation to the
> world. We could not possibly modify or reform this strong underly-
> ing message with a sprinkle of diversity. (629)

Thus, simply adding women of color to women's studies courses
cannot result in true inclusion. Rather, as Liu suggests, we must also
be attentive to how we, as feminists, "account for and explain the differences among women" (629). To her question about how feminists
have explained such differences, I might add, How do we understand
our own social locations according to such differences, not only to recognize the forms of oppression we may face but also the sites of privilege we occupy and the ways in which we may be complicit with
oppressive and exclusionary practices?

To adequately include women of color studies within women's studies, we might shift our focus to the study of gender in relation to race as well as other social categories. Such a shift enables us to focus not only on women of color as the intersection of race and gender but also on theories of whiteness and white privilege, on racialized sexuality, for example, and on notions of masculinity and femininity as racially coded constructions. Nearly a decade ago, in one of my first Introduction to Women's Studies classes, I wrote on the board for my students, "Race transforms gender" and "Gender transforms race." I asked them to discuss the possible meanings and implications of these two statements. They responded by asking me to change "transforms" to "transcends." "These are separate things," one of them explained. "It makes it too confusing for you to put them up there together like that." I responded by explaining to them that the neat and fixed separation of these two categories was exactly what I wanted them to question. Their simple resistance to thinking through social categories as intersecting, voiced so powerfully in the request to alter my two statements, continues to haunt my own pedagogical process. In all of us, perhaps, there is a need and desire to keep things simple and uncomplicated, to proceed as though "women" as a group makes sense and to believe that deep down, we are all the same underneath. But approaches that fail to take into account the ways in which race and gender (and sexuality, class, national identity, ability, age, and size, for example) all profoundly impact one another, will only continue to allow for disavowals, disclaimers, and an utter lack of accountability to consider the many differences among us.

The WS330 course and others like it have the potential to transform the ways in which we understand feminism and women's studies. At the same time, they run the risk of tokenization. As such, the course, in Lee's words, "carries the weight of a racial alibi . . . [and functions] as a synecdoche for women's studies' own blindspots" (86). Rather than infusing the entire women's studies curriculum with an understanding of women of color and issues of race, this course inadvertently creates a space in which others may be relieved of the "burden" of including women of color. Lee argues, "At the same time that heels are dug in over the necessity of maintaining a course on women of color, there is a peculiar disinvestment in the body of scholarship by and about women of color that all core faculty should be expected to know and to teach" (88). Thus, with inclusion of courses about women of color, often not required for women's studies majors or required only as interchangeable courses (e.g., programs in which students must take one course related to women of color from among Black

Women's History, Asian American Women's Literature, The Chicana/Latina Experience, and Native American Women), other more traditional courses such as Introduction to Women's Studies and Feminist Theory are not required to change. As long as classes about women of color represent the primary (and sometimes sole) sites for discussion of women of color within women's studies, power dynamics within the field will mirror the dynamics between women's studies departments and the larger university culture. Paralleling the dynamic I describe here, many mainstream university departments push examinations of women and gender onto women's studies programs, creating reservoirs within women's studies departments and relieving the rest of the university from any sense of accountability around issues of gender.

The Women of Color in the U.S. class, then, functions as a necessity within women's studies departments at the same time that it comes to symbolize—and sustain—a long history of racial exclusion within women's studies. It demonstrates the ways in which women of color are very much centrally located within women's studies while simultaneously positioned perpetually on the margins of the field. As "outsiders within," women of color (and the class itself) occupy critical, liminal sites for transformation; more and more we are calling for not simply "inclusion" but an actual reconfiguration of the field of women's studies. As Butler suggests, women of color may be "beyond the point of complete invisibility and complete distortion" within women's studies, but we must still demand that our voices be heard and that our experiences be understood from our own perspectives, just as women of color demanded thirty years ago (176).[11]

NOTES

The excerpt from Jayne Cortez's poem "There It Is" is reprinted by permission of the author.

1. Portland State University is a large, urban university located in the heart of downtown Portland, Oregon. The Women's Studies Department, while small, has a long history in the United States and is committed to student-centered, activist-oriented education.

2. Being hired as the first woman of color faculty member in a department where I would be expected to teach the women of color course resulted, in some ways, in my positioning as *the* woman of color of the department (rather than a woman of color, an Asian Pacific American woman, a queer woman, a new professor, etc.). Rachel Lee, too, found herself hired to teach the women of color course within the University of California, Los Angeles's Women's Studies Department. It was through this process, she writes, that she "became a woman of color, as opposed to an Asian

American woman, an interpreter of literature, or even a professor of women's studies" (85).

3. By this I mean that the course, while not required for the major, does occupy a central place within the department. As a specially approved "university studies" course, it is taught at least once each academic year and fulfills particular requirements for students who may choose to complete women's studies "clusters" requirements. In addition, in conducting a faculty hire for a candidate capable of teaching this course, the department has designated it as a permanent feature.

4. Portland State University, at this time, has no Asian American Studies, Native American Studies, or Ethnic Studies programs or departments.

5. Here I do not intend to suggest that all white students respond to issues raised in this class in the same way. Nor do I suggest that white students comprise a homogeneous or monolithic category. In fact, white students' experiences, too, vary by gender, class, ethnicity, immigration status, language, sexual orientation, age, and a host of other factors. White students—and white people in general—are also positioned differently in relation to issues of race and racism, sometimes through involvement in interracial or multiracial relationships or families and/or due to differing levels of awareness of issues surrounding racism and white privilege. For a critical discussion of such themes, see Frankenberg.

6. Anzaldúa links these actions to what she refers to as the "selective reality" of some white students—the ability to erase their own racial positioning as white, thereby foregoing any recognition of white privilege and resulting in racist behavior. She writes, "Whites not naming themselves white presume their universality; an unmarked race is a sign of Racism unaware of itself, a 'blanked-out' Racism" (xxi).

7. In another essay, I have described the many tactics employed by white students to divert or deflect attention away from issues of race and women of color. See Duncan.

8. Here I am referring again to my article "Decentering Whiteness: Resisting Racism in the Women's Studies Classroom" (Duncan).

9. Of course, much of this also has to do with class and classism in the university. Because race and class are so inextricably intertwined, and because poor and working-class students of all races also receive messages about not belonging in the university, it is important to note that experiences such as exclusion, isolation, and exploitation are shaped and informed by class structures in the United States. For an excellent discussion of the ways in which class shapes our experiences in the university, see Kadi.

10. See, especially, Mitsuye Yamada's essays, "Invisibility Is an Unnatural Disaster: Reflections of an Asian American Woman" and "Asian Pacific American Women and Feminism," and Paula Gunn Allen's essay, "Some Like Indians Endure," as well as her book, *Off the Reservation: Reflections on Boundary-Busting, Border-Crossing Loose Cannons.*

11. See also Nell Irvin Painter, "Regrets," published in *Feminisms at a Millenium,* in which she expresses regrets over the fact that so little has

changed in the last twenty-five years for faculty and students of color in higher education. Also, Paula Gunn Allen, in her essay "Looking Back: Ethnics in the Western Formalist Situation," writes that while people of color have been struggling to fit into U.S. academic institutions since the late 1960s, we still suffer from an extreme amount of institutional racism and exclusion (1998).

WORKS CITED

Allen, Paula Gunn. "Looking Back: Ethnics in the Western Formalist Situation." *Off the Reservation: Reflections on Boundary-Busting, Border-Crossing Loose Cannons.* Boston: Beacon, 1998. 132–44.
———. "Some Like Indians Endure." *Making Face, Making Soul / Haciendo Caras: Creative and Critical Perspectives by Women of Color.* Ed. Gloria Anzaldúa. San Francisco: Aunt Lute, 1990. 298–301.
Anzaldúa, Gloria. "Introduction: Haciendo cara, una entrada." *Making Face, Making Soul / Haciendo Caras: Creative and Critical Perspectives by Women of Color.* Ed. Gloria Anzaldúa. San Francisco: Aunt Lute, 1990. xv–xxviii.
Baca Zinn, Maxine, Lynn Weber Cannon, Elizabeth Higginbotham, and Bonnie Thornton Dill. "The Costs of Exclusionary Practices in Women's Studies." *Making Face, Making Soul / Haciendo Caras: Creative and Critical Perspectives by Women of Color.* Ed. Gloria Anzaldúa. San Francisco: Aunt Lute, 1990. 29–41.
Butler, Johnnella E. "Transforming the Curriculum: Teaching about Women of Color." *Multicultural Education: Issues and Perspectives.* 4th ed. Ed. James A. Banks and Cherry A. McGee Banks. New York: Wiley, 2001. 174–93.
Cortez, Jayne. "There It Is." *Coagulations: New and Selected Poems.* New York: Thunder's Mouth, 1984. 68–70.
Duncan, Patti. "Decentering Whiteness: Resisting Racism in the Women's Studies Classroom." *Race in the College Classroom: Pedagogy and Politics.* Ed. Bonnie TuSmith and Maureen T. Reddy. New Brunswick, NJ: Rutgers UP, forthcoming. 71–90.
Frankenberg, Ruth. *White Women, Race Matters: The Social Construction of Whiteness.* Minneapolis: U of Minnesota P, 1993.
Kadi, Joanna. "Stupidity Deconstructed." *Is Academic Feminism Dead? Theory in Practice.* Ed. The Social Justice Group at the Center for Advanced Feminist Studies, University of Minnesota. New York: New York UP, 2000. 327–46.
Lee, Rachel. "Notes from the (non)Field: Teaching and Theorizing Women of Color." *Meridians: Feminism, Race, Transnationalism* 1.1 (2000): 85–109.
Lim, Shirley Geok-Lin. "The Center Can(not) Hold: U.S. Women's Studies and Global Feminism." *Women's Studies Quarterly* 26.3–4 (1998): 30–39.
Liu, Tessie. "Teaching the Differences among Women from a Historical Perspective: Rethinking Race and Gender and Social Categories." *Unequal Sisters: A Multicultural Reader in U.S. Women's History.* 3rd ed. Ed. Vicki L. Ruiz and Ellen Carol DuBois. New York: Routledge, 2000. 627–38.
Lorde, Audre. "The Uses of Anger: Women Responding to Racism." *Sister Outsider: Essays and Speeches.* Freedom, CA: Crossing, 1984. 124–33.
Painter, Nell Irvin. "Regrets." *Feminisms at a Millenium.* Ed. Judith A. Howard

and Carolyn Allen. Chicago: U of Chicago P, 2000. 208–9.

Smith, Barbara. "Racism and Women's Studies." *Making Face, Making Soul / Haciendo Caras: Creative and Critical Perspectives by Women of Color.* Ed. Gloria Anzaldúa. San Francisco: Aunt Lute, 1990. 25–28.

Uttal, Lynet. "Inclusion Without Influence: The Continuing Tokenism of Women of Color." *Making Face, Making Soul / Haciendo Caras: Creative and Critical Perspectives by Women of Color.* Ed. Gloria Anzaldúa. San Francisco: Aunt Lute, 1990. 42–45.

Yamada, Mitsuye. "Asian Pacific American Women and Feminism" *This Bridge Called My Back: Writings by Radical Women of Color.* Ed. Gloria Anzaldúa and Cherrie Moraga. New York: Kitchen Table Women of Color, 1981. 71–75.

———. "Invisibility Is an Unnatural Disaster: Reflections of an Asian American Women." *This Bridge Called My Back: Writings by Radical Women of Color.* Ed. Gloria Anzaldúa and Cherrie Moraga. New York: Kitchen Table Women of Color, 1981. 35–40.

Patti Duncan is assistant professor of women's studies at Portland State University in Portland, Oregon. Her teaching focuses on women of color and Third World feminisms. She has published essays on antiracist pedagogies, Asian American women's writings, and the intersections of race, gender, nation, and sexuality. Her book, Tell This Silence: Asian American Women, Feminism, and the Politics of Speech, *is forthcoming from the University of Iowa Press.*

From Social Construction to Social Justice

Transforming How We Teach about Intersexuality

Emi Koyama and Lisa Weasel

Intersex is technically defined as a group of medical conditions that involve "congenital anomaly of the reproductive and sexual system." In other words, intersex people are those born with physical conditions that result in atypical internal or external reproductive anatomies or chromosomal anomalies (Koyama 3). Intersex is thus not a single diagnostic category but includes a wide range of conditions and syndromes such as congenital adrenal hyperplasia (enzyme deficiency resulting in overproduction of androgen and virilization in genetic females) and androgen insensitivity syndrome (inability for the body to respond to androgen in genetic males, often resulting in female appearance), just to name two. The estimated frequency of intersex conditions varies depending on how the definition is applied, but it is assumed that one in two thousand babies in the United States (or approximately five babies per day) are born visibly intersex, prompting early diagnosis and treatment.

Today, the standard treatment for intersex conditions involves surgical and hormonal interventions that are designed to alter the appearance of the body so as to make it more visually "normal," but do not necessarily address any particular health issues (although these may also be present). These surgeries are often performed in early childhood, when children are too young to understand or consent to what is being done to them; such children are rarely told the truth about their medical histories even after they grow older (Dreger 16).

Even though doctors have performed these surgeries for the last fifty years, there is little evidence that they are effective and safe in the long term; on the contrary, several recent studies have confirmed that early surgical treatment on genitals often results in psychological and sexual problems rather than better social adjustment (Alizai et al. 1588; Creighton 219; Creighton et al. 124; Zucker et al. 300). The social power and authority of the medical establishment combined with fear and lack of awareness in the general public allows these surgeries to go on unquestioned, inflicting lifelong pain on those defined as intersex.

In 1993, several intersex people created the Intersex Society of North America (ISNA), the first advocacy group for people with intersex conditions, to connect with other intersex people and to take back control over their own bodies. ISNA states,

> We believe that intersex is not something so shameful that it has to be concealed medically and socially. We believe that intersex people have the right to know all the information currently available about conditions we experience, and determine for ourselves what is done to our bodies. . . . We oppose the idea that eliminating our physical differences is the way to address social issues we may encounter; rather, we believe in addressing social difficulties intersex people may experience through social and psychological interventions. (1)

Intersex in Women's Studies: Where We Are Now

There has been a growing interest in and attention to the topic of intersexuality in women's studies in recent years. To investigate how intersex issues are being integrated into women's studies classrooms, we conducted a small internet-based survey of twenty-four self-selected scholars in spring 2001 on how they teach about this topic in their courses. Invitation to participate in the survey was distributed through academic mailing lists that deal with women's studies, queer studies, and other related fields. Responses were collected through a specially designed Web site and were analyzed for themes. While not relying upon a controlled research design and primarily exploratory in nature, the preliminary results of this pilot study nonetheless confirmed our prediction that intersex existence is understood and presented largely as a scholarly object to be studied in order to deconstruct the notion of binary sexes (and thus sexism and homophobia) rather than as a subject that has real-world implications for real people.

Our survey found that the approach to intersex issues taking place in women's studies classrooms is severely limited, despite instructors' good intentions. For example, only four of the twenty-four respondents use materials written or produced by known intersex people, despite the fact that these materials have become widely available in the last few years and would provide a perspective on intersexuality central to any theoretical discussion.

According to our survey, Anne Fausto-Sterling's 1993 classic, "The Five Sexes: Why Male and Female Are Not Enough," continues to be the favored text among our respondents, with fifteen instructors reporting use of it; nineteen of twenty-four instructors use this and/or other works by Fausto-Sterling. Other nonintersex scholars cited more than once were Suzanne Kessler (6), Alice Domurat Dreger (3), Judith Butler (2), and Kate Bornstein (2). Intersex writers mentioned were ISNA (3), Cheryl Chase (2), Angela Moreno (1), Morgan Holmes (1), and Martha Coventry (1).

In response to the question regarding their selection of materials, only one of the respondents reported a conscious effort to give voices to intersex people by using sources produced by intersex people themselves. A respondent who included multiple works by intersex authors reported that they were brought to her attention by her students who found them on the internet. Because few intersex people have access to publication in academic journals, incorporating nonacademic sources such as magazine articles and Web sites seems to be a good strategy.

Several respondents seem to confuse or conflate intersex issues and transsexual/transgender issues; in response to this question some mentioned works by or about transsexual/transgender individuals such as Kate Bornstein, which do not address intersex issues in depth. While it is not uncommon to associate intersexuality issues with transsexual or transgender issues, this is nonetheless a misperception that overlooks very specific ways in which intersex people's rights to self-determination and informed consent are taken away under the guise of providing necessary medical treatment.

When asked the reasons for including materials addressing intersexuality, nearly all respondents stated that one of the main purposes was to deconstruct one or more conventional understandings of human sexes, genders, and sexualities. In many cases, this revelation is then used to deconstruct gender roles, compulsory heterosexuality, and even scientific objectivity. Our respondents use the subject of intersex as a gender issue and a way to illustrate the social construction of gender, without explicitly addressing medical ethics or other issues with direct real-life implication to the lives of intersex people.

A small number of respondents indicated raising awareness of intersex issues as one of their goals, but even in these cases, there are mismatches between this stated goal and the kind of materials selected for use in the courses. For example, Fausto-Sterling had not spoken with any intersex person at the time she wrote "The Five Sexes" and thus only discusses historical cases. Rather than increasing awareness of intersex issues and affirming students who are themselves intersexed, use of such outdated materials in the absence of more contemporary materials by intersex people may further mythologize and exoticize intersex existence and make it seem like an anomaly of the past. In another example, one respondent wrote, "[Intersex] issues are marginalized and need to be given more attention. Here I often direct students to the writings of transsexuals such as Kate Bornstein and Leslie Feinberg." Although the goal is to raise awareness of intersex issues, neither Bornstein nor Feinberg is known to be intersexed and it is unclear how these writings provide more attention to intersex issues. Most likely, this problem arises from the confusion surrounding intersexuality and its distinction from transsexual/transgender issues discussed above.

Furthermore, beyond the assumption that a greater visibility will eventually lead to the liberation of a marginalized group, a carryover from lesbian, gay, bisexual, and transgender (LGBT) politics, there seems to be little thought around how advocating for intersex people might take a different form or require a different set of priorities than advocating for LGBT communities. As one intersexed speaker said during the National Gay and Lesbian Task Force's "Creating Change" conference in November 2000, "If virtually all gays and lesbians were forced to undergo reparative therapy against their will, and it was done in complete silence and secrecy so that none of them knew each other, visibility would be last on their agenda."[1] While LGBT communities can certainly provide forums for addressing intersex issues, conflating or collapsing intersexuality into LGBT agendas fails to acknowledge the specific and urgent issues facing intersex people.

Because the existence of intersex people is under pervasive marginalization and erasure, there is a concern that classroom discussion about intersexuality could wind up reinforcing exoticization and objectification of intersex people. This is particularly damaging to students who are themselves intersexed, whether or not those around them are aware of their status. We included in this survey a question about how instructors maintain a safe learning environment for students who may be intersexed because we wanted to stimulate awareness of these students' existence among instructors as much as to determine their answers.

In response to this question, nearly half (11) of respondents reported that they believed the general "ground rules" for their classes address this issue sufficiently (although these ground rules were often not explicitly detailed). In addition, six respondents said that intersex issues would not stand out because transgender issues and other gender-related issues are also discussed in the course.

Strategies specific to intersex issues included citing statistics to show
that there are many intersex people on a campus or that any of the students could be intersexed and not know it (8), as well as asking hypothetical questions like "what would you do if you had an intersexed
child?" (2). These strategies are designed to demystify and destigma-
tize intersex existence but may actually contribute to further objectification of intersex people because they seem to assume that no
students already know themselves to be intersexed or have intersexed
family members. In addition, the former approach also runs the risk
of reducing the category of intersexuality and the medical interventions to an interesting biological trivia rather than a site of intimate
physical violation.

A more troubling tendency we noticed is that some respondents (6)
actually focused in their responses on ways that they make the classroom more comfortable for nonintersex students rather than considering classroom safety issues for students who are intersexed. A
respondent wrote, "I try to connect the issue to gender, which many
are more comfortable discussing. . . . It eases them into the challenge
to their own preconceptions about sex (and gender) as fixed, binary
categories." There are two problems with this approach: First, it reinforces the invisibility of intersex people, and second, it prioritizes the
privileged group over the marginalized one. By interpreting the question to apply to nonintersex people, these respondents further reinforced the notion that the stigmatization of intersex people is normal
and legitimate. In addition, two respondents reported that they had
not had to deal with this issue because they had never had any student
come out as intersexed. The lack of disclosure by intersex students in
their classrooms merely indicates the intensity of erasure and silencing against intersex people in this society as well as in their classes,
rather than their actual lack of existence.

Four instructors admitted that they needed further education on
the issues intersex people face in order to become more sensitive to
the needs of students who are intersexed, and two reported that they
use first-person materials written by intersex people in a nonobjecti-
fying manner. These responses are compatible with the goals and priorities of the intersex movement. In response to these stated needs,
ISNA has prepared a teaching kit to help instructors incorporate intersex issues into classroom teaching in a way that addresses the lives and
realities of intersex people and the social and ethical justice issues
relating to surgical interventions. Additional resources address the
social construction of binary sex while incorporating voices of intersex individuals and organizations with a critique of the unnecessary

and traumatic impacts of medical intersex surgeries (Preves). Given the growing awareness and incorporation of intersex topics into women's studies classrooms, it is important for instructors to gain understanding of not only the theoretical dimensions of intersexuality but also the urgent practical issues facing intersex individuals.

Since virtually all respondents indicated that they introduce intersex issues in order to address theories about social construction of sex and gender, as discussed above, it is not surprising that a majority (13) of respondents reported students' learning of social construction theory as the primary result of their instruction. It is encouraging that some respondents did report that students are seriously considering the ethical "dilemma" of whether or not surgery is warranted (5), that some became interested in learning more about intersex people (4), or are appalled at the medical abuse of intersex children (3), after the initial shock.

Four respondents reported an interesting by-product of addressing intersex issues: gay, lesbian, and bisexual students felt more comfortable after discussing intersex issues in class. One respondent wrote, "Several 'out' lesbian students thought this was the coolest thing in the world—seemingly somewhat mollified." Another said, "I have had many gays, lesbians and bisexuals tell me that they feel much better about themselves after taking my course and hearing alternative views such as Fausto-Sterling's." While this is a positive side effect, it appears that discussions about intersex within women's studies often get "stuck" in such conversations, as one instructor puts it, and do not address issues and concerns specific to the lives of intersex people.

But perhaps this is an inaccurate way to describe the situation; a better way to understand it may not be to assume that discussions are "stuck" prematurely but that they are in need of a different framework that addresses issues of medical ethics, social justice, and erasure. Courses need to treat intersex people as ends and not just means, and need to start from the assumption that intersex people are experts and authorities on their own experiences; their voices should be required materials.

While it is important and encouraging that feminist and LGBT communities are beginning to recognize and embrace the issue of intersexuality, and women's studies, gender studies, and queer studies courses may be the only place where intersexuality is incorporated into the curriculum, the specific ways in which intersex issues are introduced in these classrooms should be strengthened and made more relevant to the social justice movement. Despite instructors' good intentions, a lack of awareness and attention to the realities of intersex lives biases the presentation of the topic, potentially unintentionally perpetrating the invisibility and objectification of intersex people.

Guidelines for Teaching Intersex Issues

What follows below is a list of recommendations we have developed in order to address intersex issues in women's studies courses. While it is not definitive, we believe that it provides a good starting point as it addresses some of the common problems we discovered in the survey.

- Give authority to intersex people. When teaching about intersex, introduce students to first-person narratives as well as academic writings by intersex authors, such as those found in Alice Dreger's *Intersex in the Age of Ethics* and on the Web site of the Intersex Society of North America[2] while being careful not to indulge voyeuristic attitudes. If you are using materials created by nonintersex authors, make an effort to avoid presenting intersex voices as in need of legitimizing or interpretation by nonintersex "specialists."
- Do not exploit intersex existence for gender-sex deconstruction only; make sure to address real-life issues faced by intersex people. If the social construction theory needs to be addressed, do so in the context of exposing and resisting the oppression against intersex people. In other words, use theories to support people, rather than the other way around.
- Assume that intersex people are everywhere including in your classroom. Do not ask hypothetical questions as if none of the students are intersexed or family members of an intersex person. Do not expect intersex students to "come out" in the class or interpret the absence of openly intersex students as the absence of intersex individuals.
- Recognize that the intersex movement may have priorities and strategies beyond those of the gay and lesbian or transgender movements. Do not automatically treat intersex issues simply as an extension of LGBT issues, or intersex people as a subgroup within LGBT communities.
- Draw connections to many issues, not just LGBT issues. Consider implications of the intersex movement on the (dis)ability movement (normalization of bodies marked as different); psychiatric survivor movement; medical ethics (informed consent), health activism, and feminist antiviolence movements (child sexual abuse, domestic violence, female gen-

ital cutting, etc.); reproductive rights; children's and youth rights; and so on—and vice versa.

• Recognize that it is not the responsibility of intersex people to deconstruct binary gender-sex or to be used as guinea pigs to test out the latest theories about gender. Do not be disappointed that many intersex people are not interested in becoming members of the third gender or overthrowing sex categories altogether, although we should support those people who happen to be interested in these things, whether they are intersexed or not.

• Engage yourself and your students in actual activist work in support of the intersex movement. It is essential for feminist scholars to contribute something back to the movements they study rather than merely using them as objects of academic inquiry.

• Educate yourself about intersex issues. For example, learn which words and phrases are preferred or not preferred by intersex people and why.

Conclusion

Before the second wave of the women's movement, the only published information about women's bodies and sexualities came from male doctors who claimed authority over them; the emergence of a women's health movement and the publication of literatures such as *Our Bodies, Ourselves* changed that forever. Today's feminist scholars thus have the fundamental moral and scholarly obligation to support intersex people's struggle to regain their own voices and narratives by bringing them into the classroom, while critically interrogating feminist and medical perspectives on intersexuality. Indeed, there appears to be growing interest and attention to intersex issues in women's studies classrooms, providing a potential space to educate students and encourage activism around these issues.

Yet too often, exploration of the political and practical issues relating to intersex lives have been marginalized in feminist scholars' use of intersex existence in support of their theoretical and pedagogical deconstructions. While feminist scholars have been hard at work using the existence of intersex people to deconstruct gender in their theories and classrooms, the medical profession has been busy "reconstructing" intersex bodies through unnecessary and often damaging surgeries to fit those same binary norms and standards that feminists are attempting to dismantle. As with any feminist undertaking, it is essential that theory and practice must meet, that feminist scholarship and pedagogy must engage with activist strategies that address the real-life issues that intersex individuals face.

NOTES

This article is based on the sixteen-page booklet "Teaching Intersex Issues: A Guide for Teachers in Women's, Gender and Queer Studies," by Emi Koyama and Lisa Weasel, distributed through Intersex Society of North America as part of the "Intersex Teaching Kit." For more information, visit ISNA's Web site at http://www.isna.org/ or contact ISNA at P.O. Box 301, Petaluma, CA 94953.

We would like to acknowledge and thank Cheryl Chase, Morgan Holmes, and Alice Dreger for sharing their insights with us for this project.

1. See http://www.ngltf.029/cc/index.cfm.
2. See http://www.isna.org.

WORKS CITED

Alizai, N., D. Thomas, R. Lilford, A. Batchelor, and N. Johnson. "Feminizing Genitoplasty for Congenital Adrenal Hyperplasia: What Happens at Puberty?" *Journal of Urology* 161 (1999): 1588–91.

Boston Women's Health Book Collective. *Our Bodies, Ourselves for the New Century.* New York: Free Press, 1998.

Creighton, S. "Surgery for Intersex." *Journal of the Royal Society of Medicine* 94 (2001): 218–20.

Creighton, S., C. Minto, and S. Steele. "Objective Cosmetic and Anatomical Outcomes at Adolescence of Feminizing Surgery for Ambiguous Genitalia Done in Childhood." *The Lancet* 358 (2001): 124–25.

Dreger, Alice Domurat. *Intersex in the Age of Ethics.* Hagerstown, MD: University Publishing Group, 1999.

Fausto-Sterling, Anne. "The Five Sexes: Why Male and Female Are Not Enough." *The Sciences* March/April 1993: 20–25.

Intersex Society of North America. Online, available: *http://isna.org/faq/faq-medical.html.* 2001.

Koyama, E. *Introduction to Intersex Activism: A Guide for Allies.* 2001. Booklet available from Intersex Society of North America, P.O. Box 301, Petaluma CA 94953.

Preves, Sharon E. "Sexing the Intersexed: An Analysis of Sociocultural Responses to Intersexuality." *Signs: Journal of Women in Culture and Society* 27 (2001): 523–56.

Zucker, K., et al. "Psychosexual Development with Congenital Adrenal Hyperplasia." *Hormones and Behavior* 30 (1996): 300–318.

Emi Koyama is the program assistant of the Intersex Society of North America (ISNA) and has been writing and lecturing on the topics of third-wave feminisms, domestic violence industry, and working-class sex worker feminism in addition to intersex. She maintains a Web site, http://www.emi-

nism.org. **Lisa Weasel** *is an assistant professor of biology at Portland State University, Oregon, who works in the area of feminist science studies. In addition to her work on the teaching of intersex issues, she currently directs the Global Helix Project, which focuses on ethics and equity issues pertaining to globalization and biotechnology.*

Implications and Articulations

The Ph.D. in Women's Studies

Electa Arenal

Morning, noon, and night we crossed lobbies and hallways decked out with hanging televisions, catching or avoiding voices and images of terror, fear, and war—garish, round-the-clock newscasts aimed at whipping up uncritical patriotism. Despite the trauma suffered on 11 September 2001, and the long shadow of grief it cast over all, the working conference, "The Ph.D. in Women's Studies: Implications and Articulations," got started on schedule. Sally Kitch, of Ohio State University, stated in her opening remarks that we were gathered in affirmation of thoughtful, compassionate, collaborative learning as stakeholders in women's studies development.[1] Breaking news of national and international events—the climate of vengeance, the politics of fear, the rush to war—would weave in and out of our conversations and deliberations for the four days that we were together.

Just as this summary of those days is one person's perception of the meanings of what was said, the significance of these pages will be different for each reader. I adhere to a tradition within our field that stresses having an ear to the ground of women's lived experiences, critical thinking, and the centrality of the arts. Drawing a wide-angled sketch, I have attempted to be as informative as possible while pinpointing what were for me highly dynamic and daring ideas on the Ph.D. in women's studies. Approaches based on interrogation of the very tools we use, on collaborative research, and on transdisciplinary unboundedness rather than strict disciplinarity compelled my interest most.

11–14 October 2001, Emory University's Conference Center in Atlanta, Georgia. More than eighty participants, probably the largest and most diverse group of North American women ever gathered to discuss the highest degree in women's studies offered by universities in the United States and Canada, met to try to understand its possible connections—and oppositions—to the entire educational and sociocultural enterprise. We came from almost all of the institutions that already offer Ph.D.s in women's studies, including York University;

Clark University; Emory University; Rutgers University; the University of Michigan; the University of Minnesota; the University of Maryland; the University of California, Los Angeles; the University of Washington; Ohio State University; and the Union Institute, some with free-standing programs and some linked to other disciplines or programs. We came from community colleges and research universities, private and public, ivy and cinderblock. We were graduate students; emerita, full, associate, and assistant professors. We were African, Asian, Pacific Island, and Caucasian Americans, and Latinas and Canadians as well. Privileged and less than privileged.

From the start of the working conference, the fears many people would wish to deny—of the real changes substantive diversity must bring—were subtly underscored. Superficial diversity and shallow multiculturalism were ridiculed. Frances Smith Foster, of Emory University, quoted Toni Cade Bambara's Minnie Ransom in *The Salt Eaters*, asking Velma Henry, "Are you sure, sweetheart, that you want to be well?" (3). She was referring to the shouldering of burdens and responsibilities required to engage psychic and social truths in an unjust world. To become fully, critically aware is no easy task. We were implicitly being asked to resist cooptation, to oppose gender and race hierarchies, and to embrace an ongoing, multifaceted consciousness-raising as we pursue our scholarly work. Bonnie Thornton Dill of the University of Maryland referred back to the same question, claiming that we need time to develop innovative theories and to transcend the erroneous notion that there is *one* "Feminist Theory." In so doing we might continuously put ideas from different margins and centers into conversation with each other.

Beverly Guy-Sheftall, from Spelman College, suggested we analyze the nature of our complicity in the very hegemonic structures we abhor and asked, "If the theoretical bases for the women's studies Ph.D. are inclusive and global, why do exclusionary practices persist?" If that critical (in both senses) question wasn't answered by the final session on Sunday morning, neither was it, I think, forgotten. The distortions brought about by a long legacy of undemocratic privileging were often on my mind. How many of us were thinking of the unavoidable complicities involved in being part of an academic elite?

During a lunchtime panel on diversity, Inez Martinez, of Kingsborough Community College, emphasized the capacity of the imagination to act as a pathway on which materials from the unconscious travel to consciousness. She added new bodily and cordial (meaning *of the heart*) dimensions of intelligence to those of the mind, positing and attempting to answer thorny questions such as:

Can feminist education, especially at the Ph.D. level, incorporate knowing and spread it "beyond our brains to other parts of the body?" Can we honor, along with the imagination, the "timing rhythms of body and psyche," which are different in each individual? "Can we educate not just to inform, but to transform?" Casting back into history as well as inward to the psyche, she asked, Can the most advanced women's studies education acknowledge a complex and long-standing "state of psychological fixation in unresolved historical conflicts" in order to transform race relations? Dispossession of indigenous peoples who were here before us and enslavement of those forcibly brought from Africa are the sins of a past that lives on, adhering to the collective unconscious. Central to theory courses in which that transforming mission is embraced, she claimed, are the ideas of such thinkers of color as Audre Lorde, Patricia Hill Collins, bell hooks, Gloria Anzaldúa, and María Lugones. Martinez's call to "Imagining Our Way Together" became a leit-motif, echoed in allusions to re-imaginings: multilogues rather than dialogues; theories rather than one "feminist theory"; thinking from the heart and the body as much as from the head.

At several points we practiced Lorde's lessons—given in speeches, verse, and prose—about enduring and accepting conflict for its creative possibilities. In the discussion periods that followed plenary sessions and spilled over into coffee and tea breaks, and during breakout sessions, numerous participants continued to debate. Breakout sessions covered many topics including curriculum (from redesigning it by "thinking out of the box" to getting it approved); disciplinarity/ interdisciplinarity (is "transdisciplinarity" a better term for what we seek?); undergraduate, M.A., and Ph.D. programs in women and gender and the relationships between them (how to avoid repetition, how to differentiate and articulate sensibly and flexibly); research theories and methodologies; structures and practices of the academy; and social change.[2] Stimulated and provoked, graduate student participants and others made plans for postconference follow up. Some have linked up in cyberspace. They held a fruitful discussion of differences in curriculum between an M.A. and Ph.D. in women's studies and made plans to continue and develop it at the National Women's Studies Association (NWSA) National Conference in Las Vegas in June 2002.

A poster display with details of all existing and incipient Ph.D. programs ran throughout the conference. Sign-up lists for further/future projects were on tables outside conference session rooms. "Nuts and bolts" aspects of the women's studies Ph.D. project were taken up in self-forming small groups and in larger planned sessions related to bureaucratic, administrative, and structural themes. In a session on "Construction and Implementation," representatives of six established programs related stories of beginnings, the strategies worked out and the steps taken toward obtaining approval. They shared the character of the reception in institutional, research, and academic spheres of the new Ph.D. programs and described their present status.

The way had been paved initially by poets, artists, writers, and activists in the women's movement of the last third of the twentieth century, and the hundreds of college and university students and dozens of faculty members allied with them who became founders, teachers, and graduates of women's studies courses and concentrations or majors on the undergraduate and master's level, and of certificate and other sorts of programs on the Ph.D. level (Arenal "What Women Writers?"; Howe).

In recent years, controversy attended discussions on the pros and cons of a Ph.D. in the field. Even as the earliest Ph.D. programs were actually established—at York University in Canada (1992) and Clark in the United States[3]—polemical articles emerged, feature essays (*Women's Studies Quarterly;* Shteir) and special issues of journals (*Feminist Studies*) appeared. Graduate certificate programs in women's studies had matured and come into their own—but they were not on their own. University faculty, often spurred on by students, held meetings to discuss the future. There were many questions and viewpoints. It is no surprise, then, that an intrepid group of eleven scholars became the convening team for a first national conversation on the subject—the October 2001 conference at Emory University and topic of this essay.[4] For eighteen months a core group worked in an extraordinarily focused fashion, carefully developing a rationale and formulating ideas and concerns that in themselves reflect the dynamism and diversity of women's studies and the successes and problems of new women's studies Ph.D. programs.[5]

The schedule of plenaries, panels, and breakout sessions they devised assured substantive and pithy yet open-ended discussion of major issues. The chosen topics outline historic, epistemological, methodological, and ethical, as well as pedagogical and institutional themes important to the field. During the opening session—"Why Are We Here?"—a collage of voices quoting twenty women with a wide variety of reasons for wanting to attend, proved the organizing committee's attention to process and inclusivity, and gave a sense of informal sharing by all in the very preparation of the conference.

Later, at different moments, divergence of perspective and experience and a clash of discourses made clear a need for listening, hearing, and bridging divides. Concern and disagreement were expressed about the use of accessible language, the intelligibility of some feminist writing or, rather, the lack of it—the tendency for institutionalized and professionalized women's studies specialists to become more and more abstruse and abstractly theoretical. Jacqueline Zita, from the University of Minnesota, put it this way: "We develop esoteric languages that circle 'round themselves." The antidote lies in insisting on the development of a thoughtful, self-reflexive, critical consciousness. Elizabeth Minnich of the Union Institute referred to the professionalizing tendency in historical terms, likening it to pre- and early modern periods when people were trained to copy, to repeat, to fit into molds that would entitle them to enter trade guilds. She emphasized the danger of the guild model for originality, independence, and new knowledge, as well as critical citizen building. Layli Phillips, from Georgia State University, was direct: "I say 'Just Say No' to the Ivory Tower." The point is not to isolate but to avoid moats and to create roads and crossroads rather than impediments.

How else are we to make more headway in broadening the knowledge base, in changing our institutions and our society, in routing systemic, drug and oil-slicked greed and militarism? How will we make a significantly wider citizenry aware of the political economy of knowledge production; how will we make them sympathetic to principles of academic freedom and affirmative (what in Europe is called "positive") action? At Emory, participants reaffirmed a creative, visionary, and community-minded educational politics. There an unstated but vivid demonstration took place of the significance of Black women and women of color in leadership roles. Would its impact be multiplied?

On Implications, Effects, and Possibilities

Under this rubric, the organizers printed in the program itself many of the searching questions speakers were asked to address.[6] Layli Phillips, quoted above, summarized the viewpoint of many women of color and activist scholars, among whom I count myself.[7] She made four points. Class and media were the themes of the first two[8]: "First, [w]e don't just need class analysis—we need anti-poverty action . . . to take our theory to the street—not just to identify the issues, but to publicize them, take them to the (consuming) public(s)." Second, feminist analysis must be brought to "everyday people" through the efforts of women's studies specialists "trained to use the media against itself" and to understand that every level of education merits inclusion in the weave of feminisms.

Critical education, the theme of Phillips's third point, must be reached by the feminist enterprise. She claimed, "Women's studies was born out of the streets but has abandoned the streets—kind of like the Jefferson's 'Movin' on up to the East Side.'" In presenting the fourth and final point, coordination with other movements, Phillips advocated networking and coalition-building among presently divided academic fields and splintered progressive social movements—as did other scholars in the course of the four days. In supporting her succinct arguments, Phillips cited two sources: *Feminist Genealogies, Colonial Legacies, Democratic Futures,* by Jacqui Alexander and Chandra Mohanty, and *Methodology of the Oppressed,* by Chela Sandoval. The title of Phillips's own talk—a self-conscious, at once serious and humorous throw back to more radical times, not unlike that of some in-your-face political rap/hip-hop lyrics I heard recently on WBAI—is "Bringing Decolonial Democratic Globalization to the Masses." Hopeful; a smiling, clarifying connect, not a joke.

Mary Hawkesworth, from Rutgers University, put in clear perspective the exciting contributions made by women's studies scholars over the last three decades, despite the fact that "many disciplines continue defective research strategies as if feminist scholarship did not exist." Offering two long lists, one of modified topics and another of newly created concepts, she impressed us with our own achievements. Indeed, by using transforming lenses, feminists have changed the modes in which we view all manner of themes, from the social constitution of subjectivity, to patterns of production and consumption, to the dynamics of diaspora and decolonization, to the twenty-four others she enumerated. She spoke of the many innovative concepts devised within women's studies, such as standpoint theory, gynocriticism, mestiza consciousness, technologies of gender, heteronormativity, and thirty-three more.

We who before the era of women's studies were able to raise our consciousness by "disidentify[ing]" from our intellectual fathers, went on to create the field of women's studies in spite of, and in opposition to, entrapment in the "traditional disciplines and androcentric/phallogocentric paradigms of the master's house."[9] The picture has changed. The new generations come up using the tools of gender and intersectionality to "interrogate the creation and accreditation of knowledge, the range of cognitive practices and explanatory frames." Hawkesworth shared the satisfaction that stems from teaching students to fashion analytical tools that lead to new research questions by "problematizing the given and denaturalizing the taken-for-granted." In *Three Guineas* (1938), she noted, Virginia Woolf

visualized a revolutionary flowering of an alternative women's education if—that is, providing—the "hierarchy, competition, self-inter-
estedness and aggression typical of male dominant institutions" could
be rejected. Hawkesworth urged us to follow Woolf's lead in our new
Ph.D. programs: to "promote an ever changing, ever responsive
action-oriented agenda for women's freedom and empowerment."

Deborah Rosenfelt of the University of Maryland and Rosemarie
Garland-Thomson of Howard University replied to some of the following questions on the program sheet regarding research on women
and gender: "How will the existence of the Ph.D. in women's studies
change the subjects considered worthy of research? How will gender-
based research intereact with research on race, ethnicity, class, sexuality, disability? How should the field integrate discipline-based and
interdisciplinary research?"

Underscoring the need to link the study of language and power, of
epistemology and ethics—to structurally link the study of race, gender, and ethnicity—and referring metaphorically to the institutionalization of *This Bridge Called My Back,* Rosenfelt called for the forging
of a different academy for a different, transnational world (Moraga
and Anzaldúa). It would be one where people could pursue a special-
ization in African diasporic studies, for instance, that fully encompasses
gender, or, in a deprovincialized Latina studies, take classes that both
cross borders and acknowledge how important a role nation and
nationality continue to play. She also mentioned as exemplary
women's human rights campaigns—spearheaded early on by feminist
scholars of color—committed to a strategic universality that does not
excuse the need to give meticulous attention to diverse experience.

Garland-Thomson used a disability model and the framework of
feminist pedagogy to posit making women's studies a universally useable field capable of transforming society as well as the university, both
of which are dominated still by an ideology of ability that insists on narrow definitions of the "normal." She spoke of intercorporeality,
removal of barriers, and time and standards accommodation for a variety of abilities.

At another point in the program, defending ambiguity, risk-taking,
and the concept of compound spaces—including the spaces of not
knowing—Vivian May from William Patterson University cited Simone
de Beauvoir's critique of fascism and warned against the reinstatement
of canons, strict methodical coherence, and bounded space.

I was among those asked to think about the multiple ramifications
of the following question: "What are the implications of the women's
studies Ph.D. for social justice issues and movements, the formation

of gender-related public policy, the communication of women's studies and the dissemination of research results to a wider public, and the promotion of changes in basic American cultural values and popular culture?" It depends (I answered, in part) on a reshuffling of relationships, on promotion of thinking, research, and writing that whenever possible includes and consults with its subjects; that always subsequently gets translated (into plain English as well as when appropriate into other languages) and *divulgado* (divulged), as we say in Spanish—widely circulated, mainstreamed. Too many academic research projects continue, subtly or grossly, to appropriate information, to treat informants or a community serving as a resource as "them" (other), and to lack a respectful reciprocity and follow-through. Therefore we must insist that findings be divulged to—shared with—the communities of which they treat and made available also to other possibly interested nonacademic parties.

It depends also on our effectiveness in gaining a chance for women and men in society at large to become transformed by feminist perspectives (inclusive and transnational in the spirit of Audre Lorde), and on being able to counterbalance the pervasiveness of masculinist studies, so that women's (and girl's) and gender studies are included in teacher training and K–12 curricula. Finally, it depends on increasing the stake advanced women's studies scholars claim and can inspire fellow citizens to claim, for implementation of the twelve points of the Beijing Platform for Action of 1995.[10] Cultural values and popular culture change when physical and material conditions change, when there is a shift in consciousness and in the creative expressions of that shift.

To underscore the importance of including the study of women writers and artists of other cultures and of periods prior to the nineteenth and twentieth centuries in our curricula and bibliographies, I used the example of Sor Juana Inés de la Cruz (Mexico, 1648/51?–1695). To demonstrate the advanced consciousness of this seventeenth-century poet, playwright, thinker, and nun that earned her the appellation "first feminist of the America's," I read verses from her "Philosophical Satire." Its first two lines are famous in the Spanish-speaking world. She writes, "You foolish and unreasoning men, / who cast all blame on women." The seventeen-stanza poem wittily exposes the social position of women, marked by a thorough-going double standard, showing it to be historical and ideological.[11] It seemed fitting to end with a selection from another poem in which, while criticizing human sacrifice among the Aztecs, Sor Juana denounced the bellicosity of her Spanish and *criollo* (Spaniards born in the Americas) compatriots and censured men for encouraging animosity to turn into brutality:

for men themselves
are crueler to the marrow
than the cruelest beasts—
for beasts you'll find not one
who'll turn his fearsome claws
against another of his species;
whereas among men we see
not only hate, but enmity
become a trade
and cruelty an art.[12]

A Ph.D. Program in Global/Transnational Women's and Gender Studies

I did not get to speak in Atlanta of a projected Ph.D. for the City University of New York (CUNY) in global/transnational women's and gender studies but want to here. As director of the Center for the Study of Women and Society and coordinator of the Women's Studies Certificate Program, CUNY (1997–2000), I was able to set up both informal and formal discussions of the subject and to mull over a proposal for a "wide spectrum" doctoral program drawn up earlier by a committee of colleagues. While I hesitated to carry the project forward in its original form in the face of resistance from within as well as from without our ranks, I began to think about a different sort of Ph.D. for CUNY, given its proximity to the United Nations (U.N.), its international student body, and its commitment to diversity—a Ph.D. program that would also be appropriate for other urban universities and universities with strong international studies components or broadly international student bodies.

Transnational in focus, it would bring together women who have already spent years in the field—in policymaking posts, U.N. and nongovernmental organization (NGO) offices, and grassroots organizing—and now need time, space, and academic and technical support to think, theorize, and "multilogue" in an intellectual environment. An advanced degree for women working at and around the United Nations, in the international arena, in "development," and for women involved in community service and the nonprofit sector has been lacking for some time. Numerous such women with whom I have spoken informally say they would welcome the opportunity to reflect on where they have been and what they have done and to organize their thinking and their materials in order to share them with others. Through seminars and study they could gain theoretical contexts, learn to tweak their discursive skills, and be enabled to produce a document or thesis about their work.

One of the dilemmas such a program might help ameliorate is that of finding expert transnational, comparative, decolonialist women's studies and gender specialists. Such specialists would be able to serve as resources and prepare personnel in international (and some national) bodies for new tasks. Charged with bringing women's and gender perspectives to each and every one of their organization's agencies, offices, and programs, and the documents they produce, well-meaning employees often flounder. U.N. officers neglected to fully consider the issue of effective implementation when they mandated the much-needed inclusion. Verónica Vásquez García documents the disappointing and sometimes disastrous effects of the failure in three sustainable development projects in Mexico in the spring-summer 2001 issue of *Women's Studies Quarterly*.

Women and men who are assigned to help international (and national) bodies add a gender perspective to all their work would greatly benefit from training by people thoroughly knowledgeable and experienced in women's studies as well as in creating environments propitious for consciousness-raising. In addition, of course, there is a crying need in this country for resituated—nomadically situated—knowledge about ourselves and the rest of the world. Feminist philosopher Rosi Braidotti uses "nomadic" to identify the capacity of specific, particular, located knowledges to be appropriately adopted and adapted, to move from place to place.[13]

Recently, Linda Basch, executive director of the National Council for Research on Women (NCRW); Patricia Clough, current director of the Center for the Study of Women and Society (CSWS) of the Graduate Center of CUNY; along with Kristin Timothy, formerly of the United Nations and now a senior researcher at NCRW, designed a three-year program entitled "Facing Global Capital, Finding Human Security: A Gendered Critique." It won support from the Rockefeller Foundation for 2002–04 to bring activists, policymakers, and scholars from different parts of the world together to delineate a gendered interpretation of human security. They will examine "the new configurations of global and local forces that contribute to the tenuous nature of the majority of women's lives and to the personal and state violence in which women's bodies become a battlefield" (Basch et al).[14] The project may well prove a fitting and timely platform for the launching of a CUNY Ph.D. program in transnational/global women's and gender studies (or comparative women's studies). Gaining much from all of those who participate in the activities of this Rockefeller grant period and from Ph.D. programs already in place elsewhere, it might in turn serve as a model for programs at other universities.

I left Emory mulling over the distance between aggressive doublespeak offered to the North American public through those pendant lobby televisions and the thoughtful deliberations of which I'd just been a part in the rooms at the conference center. Science and technology, the social sciences, and the humanities revisioned by members of women's studies Ph.D. programs (interested in education in the broadest sense) could well provide responses and alternatives for those that, throughout the country, indeed throughout the world, call for redefinitions of human and planetary health and welfare.

NOTES

I would like to thank Beatrix Gates, Ann Hoff, and Martha T. Zingo for their comments and editorial assistance.

1. Kitch, chair of the Department of Women's Studies at Ohio State University, 1992–2000, is a feminist theorist and has worked to promote interdisciplinary women's studies research "as a way to solve gender related problems that lie beyond the focus of existing disciplines" (Ohio State University Web site). In listing the interests represented Kitch said, "We are feminist, womanist, Africana, Asian-American, Xicana, Latina, disability, ethnic, lesbian, and queer studies scholars." For information on other scholars mentioned in this article, I suggest browsing the Web sites of their respective institutions. Links to all of the existing Ph.D. programs can be found at http://www.depts.drew.edu/wmst/WS_PhD/Links.htm.

2. "Thinking out of the box" is a phrase used by Ruth Perry of the Massachusetts Institute of Technology in describing a faculty research seminar designed to tap a wide variety of knowledge bases in preparing university teachers for collaborative, interdisciplinary thinking and teaching.

3. The Union Institute, without having programs or departments, was one of the first institutions to award Ph.D.s in women's studies.

4. They are Frances Smith Foster (Emory); Beverly Guy-Sheftall (Spelman); Sally Kitch (Ohio State); Wendy Kolmar (Drew); Inez Martinez (Kingsborough Community College); Vivian May (William Patterson); Claire Moses (Maryland); Jean O'Barr (Duke); Stephanie A. Shields (Penn State); and Bonnie Zimmerman (San Diego State). Also, Paula Jayne, a graduate student at Emory, was recognized for inestimable assistance in organizing the conference.

5. The organizers of the Emory working conference sought financial support from universities and foundations. Major grants came from the Ford Foundation and Emory University; funds were also provided by Nag's

Heart for planning sessions. Other financial assistance came from City University of New York, Drew University, Duke University, University of Maryland, Ohio State University, Penn State University, San Diego State University, Spelman College, and Texas Woman's University.

6. In the pages of this essay I have already referred to several of the questions raised and will cover almost all of them by the end of it, although it is impossible to include the full brilliance, incisiveness, and range of the proceedings in this selective report and commentary. In regard to women's studies, the program listed the following questions: How will existing undergraduate degree programs and Ph.D. certificates and "concentrations" in women's studies change as Ph.D. degree programs develop? In regard to the academy: How will doctoral-granting programs in women's studies articulate with existing fields, including traditional disciplines as well as sister interdisciplines, such as African American studies, gay and lesbian or queer studies, Asian American studies, Native American studies, Latino/a studies, disability studies, and so on.? Should women's studies Ph.D. programs be concerned with transforming institutional politics and values, both internal and external, as well as the conventions of Ph.D. education itself? The other two categories, research on women and gender and society at large, are quoted in the text itself.

7. Phillips was asked to address the implications of the women's studies Ph.D. for research on women and gender and/or society at large.

8. Mentioning global shifts—bifurcation and polarization—resulting from neoliberal economic policies, she stated, "We need to bring attention to class front and center—but when I say class, I really mean poverty, because poverty is the #1 impediment to women's and human well-being in our times." Overshadowing issues of religion and culture as root causes of terrorism and war, for me, is the undemocratic distribution of the world's resources—the overwhelming poverty of the overwhelming majority in all its differing specificity.

9. Hawkesworth was citing Rosi Braidotti (207).

10. The Beijing Platform for Action delineated "12 Areas of Concern," the second being education and training of women. For details of the platform, see http://www.un.org/womenwatch/daw/followup/session/presskit/presskit.htm.

11. Sor Juana's popular and oft-repeated opening stanza accuses *"Hombres necios que acusáis / a la mujer sin razón / sin ver que sois la ocasión / de lo mismo que culpáis"* (You foolish and unreasoning men / who cast all blame on women, / not seeing you yourselves are cause / of the same faults you accuse) (Cruz, *The Answer* 156–59).

12. Translated by Amanda Powell. Cited in the introduction to my play "This Life Within Me Won't Keep Still" (Arenal "This Life Within Me" 162). For the Spanish, see Sor Juana Inés de la Cruz (*Obras completas* 186). I circulated two sheets with passages that exemplify Sor Juana Inés de la Cruz's concept of reason, wisdom, and conciliation; her psychological insights; and her questioning, independent, woman-centered

vision. Conversations about this figure, new to many, continued that evening and between sessions the next day after people had had a chance to read them through. The same was true about many other subjects brought up during the working conference—the conversations went on nearly round the clock.

13. See Braidotti.

14. From "Facing Global Capital, Finding Human Security" (Basch et al.), distributed at a recent meeting of the board of advisors on which I serve. Information about the fellowship program is available through http://www.ncrw.org.

WORKS CITED

Note: I do not cite quotations from conference proceedings, including the drafts of Hawkesworth, Martinez, and Phillips conference papers that were sent to me. They can be consulted at http://www.depts.drew.edu/ WMST/WS_PhD/Sessions.htm#why.

Alexander, Jacqui, and Chandra Mohanty. *Feminist Genealogies, Colonial Legacies, Democratic Futures.* New York: Routledge, 1997.

Arenal, Electa. "This Life Within Me Won't Keep Still." *Re-Inventing the Americas: Comparative Studies in Literatures of the United States and Spanish America.* Ed. Bell Chevigny and Gari LaGuardia. New York: Cambridge UP, 1986. 158–202.

———. "'What Women Writers?': Plotting Women's Studies in New York." *The Politics of Women's Studies: Testimony of Thirty Founding Mothers.* Ed. Florence Howe. New York: Feminist, 2000. 183–93.

Arenal, Electa, and Amanda Powell. Critical edition and translation. Sor Juana Inés de la Cruz. *The Answer/La Respuesta, Including a Selection of Poems.* New York: Feminist, 1994. 158–202.

Bambara, Toni Cade. *The Salt Eaters.* New York: Vintage, 1981.

Basch, Linda, Patricia T. Clough, and Kristen Timothy. " Facing Global Capital, Finding Human Security A Gendered Critique—A Summary." *http://www.ncrw.org.* 2001.

Braidotti, Rosi. *Nomadic Subjects: Embodiment and Sexual Difference in Contemporary Feminist Theory.* New York: Columbia UP, 1994.

Feminist Studies. Special issue: *The Ph.D. in Women's Studies.* 24 (Summer 1998).

Howe, Florence, ed. *The Politics of Women's Studies: Testimony from Thirty Founding Mothers.* New York: Feminist, 2000.

Moraga, Cherrie, and Gloria Anzaldúa, eds. *This Bridge Called My Back: Writings by Radical Women of Color.* Watertown, MA. Persephone, 1981.

Ohio State University Web Site. *http://womens-studies.ohio-state.edu/personnel./ corefac.htm.*

Sandoval, Chela. *Methodology of the Oppressed.* Minneapolis, MN: U of Minnesota P, 2000.

Shteir, Ann B. "The Women's Studies Ph.D.: A Report from the Field." *Women's Studies Quarterly* 25 (spring–summer 1997): 388–403.

Sor Juana Inés de la Cruz. *The Answer/La Respuesta, Including a Selection of Poems.*

Ed. and trans. Electa Arenal and Amanda Powell. New York: Feminist, 1994. 158–202.

———. *Obras completas*, vol. III. Ed. F. Méndez Plancarte. México: Fondo de Cultura Económica, 1951–57.

Vásquez García, Verónica. "Taking Gender into Account: Women and Sustainable Development Projects in Rural Mexico." *Women's Studies Quarterly* 29 (spring-summer 2001): 85–98.

Woolf, Virginia. *Three Guineas.* New York: Harcourt, 1938.

Women's Studies Quarterly. Special issue: *Looking Back, Moving Forward: 25 Years of Women's Studies History* 25 (spring/summer 1997).

Electa Arenal is a writer, translator, activist, and professor emerita of Spanish and Women's Studies, City University of New York (CUNY) Graduate Center and the College of Staten Island. She directed the Senter for Humanistisk kvinneforskning (Center for Feminist Research in the Humanities), University of Bergen, Norway (1992–94) and CUNY's Center for the Study of Women and Society (1997–2000).

Choose Your Own Critical Adventure in (Cyber)Space

How2 and the Impact of the Online Medium

Julie O'Neill Kloo and Laurie McMillan

In 1983, Kathleen Fraser began a small journal of innovative women's poetics called *HOW(ever)*. It ran through 1992 and in 1999 was reinvented as the online journal *HOW2*, explicitly committed to "extending *HOW(ever)*'s original spirit of inquiry into modernist and contemporary innovative writing practices by women" (*HOW2*). *HOW2* includes not only innovative poetry by women but also critical scholarship, informal exchanges between readers and editors, self-reflective essays on the journal's mission, and archives of past issues of both *HOW2* and *HOW(ever)*. Fraser explains in "The Tradition of Marginality" that *HOW(ever)* was meant to fill a gap in poetic circles: Much experimental poetry by women was rejected by male-dominated journals and publishers, but the women-based journals that arose from the feminist movement tended to "call for the immediately accessible language of personal experience as a binding voice of women's strength" (31). Thus, *HOW(ever)*'s purpose was not "to displace or replace anything or anyone" but "instead to be an added source of information and stimulation" for poets and scholars (36).

HOW2's launch into cyberspace is just one example of an embracing of technology by those involved in teaching and writing, feminism and women's studies. The new and developing online format is full of opportunities for those interested in exploring and challenging traditional forms and institutions. Lyn Hejinian's description of the "open text" highlights the ways "arrangement" and "rearrangement" can affect a text's reception:

> It [the "open text"] invites participation, rejects authority of the writer over the reader and thus, by analogy, the authority implicit in other (social, economic, cultural) hierarchies. It speaks for writing that is generative rather than directive. . . . The "open text" often emphasizes or foregrounds process, . . . and thus resists the cultural

tendencies that seek to identify and fix material and turn it into a product; that is, it resists reduction and commodification. (43)

HOW2 exemplifies the "open text," and in doing so, it suggests that the internet format can contribute to the feminist challenging of traditional hierarchies by allowing more inclusiveness and encouraging a dialogue between reader and writer.

The temptation that comes with the online form, however, is to try to make feminist endeavors all things to all people; after all, internet journals are potentially available to anyone, and feminism can only grow and prosper from the inclusion of different voices. Yet *HOW2*, eclectic though it is, neither appeals to everyone nor can be accessed by everyone; like all journals, factors of time, class, and education affect readership and contributions. The greatest strength of *HOW2*, then, may be its own acknowledgment of its limitations—and in this it can provide a sound model for other feminist online ventures.

The dynamics—the impossibilities—of the feminist online journal are what interest us. We have taken a bit of a critical adventure in order to help us discover through performance what *HOW2* and similar journals stand to gain and lose, not only in terms of the online format but also in attention to space and form, the juxtaposition of poetry and scholarship, the use of biographical notes, and the combination of formal and informal modes of writing. We do not, of course, completely mimic the journal (not least because we are translating to print form), but we imagine that the experience of reading this "essay" will tell you as much about *HOW2*'s effect as our observations will. While we have been very critical of *HOW2*, it is because we value the journal and its mission. *HOW2* is doing and publishing exciting work as it provides a place for women to experiment and explore in a critical but welcoming environment.

To begin the critical adventure,
please choose from among the following options:

PARTY LINE POSSIBILITIES   WORKING & PLAYING NOTES
dialogism in cyberspace   ~B~
~A~

POETIC ADVENTURES
HOW2 READ in Cyberspace
~C~

BREAKING THE CODE   EXPLORER BIOGRAPHIES
the materiality of language   ~E~
in cyberspace
~D~   PAST ADVENTURES
archiving a women's tradition
~F~

HOW2
http://www.departments.bucknell.edu/stadler_center/how2
~!~

~A~
Party Line Possibilities
dialogism in cyberspace

A feminist poetics that seeks to question patriarchal values and norms without creating a new, often reversed, hierarchy must rely on some degree of dialogism (an interplay of multiple perspectives in which no single point of view is completely privileged). In this approach, hierarchies do not disappear completely, but they are recognized as temporary while differences are acknowledged and celebrated. The goal, then, is not to reach a final solution to problems of oppression; instead, solutions are always provisional and the ongoing *process* of an interactive exchange of ideas is emphasized. The online format of *HOW2* contributes to this style of feminist poetics by widening its readership and its pool of contributors and utilizing a Web design that reduces hierarchical relationships, invites an active readership, and emphasizes process.

One of the major advantages of an online journal is its ability to bridge geographical distances. Kathleen Fraser explains that many recent women-edited journals "have tended to circulate within discretely separate geographic, academic and special-interest circles" ("Intentions & Needs"). However, as Meredith Stricker states, "The current *HOW2* exchanges will be available to anyone on the planet who has access to the Internet and perhaps keys in 'women,' 'writing,' or 'innovative.'" This degree of accessibility creates a network that many female poets of Fraser's generation missed hav-

however . . .

"A cyberspace community is self-selecting, exactly what a real community is not. . . . The essence of real community is its presumptive perpetuity— you have to worry about other people because they will always be there. In a cyberspace community you can shut people off at the click of a mouse" (Calcutt 23).

Editing still takes place in *HOW2*, despite the presence of guest-editors and multiple contributors. Voices are still left out, and who you know and where you are still matters— the virtual world does not leave all of the dynamics of the material world behind.

"The Internet allows its dominant users— middle class, suburban Americans—to ing (Fraser, "Traditions" 35–38). *HOW2* thus "mak[es] [internationally] available often privileged information through creating a bulletin board of public conferences; a list of women-edited English language journals and books; and a place for an informal 'postcard' exchange among readers" (Fraser, "Contribution"). By creating an opportunity for virtual conversation, furthermore, *HOW2* may relieve some of the limits of real-time exchanges, such as "not having enough time to formulate a reply" (Calcutt 22). The internet format thus invites a wider circulation and facilitates a thoughtful and supportive conversation among participants.

The spatial aspects of the online journal further encourage dialogism. On a very basic level, cyberspace is practically unlimited, so an online journal can afford to be much more inclusive than a print journal.

Additionally, the Web configuration disrupts hierarchical structures implicit within a print text. The linear nature of print texts suggests that the reader is progressing toward a final answer or resolution; the online reader, on the other hand, must decide both the order in which the pages will be read and at what point the reading is "finished." In this medium, then, no page is in a "superior" position, reader participation is key, and reading is always in process. Meghan Quinn points out, "It is the *visual* manifestation of collaboration that makes hypertext so exciting. Electronic texts expose the patchwork of our lives, and it is this very mutability and fragmentation that hypertext readers and writers seem

keep in touch with carefully screened groups of similar people, right across the world, from the safety of their increasingly fortified homes" (Stephen Graham, qtd. in Calcutt 25).

In a world that provides more and more information all the time, is a journal the size of *HOW2* practical? Who has time to read it all (especially considering how long it takes for pages to load for those of us whose internet connections are—literally— not up to speed)? How many people are daunted by its size? What percentage of the world's population speaks English?

Computer programs are based on a language with exactly two components: 0 and 1. Every code on the computer can be reduced to this basic binary.

to find compelling." In other words, readers collaborate and multiple voices come together to make meaning in every text, but these dynamics are especially foregrounded in cyberspace.

Finally, *HOW2* itself is always in process because updates are made between issues ("postcards" and conference announcements). A print journal cannot accommodate excess or overflow; an internet journal, however, has space and time to be always growing and changing outside of its initial boundaries (such as volume and issue). The updates seem vital to *HOW2*'s commitment to conversation, for responses to the journal (and to others' responses) do not take place over months through letters to the editor but instead with something close to immediacy, keeping the exchange active and relevant.

"Many cybercitizens are concerned that the population of the world is set to be redivided into the information-rich and the information-poor. In a world where participation is dependent upon access to information, it is feared that the 'information-poor' will simply not exist in the same social realm as the 'information rich'" (Calcutt 36–37).

Continue to explore: A: PARTY LINE POSSIBILITIES / B: WORKING & PLAYING NOTES / C: POETIC ADVENTURES / D: BREAKING THE CODE / E: EXPLORER BIOGRAPHIES / F: PAST ADVENTURES / HOW2: http://www.departments.bucknell.edu/stadler_center/how2

~B~
Working & Playing Notes

- It is no accident that many of the ideas and most of the quotes for our project came from HOW2; its self-consciousness about the work it is doing and its awareness of its own complicity with structures of oppression render it open, dynamic, and exciting. It is rare to find self-critique within an academic journal, a genre that tends to evaluate everything except itself.

- We decided not to have one unified format because exploring different material requires the use of different forms. This approach allowed us to make many independent decisions, but we also agreed on the way the project as a whole would appear.

- Working collaboratively = a project similar to that of *HOW2:* coming together in conversation, building upon one another's ideas, creating an excitement about our work because each of our voices has value.

- Also, the risks in collaboration—ours and that of *HOW2*—became apparent. From seeking out a partner to offering ideas, fears of being rejected or being too controlling were often present. Yet these risks are important to learning about what it means to remain in conversation with others. *HOW2* provides a place for women—like us!—to learn to take such risks.

- Much of our thinking about the way the journal operates within cyberspace was played out as we tried to adapt the print form to enact many of the positive aspects of the Web form. Our thoughts thus developed through the creative process; performance became key to our learning about possibilities and limitations of the internet and print texts—placing an emphasis on process that informs our entire project.

- Allowing our critical ideas to take on creative dimensions has been freeing; substantive thought does not appear in 1 form—and traditional scholarly papers may sometimes limit substantive critical thinking. This calls attention to restrictions of traditional critical forms that had seemed transparent and begun to feel "natural."

Continue to explore: A: PARTY LINE POSSIBILITIES / B: WORKING & PLAYING NOTES / C: POETIC ADVENTURES / D: BREAKING THE CODE / E: EXPLORER BIOGRAPHIES / F: PAST ADVENTURES / HOW2: http://www.departments.bucknell.edu/stadler_center/how2

~C~
Poetic Adventures
HOW2 READ in Cyberspace

Sit at your desk (do not lie in bed
 do not go to the beach
  do not sit on the porch with lemonade
   at your side)
Turn on the computer (and wait and wait)
The monitor comes to life and a program checks for viruses
 (you wait and wait)
Enter your password to get online (and wait and wait) (and reflect on
 passwords: you used to associate them with spies and secret
 agents, but now they are so common that you have many
 passwords despite the little you might want to hide)
Go to "Bookmarks" and click *HOW2* (and wait and wait)
"Enter *HOW2*"
  and choose current issue
   or choose archives
    or choose . . .
     or choose . . .
      or choose . . .
  and read or scan and choose again (and wait
  hit down arrow hit up arrow move and think
  back move forward return home and wait
  return to contents go to postcards and think)

be impressed with the graphics ("this isn't some rinky-dink Wayne's
 World of a journal created in somebody's shady basement")
be impressed with the university affiliation in the address ("academic—
 important—worthy—professional knowledge—*contacts . . .*")
be impressed with the archives of the print journal *HOW(ever)*
 ("print = funded = respected/respectable and, once again,
 worthy")
be impressed with the biography of the poet or critic who is associated with an academic institution and has been published in
 such-and-such a journal or has edited or written a book in
 real space that is more valid than this virtual democratic
 chaotic mess that I cannot trust because who will judge for
 me who will sanction the words how shall I choose whom to
 believe and whom to dismiss as the latest crackpot bigot who
 continues to deny the Holocaust????

And look at yourself as you   (and notice the self-
Wait and wait   consciousness of the
And be conscious of   journal—a tendency you
Choices and non-choices   respect beyond all poems)

And be filled with shame at the validations you still seek out despite
    your revolutionary-anti-Establishment-distrust-all-authority-
    especially-that-of-institutions training

    (and admit that you don't trust your own judgment; that you
    don't know what is "good," what is "bad," that you have
    learned to speak out assertively against littering but that
    almost everything else leaves you aware of complications
    hesitating   before any act of speech

Continue to explore: A: PARTY LINE POSSIBILITIES / B: WORKING
& PLAYING NOTES / C: POETIC ADVENTURES / D: BREAKING
THE CODE / E: EXPLORER BIOGRAPHIES / F: PAST ADVEN-
TURES / *HOW2*: *http://www.departments.bucknell.edu/stadler_center/how2*

~D~

Breaking the Code
the materiality of language in cyberspace

Much recent innovative poetry has focused on language's materiality because language that seems transparent hides its role in the perpetuation of oppressive structures; in other words, both language and cultural systems can appear natural and stable rather than open to change. *HOW2* can contribute greatly to a poetics interested in denaturalizing language because it relies on cybertext. Reading from a computer screen defamiliarizes the process to an extent, so that reading and language appear less natural and transparent than they do when reading from a book. As Meghan Quinn explains, "In cyberspace, any presence is potentially tenuous, prone to (or even dependent upon) trickster shape-changing and transformation." This suggests that cybertext emphasizes its own instability while print text has become so familiar that it appears stable. The space between reader and the words on the screen emphasizes the way that the positionings of reader, text, and writer impact the activity of reading; process rather than product is highlighted. Cybertext's ability to expose the limits and possibilities in words and structures is central to *HOW2*'s potential impact on real-life situations.

however . . .

The computer monitor is inconvenient in terms of where and when it can be read or accessed. While I am inclined to read a book on a bus, in bed, or even while standing in line to vote, most people do not have the technology to read an online journal without sitting down at a computer table. This minimizes the time many of us will spend perusing the journal at any one time, and it also creates a very specific physical positioning of the journal's readers. I wonder if this physical positioning has an impact on the activity of reading—it may make it feel formal

While recognizing the instability of language and texts is important, this cannot mean ignoring the ways the body and material conditions are affected by linguistic and textual practices. Cybertext may promote such a strong feeling of distance between readers, writers, and texts that the referentiality to material conditions is downplayed. The very physical act of holding a book and turning its pages—in a sense, much more interactive than clicking a mouse on words, images, or arrows—may serve as a reminder of the immediacy of concerns and academic, or it may have the opposite effect, promoting a casual, even cavalier reading, as if journal pages are clever e-mails forwarded from one friend to another.

expressed in poetry, criticism, or other genres. (I have rarely cried in front of the computer screen, but I've read many a book through a stream of tears as I've realized that the book refers to pain that people have actually suffered—in ways that cannot ever be fully communicated or made transparent to me.)

Continue to explore: A: PARTY LINE POSSIBILITIES / B: WORKING & PLAYING NOTES / C: POETIC ADVENTURES / D: BREAKING THE CODE / E: EXPLORER BIOGRAPHIES / F: PAST ADVENTURES / *HOW2*: *http://www.departments.bucknell.edu/stadler_center/how2*

~E~
Explorer Biographies

BIO: Laurie McMillan has worked as a waitress, a telemarketer, an encyclopedia sales representative, a hotel maid, a 7–11 clerk, a salesperson at "The Limited," and an elementary teacher at the Red Sneakers School. She published a poem in her undergraduate literary magazine.

BIO: Julie Kloo lives in a suburb of Pittsburgh. She is very tenuously affiliated to Duquesne University by means of a teaching assistantship renewable annually. Her exam reading list is forthcoming. She is currently beginning to think about writing a dissertation.

BIO: Julie Kloo is the daughter of Paul and Nancy. She is the wife of Juergen and the mother of Jay and Ian. She is the sister of Patti, Margaret, and Paul. She is the sister-in-law of Andy, Phil, Celine, Manuela, Joe, Anton, Lisa, Anita, and Doug. She is the aunt of Nancy, Michael, Alex, Vicki, Philip, Sarah, Drew, Evan, Reilly, Jack, Stephen, Brooke, Megan, Natalie, Hans, and Tori.

BIO: Laurie McMillan is a white woman with parents who have moved between blue-collar, pink-collar, and white-collar jobs. She

Kathleen Fraser writes, "It is time for life itself to matter again. That is, the life of the poet" ("Contribution"). While Fraser's hope for a return of the "stench of reality that used to cling to certain works/words" ("Contribution") is valid, as is the self-conscious positioning of the poet, the biographies in *HOW2* often serve instead as a means to validate/authorize the contributions and the journal itself.

On the internet, every site is on a level playing field. Hierarchies break down, but readers also rely on subtle markers that lead them to take *HOW2* seriously. The university affiliation, the *HOW(ever)* affiliation, and the sophisticated appearance of the journal are all coded displays of prestige.

Within the journal, furthermore, authority is regularly established through the biographies. Speaker authority can come from many places depending on context: financial success, contacts, family name, profession, social position (including both dominant and oppressed positions, at different times), was raised Catholic in a middle-class Boston suburb, and she had her first and only long-term experience of being a minority when she attended Brandeis University (which is 70% Jewish) in a nearby town.

BIO: Julie Kloo lives in a house with a mortgage. She has two cars. She has a checking account and money market account. She has Visa, MasterCard, and American Express cards. She currently has $27.84 in her wallet and approximately $3.00 in change in the cup holder of her car.

BIO: Who is Laurie McMillan? Reader writer teacher student mother daughter wife friend sister cousin aunt leader follower thinker doer child adult virgin whore audience performer— these are just a few of the socially constructed roles she has occupied—or refused to occupy—at various moments in her life. Fluid. Multiple. Legion. Changing. The language that constructs the woman cannot contain her.

BIO: Julie Kloo Laurie McMillan

and education—to name only a few. *HOW2*'s biographies establish institutional affiliations and publications, relying on traditional academic and professional/writer-ly tags of authenticity. These means of validation may weaken the questioning of dominant institutional structures that the writing in *HOW2* so often enacts. How "on the edge" can a poetics be that receives so much endorsement? Yet, without markers of authority, how is credibility established?

Continue to explore: A: PARTY LINE POSSIBILITIES / B: WORKING AND PLAYING NOTES / C: POETIC ADVENTURES / D: BREAKING THE CODE / E: EXPLORER BIOGRAPHIES / F: PAST ADVENTURES / *HOW2*: http://www.departments.bucknell.edu/stadler_center/how2

~F~
Past Adventures
archiving a women's tradition

Having *HOW2* online allows access to an archive of past issues. This record of poetry and prose makes denying a tradition of experimental women's writing impossible. Hannah Mockel-Rieke sees the archive as "a place to look for literary prefigurations," hoping that to "recontextualize one's own writing in such a context might bring out aspects previously not emphasized" (Mockel-Rieke). She comments, "I was just reading what Derrida has to say about archives and patriarchal power and that reminded me how important it is to disturb, disperse and distribute this control." The archive serves as a reminder that, although the material published in *HOW2* is new and/or different, it is not without a significant, historic foundation.

and . . .

The online archive is more user-friendly than print archives. With past issues on the internet, reading a particular article does not involve interlibrary loans, which require time and money. Interested readers will not have the experience of finally tracking down a bound collection of volumes to find the one article they wanted has been ripped from the binding. The articles that the reader finds online are not damaged—pages torn, missing, or written all over. There is no need to copy whole articles, again requiring time and money. The reader can print out any essential material.

however . . .

Just because the archive is "out there," will people find it? Meredith Stricker asks, "What happens if increasingly diverse work by women is available, but no one can find it?" (Stricker)

> 10:19—The search begins.
> I go to Yahoo's search engine, click on "literature"
> and then "Feminist Poetry." I find a page called
> "Writings and Cryings" and from there find "web ring
> links"—all sorts of online journals have formed a
> community in which they all link to one another to
> become more accessible to people interested in fem-
> inist poetry. As I peruse the titles of journals and

attempt to continue my search, the program per-
forms an illegal operation and Netscape shuts down.
I have not found *HOW2*, although I now know that
great numbers of feminist and lesbian poetry Web
sites exist.
10:28—The search pauses.
10:29—The search resumes.
I go to the Lycos search engine. I click on Arts >
Literature > Poetry > Magazines and E-Zines. I find
"John's e-zine index," a site that seems to describe
and categorize every magazine on the internet with
an impressive list of keywords. I do not find *HOW2*. I
see "How to Promote Your Site," "How to Really Make
Money," and "The How To Web Update." (I wonder
if *HOW2* could learn something from the first of
these?) I'm not sure if an internet journal is different
enough from a "magazine" to explain *HOW2*'s
absence. However, I notice that a journal of language
poetry has made John's index, and I don't quite buy
the excuse.
10:43—I give up. There are plenty of other things to
read.

Continue to explore: A: PARTY LINE POSSIBILITIES / B: WORKING
& PLAYING NOTES / C: POETIC ADVENTURES / D: BREAKING
THE CODE / E: EXPLORER BIOGRAPHIES / F: PAST ADVEN-
TURES / *HOW2*: *http://www.departments.bucknell.edu/stadler_center/how2*

WORKS CITED

Calcutt, Andrew. *White Noise: An A–Z of the Contradictions in Cyberculture.* New York: St. Martin's, 1999.

Fraser, Kathleen. "Contribution to 'Postcards.'" *HOW2* (December 1999). Online, available: http://www.departments.bucknell.edu/ stadler_center/how2/postcard.html. June 2000.

———. "Intentions & Needs." *HOW2* 1.2 (September 1999). Online, available: http://www.scc.rutgers.edu/however/v1_2_1999/current/endnote.html. June 2000.

———. "The Tradition of Marginality . . . and the Emergence of *HOW(ever)*." *Frontiers* 10.3 (1989): 22–27. Rpt. Fraser, Kathleen. *Translating the Unspeakable: Poetry and the Innovative Necessity.* Tuscaloosa: U of Alabama P, 2000. 25–38.

Hejinian, Lyn. *The Language of Inquiry.* Berkeley: U of California P, 2000.

HOW2. Homepage, September 2001 http://www.departments.bucknell.edu/ stadler_center/how2.

Mockel-Rieke, Hannah. Response in "Forum." *HOW2* 1.1 (March 1999). Online, available: http://www.scc.rutgers.edu/however/ v1_1_1999/forum. html. June 2000.

Quinn, Meghan. "Quotidian Shatterings . . . Nonetheless Grouped Coherently." *HOW2* 1.3 (February 2000). Online, available: http://www.scc.rutgers.edu/however/v1_3_2000/current/forum/more-forum.html#Quinn. June 2000.

Stricker, Meredith. Response in "Forum." *HOW2* 1.1 (March 1999). Online, available: http://www.scc.rutgers.edu/however/v1_1_ 1999/forum.html. June 2000.

Julie O'Neill Kloo is a Ph.D. candidate in English at Duquesne University in Pittsburgh. She is exploring issues of gender and economics in postcolonial novels for her dissertation. Laurie McMillan is a Ph.D. candidate in English at Duquesne University. She is currently working on her dissertation, which investigates innovative feminist literary criticism.

Women's Studies Online

An Oxymoron?

Pamela Whitehouse

Over thirty years ago now, the first women's studies courses tentatively made a space of their own in the curriculum of the social sciences in higher education. The women academics that taught were on the cutting edge of developing a feminist pedagogy that challenged the traditional notions of experience, objectivity, the definition of theory, and rationality as the cornerstones of pedagogy. They demanded herstory as well as history, honored personal experience as part of the learning and writing process, and breathed vibrant life into Gloria Steinem's radical declaration, "the personal is political." Women academics joined in and celebrated through their writing and teaching the women's liberation and civil rights movements, and explored the implications of birth control—preparing a generation of college women to ask for it all, to be a person, a mother, a worker. The courses were discussion-based inquiries defined by consciousness-raising and healthy skepticism of the status quo, with the professor acting as facilitator to allow women students to find their own voices and their own paths to new ways of knowing through connecting personal experience with feminist theory and activism. It was an invigorating and validating experience for many women who had been silent in the classroom and settling for what they could get in the workplace.

Today, distributed learning environments (teaching and learning occuring both online and in the classroom) can better prepare our students to be activists by using technology-driven innovations in teaching and learning, as well as prepare them for high-end jobs in the global workplace. Distributed learning environments can promote student-centered learning (learning through doing) and constructivist teaching (guided learning through doing) by offering students "experiences that are delivered on demand in a real world problem-solving context." All traditions of teaching are now challenged by new ways of thinking, knowing, and learning through the technology innovation that permeates our school system from kindergarten to higher education. It is time for women's studies scholars and teachers to lead the way through another time of significant social change and workplace reformation (just as they did in the 1960s) to find the connections between women's lives and experiences in the "Information Age." The purpose of this essay is to explore the notion of teaching women's studies in a distributed learning environment and to think what that would look like. But first, why do it at all?

Is women's studies online an oxymoron? How can we and why should we teach a discussion-based class that honors personal experience in an online environment to a student population that generally conceives of computing as a male domain and specifically is doubtful of the efficacy of computers in their own lives? Among the key recommendations offered by the American Association of University Women (AAUW) Educational Foundation Commission on Technology, Gender, and Teacher Education, chaired by Sherry Turkle of the Massachusetts Institute for Technology and Patricia Diaz Dennis of SBC Communications, was the need for professional development for teachers to shift from "mastery of the hardware to the design of classroom materials, curricula, and teaching styles that complement computer technology." There is compelling evidence that women educators are building effective learning communities online that are both formal and informal venues for adult education.[1] I propose that the distributed learning course (taught both online and in the classroom) in particular offers multiple entry points to learning that are very effective in reaching the goals of feminist pedagogy and may offer some insight to quality learning experiences for all students in a distributed learning classroom.

A substantial but not exhaustive review of the literature on women, online learning, and technology reveals a mixed bag of discussion from postmodern theoretical work about feminism and the cyborg to discussions of how to make cyberspace more hospitable to women . There is also a political/social discussion that purports single mothers may now enjoy easier access to higher education despite their multiple roles of mother, worker, and person . Other work takes a feminist pedagogical turn and explores women's experience in distance learning courses that were combinations of television, telephone, and e-mail, and reveals that the women students understood their experience in pragmatic terms—they could not have taken the course in the traditional classroom and access through these means was better than nothing .

Women's actual experiences in taking online courses are not readily found in the literature because the differences between male and female students are often measured in terms of expertise rather than

quality of experience. Many studies have shown that women's technical expertise becomes equal with that of men as they become more
experienced computer users, and some researchers and academics
have asserted that that is the extent of the technology gap. There is
evidence that this is an oversimplification and the fuller story is much
more revealing . Other studies find a different sort of technology gap
between men and women. This gap is not limited to stereotypical
explanations that run the gamut from biological factors—boys just
being better at math and science—to powerful agents of socialization
that push girls away from computers. These studies reveal that the
important issue is not whether girls can achieve skill parity with boys
(they do), but that girls "opt out" and the skills and usage gap grows
as we trace the girls and boys to adulthood. The emerging literature
on computer self-efficacy illuminates another side of this issue: Girls
feel that women in general are effective using computers but do not
apply this belief to themselves . What does it all mean? It means that
young women coming to college will have lesser skills in computing
than young men (in general—there is a further gap between public
and private education), less confidence in themselves as users of computers, less inclination to work in computer sciences, be at a disadvantage in college courses that use technology for teaching and
learning, and ultimately not competitive for the highest-paying jobs in
the ever growing technology job market.

There are increasingly a number of voices in the literature pointing
out that after decades of economic and social gain, women will
become marginalized academically and in the job market (see
Kirkpatrick and Cuban, for example). Their lack of training in networking and computing skills associated with the systems thinking that
is now part of corporate planning and implementation in the business
of making money will result in women remaining in lower skilled jobs
(Berge). The U.S. Department of Labor reported that jobs in the technical sector (computer analysts, scientists, etc.) will double by 2008,
and there is already a shortage of skilled workers. Women are needed
to fill this gap but there is no reason to believe at this point that there
will be enough women to fill the jobs .

The implications for academia are important and currently shape
the stampede for developing online learning programs in growing
numbers of universities. The implications are particularly important
for women, whose disaffection with new technologies and computing
may push them to the edges of the global economy rather than freeing them from the space and time boundaries of the traditional workplace. Or, as Kramarae suggests in her recent report for the AAUW,

new technologies could create a "third shift" for women as they work, parent, keep house, and then take online courses at night.[2]

Women in Higher Education

"College education, whatever its form, has always carried with it a consciousness of possibilities for women"(Solomon xx). I do believe that teaching in distributed learning environments can accomplish something valuable for women students, and that the skills gained from the experience will stay with them in the workforce—a "consciousness of possibilities" (xx). Belenky et al. argued in their seminal work *Women's Ways of Knowing* that women come to the classroom with a range of "epistemological perspectives" that frame their ways of knowing and learning. Their research revealed that women respond better to pedagogical practices that allow for connected knowing, rather than separate knowing (15). Teaching that honors these ways of knowing should result in effective learning experiences for women students, particularly if the goal is not only to open up new areas of thought but to encourage activism. If new technologies are not used as delivery systems for mastery of content, but instead as multimedia learning environments that support different types of learners, then instructors can model sophisticated uses of new technologies that do not lead to data-entry jobs.

The traditional feminist classroom opened up new entry points for women coming to higher education with diverse frames of reference. It gave women voice in the traditional university setting and taught them how to move from the margins of the workforce to the center. Now it is time to give energy to the discourse on gender equity in new technologies and examine how feminist pedagogy can assist women in becoming more comfortable in the culture of computing.

First, I will discuss some of the course designs used by institutions of higher education, and then demonstrate my vision of a feminist constructivist distributive learning design. Online course design in higher education takes on many guises, from the simple replication online of the traditional class—posting the syllabus and the e-mail address of the instructor—to more elaborate, theory-based models. There are some recurring themes, however, and an emerging body of literature that explores each of them. The theoretical design models that I will discuss are *behaviorist, community of learners,* and *constructivist.* These were chosen to give a general flavor of online and distributed learning course design, but I do not claim that these are definitive of the field. I will begin with the online course design that feels furthest from feminist pedagogy to me and work toward constructing a base for comparison and reflection for the distributed learning design that I offer as a fourth model for reflection: a feminist distributed learning model.

The behaviorist model of online learning is often based on mastery of content. For example, Texas Tech is using a modified version of the "Personalized System of Instruction" (PSI) to design their Web-based courses. Robert Price described this model as "based on behaviorist and cognitive psychology and encourages mastery of course content" (2). In addition to course information and the syllabus, each self-paced course offers an introduction, lesson objects, step-by-step instructions (in order), discussion (text), self-help exercises, and a lesson assignment section that requires each student to pass a multiple-choice quiz to demonstrate their "mastery" of the subject matter. Price opined that this model is probably best for skills building or informational courses, not for courses that require group interaction.

In "The Ideal Online Course," Alison Carr-Chellman and Phillip Duchastel offer a more flexible view of the behaviorist approach and write of the value of "distributed learning" or the blurring of the boundaries between class time and Web time. They further argue that "online education is a specific medium in its own right and thus, it will have its own design considerations for effective instruction" (232). Their ideal online course has a study guide as its central element. Lecture notes and audio or videotaped lectures should be there to "enhance the student's identification with the course," not just to deliver content (234). Assignments may be either individual or collaborative—the main point is that the learners must actively seek the knowledge they need through texts and the class Web site, and the assignments must have real-world applications (authentic assignments is a recurring theme in the literature on online course design). Feedback, examples of exemplary work, and discussion as a class and as individuals are also considered important elements of the online classroom so that students will know whether they have correctly mastered the material or need to do further work.

The main issues that arise for feminist online classrooms using the PSI model is the lack of space for discussion and the use of *mastery*, a term that implies a single, correct perspective of understanding. This is truly an individualized model for skill building and therefore has little connection with many feminist classrooms. The second model is more aligned with a constructivist model but does not offer a sense of building a community of learners, a key ingredient for many women's studies courses. It is limiting in that "mastery" of the material is required, and that implies there is only one way of knowing the material as determined by the instructor, a sage on a new virtual stage, if you will.

At the other end of the online learning spectrum are learning communities, built for exploring particular issues. Linda Harasim argues that the internet is more than a network of connections—it is a place, and learning communities can be built there . Rena Palloff and Keith Pratt argue that cyberspace learning communities are more than a place: "They are formed around shared issues of identity and shared values; they are not place-based" (25). The link between the two notions is that the learning space is real and that people create this space deliberately. The learning community model could be constructivist, but not necessarily. The main criterion is that a group of people come together to work toward some goal that is both shared and individual, which leaves much space for individual interpretation.

In the case of an online class, Palloff and Pratt define the characteristics of online community as:

- Active interaction of both course content and personal communication;
- Collaborative learning—the evidence is dialogue among students, not just questions and comments addressed to the professor;
- Socially constructed meaning built through dialogue and agreement;
- Students share resources; and
- Students encourage and support each other.

These criteria also delineate the difference between a social community and a learning community because of the connection between discussion and course content.

Moller argued that Web class design should be understood through the perspective of learning communities whose main functions are to provide information and social reinforcement. This asynchronous learning environment (a threaded discussion place where participants post and read posts at their convenience, for example) provides the learner with academic, social, and personal support that are further bolstered with collaborative assignments using real-world problems both to actively engage the learners and foster community-building .

The main similarity between the online community frameworks is that they are student-centered, with faculty acting as facilitators in most cases. An important difference between the learning communities models and the other models is that although learners are actively involved in making meaning of the material presented to them, they may be ability-centered rather than effort-centered, which is not necessarily conducive to the connected knowing experiences that distributed learning design can offer women students.

The constructivist approach to online learning also defines the learner as an active agent, but the focus is on student effort rather than just rewarding ability. I will concentrate on the work done by Michael Hannafin et al. because their model is abstract and generalizable to a variety of constructivist approaches rather than falling prey to the long-standing debates on the exact definition of *constructivist*. Hannafin et al. argue that a "grounded learning systems" design is most effective in overcoming some of the problems associated with the academic disputes on what is constructivism, by providing a framework that is "rooted in corresponding foundations and assumptions," not by which epistemology is assumed to be inherently correct. It also offers a solution to the on-going problem of how to define what "good" online education looks like. Grounded learning systems design approaches ensure that, by design, methods are linked consistently with given foundations and assumptions" (104). The authors define the foundations as psychological, pedagogical, technological, cultural, and pragmatic. The assumptions will change with content.

They cite three examples of grounded-constructionist designs that each use different assumptions and demonstrate the flexibility of the grounded learning system approach. I will limit mention of these to the Jasper series,[3] based on cognitive theory and anchored instruction, which offers problems through stories on video. The information needed to solve the problems is within the story, and student groups must sift through all the information to find what information is relevant to the problem they are endeavoring to solve. This is a model of authentic problem-based collaborative learning, where students are involved with not just mathematics but also the ways in which mathematics intersects with our lives in a messy, real-world context. In summary, the importance of using grounded learning systems is evident—it does not advocate one best way for teaching online but instead offers a way to link theory and practice in meaningful and organizing forms that allow more, rather than less, academic freedom for instructor and student alike.

To take this thinking a step further, we can make the connection to using new technologies. Hannafin and Susan Land describe a student-centered learning environment (SCLE) approach to online course design in a recent article published in the *Journal of Computing in Higher Education*. They attribute the rise in popularity of this approach to "shifting beliefs and assumptions about the role of the individual in learning" (5). The design is focused on the notion that technology allows "sophisticated partnerships among learners, experience, discourse, and knowledge" (5–6). Hannafin and Land describe two examples of SCLEs. The first, Problem-Based Learning (PBL), or authentic assignments, allows students to engage in real-life problems and use the structure of individual and group assignments to "learn by doing." For example, Hannafin and Land cite Hmelo and Day, whose article described a medical school that used a multimedia package which allowed students to work through the case of a woman diagnosed with breast cancer. The students use technology to hold simulated interviews with the patient, watch a breast biopsy, and conduct their own physical exam. Project-based designs are another form of SCLEs and allow students to pose their own questions, produce products, and publicly post and discuss their projects. This type of model is useful for professional development as well, and offers teachers multiple entry points to reflecting upon and designing new curriculum with new technology (Hannafin and Land).

Sharon Smaldino describes instructional design principles that must achieve balance between four elements—learner, content, method/material, and environment. She argues that none should take precedence over the other, although student needs should take precedence over the convenience of the instructor. Her main idea is that using these four elements as the framework for design will lead to an online learning environment that is well-conceived and effective for student and instructor alike .

A couple of recurring themes are worth noting for each theoretical perspective offered to this point. All advocate active learning as a way to provide the student with extrinsic motivation to do the work, but it is important to note that the definition of active learner shifts from an individually based effort in the behaviorist section to a more communal/collaborative definition in the learning community and constructivist sections. There is an even finer shift here. Learning communities may focus on student ability or student effort while constructivist models tend to focus on effort-centered learning approaches. The second common theme is that all, to a greater or lesser degree, advocate for authentic or real-world learning that will engage the learner. All use technology as the means to bring that "real-world" connection to the learners. This is a key point of interest for a women's studies course because personal experience and personal history (real world) are the main connectors from theory to practice.

There are two important omissions that I will explore in more detail in the following section. The first is that there is little concern with offering multiple entry points to different learners, or in some cases for transforming online courses from delivery systems to learning communities that offer multiple entry points for different types of learners. In fact, there is a whole body of literature emerging from researchers attempting to define the "ideal online learner," essentially a search for ways to weed out those who do not fit the mold. The second important omission is the assumption that the online environment is set, and the students must fit the environment—the environment need not fit the students. David Jonassen et al. argue that "the most productive and meaningful uses of technology will not occur if technologies are used in traditional ways—as delivery vehicles for instructional lessons. Technology cannot teach students. Rather, learners should use technologies to teach themselves and others" . This brings us to the fourth online course design model that I offer for consideration—the feminist distributed learning model.

How does one draw in women students and create a learning environment that builds a community of active learners who, as most students indicated in recent course evaluations of my Introduction to Women's Studies distributed learning course, "never felt so responsible for their learning," "never worked so hard," and "would definitely take another online course"? The feminist distributed learning design I propose for reflection draws from traditional feminist pedagogy and the research literature about distributed learning design (particularly David Jonassen), as well as the "teaching for understanding" concepts developed by David Perkins to design a distributed learning environment for women's studies students. This model is intended to continue the discourse on gender equity and teaching in the information age and is not intended as the definitive feminist model. The course design incorporates virtual and face-to-face advantages that include synchronous (online but in real time) and asynchronous tools (threaded discussions, bulletin boards, class Web site).[4] Its flexibility both temporally and spatially and its use of multimedia offer multiple entry points for different learners and seem particularly well-suited to the needs of a feminist constructivist classroom.

So what does that look like? I teach women's studies at a state university and most of my classes are populated by women students who work (often full time), who are mothers (often single mothers), and who often have little social support. The first challenge is to design a space where students begin forming their own questions about why they are taking the course and what they want to learn. This begins in the classroom in the form of introductions and warm-up exercises but extends beyond this to the class Web site. The class Web site has a page called the Who's Who page, and it gives the students a template for constructing a simple Web page about themselves. I posed questions for the students to answer: What did they hope to learn; why were they taking the course; what favorite quotes and books would they like the class to know about them? Students had the option of posting their photographs on their pages.

The Who's Who page offers a new entry point for students who cannot "think fast on their feet" and who may have left the class feeling they did not acquit themselves well in describing themselves or their learning goals. The Who's Who page can be edited all through the semester, and many students make changes in their pages to reflect progress in their thinking. I found that students were periodically going back to check on their classmates' pages, looking for changes. The Who's Who page allows students to extend the notion of the self beyond the first face-to-face impression and to change and grow as they explore new territories of thought and learn to challenge the status quo.

The challenge of offering multiple entry points for different kinds of learners runs through the rest of the course design. It is perhaps best exemplified by the introductory page of the class Web site where students are welcomed and offered several ways to communicate with each other through the Discussion Forums, America Online (AOL) Instant Messenger, a section for questions that come directly to the instructor, and a question-and-answer archive for frequently asked questions. The students also have the option of waiting until face-to-face class time to ask questions or voice concerns, but there is an immediacy about sending off an e-mail to a fellow student or instructor that can be very satisfying.

Students have immediate access to several ways of communicating synchronously (face to face or in a chat room) or asynchronously (through posting on the discussion forum or class listserv) with their classmates or the instructor. Discussion or comments on the reading assignments or thoughts that come up while writing journals can be shared almost immediately, and in my experience builds a sense of community as other students respond to the urgency of the student posting in the discussion group. I post PowerPoint "mini-lectures" that are intended to expand on the ideas presented in the readings in a summary form. I used PowerPoint to illuminate issues of identity, and through the slides and links to Web sites, take students step by step through answering questions about themselves at the home, local community, state, national, and international levels. We then discuss, both face-to-face and in asynchronous discussion forums, what they have learned. Distributed cognition, the "dispersal of intellectual functioning across physical, social, and symbolic supports," creates a complex interplay between student and the affordances of the internet and the classroom that cannot be achieved through the traditional classroom alone, and supports diverse learning styles. On a more practical note, students who usually emerge as "natural" leaders in face-to-face discussions cannot dominate the asynchronous discussions any more than the shy or timid student can dominate the face-to-face discussions.

The women students in my Introduction to Women's Studies course were very challenged by the technology, and according to a self-assessment survey of their skills, few had much confidence in their ability to overcome technical barriers and computer glitches. Our Computing Information Technology Services provided a "Just in Time" learning section for the class Web site. The tutorials were designed for a face-to-face workshop and then were redesigned to offer step-by-step instructions on the site as an immediate resource. These resources could be thought of as information vehicles that provided timely access to information needed to function within the online portion of the course and available at any time the students had internet access (Jonassen et al.).

Our face-to-face classroom was a state of the art Macintosh laboratory designed for small group work as well as individual work on the computers. The students learned to use the Web site in the first two weeks of face-to-face class time by collaborating in pairs to work through the tutorials provided for each section of the Web site. The workshop atmosphere fostered a sense of camaraderie and "we're all in it together" that provided successful models of women using computers which might not have evolved so quickly if the course were either totally online or face to face. At the same time, course content was not neglected as students used the course readings and other materials to demonstrate their ability to post resources to the discussion groups.

The references section of the Web site offers some insight into other ways that students construct meaning and take charge of their learning through the online environment. Students initially saw only the online links that I provide for them. These range from the fun (Museum of Menstruation) to the political (Women's Bureau Online and the Institute for Women's Policy Research).[5] After students had had time to familiarize themselves with the range of links I provided, they were then given a rubric to guide them in choosing sites that they felt were important or funny to share with their classmates. This section quickly grew to more than three times the length of my own offerings. Student discussion in the Forum and by private e-mail demonstrated that not only were the students connecting the links they provided with their reading, but they were connecting with their own and their classmates' experiences. Students built their own knowledge base from which to co-construct knowledge and new understandings about women's place in American society .

The asynchronous discussion forum became the heart of the class and our face-to-face meetings shifted from discussion to procedural issues and how their online discussion experiences changed their views of the world over the course of the semester. The classroom became a place for reconnection with each other, and the discussion forum became the center for expanding one's thinking. As Jonassen et al. have argued, we as instructors can support discourse in a knowledge-building community by using technology as a social medium that allows a safe controllable place for student thinking and discussion. The online conversation ranged from consideration of readings to discussion of assignments. For example, each student interviewed a woman from another culture, using the social status indicators from a United Nations Web site to take with them to the interview as discussion points with their interviewee. This formed the basis for some really fascinating interview results and vigorous discussion on the Forum about their experiences doing the assignment, as well as connections with the readings.

Students soon used the Forum as their own space, often talking about me as if I were not there and confiding personal experiences or memories that were raised by the reading and the discussion. The Forum became a safer place than the classroom for many students although some found that their best discussion and engagement still remained in the classroom setting. The point is that the students had a choice in the matter and more control over content. Although many teachers and students have pointed out that the online asynchronous forum is invaluable for shy students or for students who need time to think, little is said about the students who tend to take over a discussion and become "leaders" in a course that should honor all experiences and voices. In the Forum, no student can take over the discussion—one does not even have to read her posts. Students who naturally "take over" soon learn to join the discussion, although there are certainly times when one student's voice is clearly leading the discussion forward. Another portion of the Forum revealed the help that students gave each other over the course of the semester, from advising on where to look for online sources to where to apply for a job. Students also used AOL Instant Messenger to talk about class issues and develop friendships in "real time." Palloff and Pratt argue that a key characteristic of an online learning community is evidence of collaborative learning and socially constructed meaning built through dialogue and agreement, and the asynchronous discussion forum and resources Web page certainly became such places.

To review the teaching design issues:

- The technology becomes less visible and barrier-like for two reasons: easily accessed technical support both online and off and constant use makes procedure less visible.
- The individual and group ownership of the class is demonstrated through the Who's Who page, the Resources page, and the Discussion Forum.
- Creating a safe place is evidenced by student participation in the discussions, not only through the posts but through the content of the posts, which reveal collaboration, meaning making, and agreement.
- Building a community of active learners is evidenced by the Resources page, where students co-constructed a knowledge base. All of the students chose their own research paper topics, discussed their choices in the Forum, and mutually agreed to post their papers before the end of term so they could read and discuss them.

The student learning challenges were met in the same ways. They helped each other reduce the technological barriers by giving each other advice and offering support. The hybrid course offers multiple entry points for different types of learners and has the added value of teaching women students to understand technology from a systems thinking perspective that is similar to the modern workplace. Students learned to use materials posted online, develop their own online material, share their thoughts and their work effectively, and make decisions using the most appropriate form of communication for a given situation. In other words, new technologies provided a context to support learning by doing . The main differences between the feminist constructivist model and the other models are rooted in the differences listed earlier: There is more scope for welcoming different types of learners at multiple entry points. The definition of active learner remains broad, effort-centered, and can handle both collaborative and individual work. The authentic or real-world learning that has always been a part of women's studies remains and is broadened in scope because students can relate their personal experiences

through multiple avenues of communication and through constructing their own space on the Web site.

Reflections

I hope that this model of what a feminist distributed learning environment could look like invites further discussion not only about what
is missing here, but what we can gain from modeling how new technologies can be used in ways that make the culture of computing accessible to women. Even more than making the culture accessible,
however, this discussion hopefully demonstrates how we can use it to
create "technology fluency" for women that includes the "ability to use
technology proactively, understand design issues, and be able to interpret the information that technology makes available."

There are two issues that I feel need further reflection, and each
leads to larger issues that concern distributed learning environments
in general. The first is the problem of fitting the learner to the learning environment rather than fitting the learning environment to the
learner. Many institutions of higher education have spent much time
and money to define the profile of the successful distance learner
rather than creating distance learning environments that provide
affordances for multiple entry points for different learners. I think this
is worth further consideration for all distance education courses but
it is especially necessary for women's studies courses online. It may be
that instead of analyzing more surveys in an effort to define the type
of student most likely to succeed online, we should instead be asking
students what they need from an online environment. The idea of distributed learning, or using a combination of face-to-face class meetings, multimedia, and virtual environments, is taking hold on many
campuses. Distributed learning models may truly offer a new paradigm
for teaching because they are not limited to thinking about one teaching and learning space but open up the possibilities for authentic
learning experiences in a variety of places beyond the traditional .

The second issue arises from the first—the assumption that online
learning and new technologies are neutral in terms of race, class, and
gender. Although race and class issues were beyond the scope of this
essay, they are important factors to consider because a growing body
of literature reveals that African American boys and Hispanics have
not embraced new technologies either, and these groups may also face
economic marginalization as well. Marcia Linn, co-author of *Computers,
Teachers, Peers: Science Learning Partners,* from the University of
California, Berkeley, said, "The most important aspect of equity is to

have effective teaching that motivates the students." Equity means offering new technologies that provide multiple entry points for different learners, as well as equality of access.

In conclusion, I have offered a model of a distributed learning design for the feminist classroom in the hopes that it will contribute somewhat to the discourse on women and new technologies. As Chris Dede so aptly noted, "The most significant influence on the evolution of higher education will not be the technical development of more powerful devices, but the professional development of wise designers, educators and learners" ("Emerging Technologies" 25). Computer literacy and computer fluency are both important issues for women in the new millennium, but I think even more important is for feminist teachers to find effective ways to model and teach using the affordances of new technologies, not only because it is good for women's potential in the workplace but because it is a blueprint for creating "communities of practice" that can support and uplift women for all of their lives (Wenger).

NOTES

I would like to thank David Perkins for his wise and always thought-provoking feedback during the writing of this essay. Any mistakes or "puzzles" are entirely of my own making.

1. For example, see Joan Korenman's syllabi on the Web at http://www.umbc.edu/cwit/syllabi.html.
2. See http://www.aauw.org/2000/3rdshift.html.
3. The Jasper series is an innovative math program that uses a real world setting for solving problems. Students watch a short video, then work in groups to answer a set of math questions based on the events in the video.
4. For example, chat rooms, shared learning environments like Groove (see http://www.groove.net), or multiuser virtual environments (MUVES) like Tapped In, a MUVE for educators (see http://www.tappedin.org).
5. For the Museum of Menstruation, see http://www.mum.org/. For the Women's Bureau Online, see http://www.dol.gov/dol/wb/. For the Institute for Women's Policy Research, see http://www.iwpr.org.

WORKS CITED

Arbaugh, J. B. "Virtual Classroom Versus Physical Classroom: An Exploratory Study of Class Discussion Patterns and Student Learning in an Asynchronous Internet-Based MBA Course." *Journal of Management Education* 24.2 (2000: 213–33.

Belenky, Mary Field, Blyth McVicker Clinchy, Nancy Rule Goldberger, and Jill Mattuck Tarule. *Women's Ways of Knowing*. New York: Basic, 1986.

Berge, Zane L. *Sustaining Distance Training*. San Francisco: Jossey-Bass, 2001.

Burge, Elizabeth, and Helen Lenskyj. "Women Studying in Distance Education: Issues and Principles." *Journal of Distance Education* 5.1 (1990): 20–37.

Canada, K., and F. Bruscha. "The Technological Gender Gap: Evidence and Recommendations for Educators and Computer-Based Instruction Designers." *Education Technology Research and Development* 39.2 (1991): 43–51.

Carr-Chellman, Alison, and Phillip Duchastel. "The Ideal Online Course." *British Journal of Educational Technology* 31.3 (2000): 229–41.

Cook, Sarah. "The University of Phoenix—A New Way for Women to Learn." *Women in Higher Education* 8.5 (1999): 8.

Dede, Chris. "Distance Learning–Distributed Learning: Making the Transformation." *Learning and Leading with Technology* 23.7 (1996): 80–88.

———. "Emerging Technologies and Distributed Learning." *The American Journal of Distance Education* 10.2 (1996): 61–93.

Dyck, J. L., and J. A. Smither. "Age Differences in Computer Anxiety: The Role of Computer Experience, Gender, and Education." *Journal of Educational Computing and Research* 10 (1994): 239–48.

Hannafin, Michael J., and Susan Land. "Technology and Student-Centered Learning in Higher Education: Issues and Practices." *Journal of Computing in Higher Education* 12.1 (fall 2000): 3–30.

Hannafin, Michael J., Kathleen M. Hannafin, Susan M. Land, and Kevin Oliver. "Grounded Practice and the Design of Constructivist Learning Environments." *Educational Technology, Research and Development* 45.3 (1997): 101–17.

Harraway, Donna. "A Cyborg Manifesto: Science, Technology and Socialist-Feminism in the Late Twentieth Century." *Simians, Cyborgs and Women: The Reinvention of Nature.* New York: Routledge, 1991.

Jonassen, David H., Kyle L. Peck, and Brent G. Wilson. *Learning with Technology: A Constructivist Perspective.* Upper Saddle River, NJ: Merill, 1999.

Kelinson, Jonathan W., and Patricia Tate. *The 1998–2008 Job.* U.S. Department of Labor 2000. 10 December 2000. http://www.bls.gov/opub/ooq2000/2000spring/art01.pdf. Kelly, Karen. "The Gender Gap: Why Do Girls Get Turned Off to Technology?" *The Digital Classroom.* Ed. D. T. Gordon. Cambridge, MA: Harvard Education Letter, 2000. 154–60.

Kirkpatrick, Heather, and Larry Cuban. "Should We Be Worried?" *The Jossey-Bass Reader on Technology and Learning.* Ed. J. B. Publishers. San Francisco, Jossey-Bass, 2000.

Kramarae, Cheris. "Technology Policy, Gender, and Cyberspace." *Duke Journal of Gender Law and Policy* 4.1 (1997): 149–58.

Kramer, Margaret Strauss. *Tech-Savvy: Educating Girls in the New Computer Age.* Washington, D.C.: American Association of University Women, 2000.

May, Susan. "Women's Experiences as Distance Learners: Access and Technology." *Journal of Distance Education* 9.1 (1994): 81–98.

Moller, Leslie. "Designing Communities of Learners for Asynchronous Distance Education." *Educational Technology, Research and Development* 46.4 (1998): 115–22.

Palloff, Rena M., and Keith Pratt. *Building Learning Communities in Cyberspace.* San Francisco: Jossey-Bass, 1999.

Perkins, David. *Smart Schools.* New York: Free, 1992.

Price, Robert V. "Designing a College Web-Based Course Using a Modified Personalized System of Instruction (PSI) Model." *TechTrends* 43.5 (1999): 23–28.

Siann, Gerda. "We Can, We Don't Want To: Factors Influencing Women's Participation in Computing." *Women in Computing.* Ed. R. Lander and A. Adam. Wiltshire, Great Britain: Cromwell, 1997.

Smaldino, Sharon. "Instructional Design for Distance Education." *TechTrends* 43.5 (1999): 9–13.

Solomon, Barbara Miller. *In the Company of Educated Women.* New Haven, CT: Yale UP, 1985.

Thornton, Carla. "Back to School, Web Style." *PC World.* July 1999: 39–40.

Wenger, Etienne. *Communities of Practice: Learning, Meaning, and Identity.* London: Cambridge UP, 1998.

Young, Betty J. "Gender Differences in Student Attitudes Toward Computers." *Journal of Research on Computing in Education* 33.2 (2000): 204–16.

Pamela Whitehouse is the research coordinator for WIDE World, an online professional development program for educators, at the Harvard Graduate School of Education. She is also adjunct faculty at the University of Massachusetts, Dartmouth, where she recently received two outstanding online teaching awards. She is completing her doctoral work at the Harvard Graduate School of Education, with research centering on design for online learning environments.

Water

Josey Foo

For Tess

The next day I am light, transparent, clear; and the sacred places
will have flowed in affirming tides, from one vessel to another.

The next day will reproduce my transparent hand in blue
and send it forward on the San Juan.

What carries its weight, same light and color, wood in the fire,
has always carried its spine if not the life of a woman—

whose language, swift that she is, slides smoke on the land,
whose religion cannot be contained indefinitely.

*Josey Foo, a Chinese native of Malaysia, immigrated to the United States in
the early 1980s. She is a lawyer-advocate in Shiprock on the Navajo Nation.
Her writing has been included in* The Best American Essays 1995,
Premonitions, *and various journals. She is the author of two books*—Endou
(Lost Roads, 1990) and Tomie's Chair *(Kaya Press, forthcoming). She lives
in Farmington, New Mexico, where she and her husband, Richard Ferguson,
run Crooked Shelf Books (http://home.earthlink.net/~fergusbooks).*

At 4:30 in the Morning

Teresia K. Teaiwa

This little coconut[1]
    went to market
This little coconut
    stayed home
This little coconut
    had roast pork
This little coconut
    had none
This little coconut
    went . . . BAD

A single mother
    is an ABOMINATION
Before the Lord
    of coconuts

A single mother
and child
Living in a three bedroom house
    is an ABOMINATION
Before the Law
    of coconuts

I can't help it
When I hear footsteps outside my window
In the middle of the night
Only one language
Leaps to the tip of my tongue
Chest filled with heart
Throat choked by oxygen
Fear and loathing
Do not translate
Into
"Sala chuttiya"[2]
I can't help it
Fear and loathing
Translate into
"Magaitinana,[3]
O cei tiko oqori?
Na daubutako?
Mai, mai!
Mai, tovolea.
MOTHERFUCKER!"
(Hollywood-bravadoisms
offer the best punctuation
in these situations.)

When I hear footsteps
Outside my window
In the middle of the night
Only one language
Leaps to the tip of my tongue

ONE BAD BUNCH
    SPOILS THE COCONUT

The security guard asks to borrow my torch (hello?). After he inspects
the backyard, finding no evidence of prowlers, he inquires innocently
about who else is at home with me. My son, I say, stupidly. The security
guard, chivalrous, then suggests that he could spend the night sometimes. Because "it's dangerous" to live alone in a big house like this.
"You need a man."

ONE BAD COCONUT SPOILS THE BUNCH

Like the prowler or the thief or the rapist or whatever he is will give a
shit if another man is in the house. Like, let's say I got a man to live
with us, like he wouldn't be afraid of another man prowling, thieving,
raping. Like, give me a break. I wouldn't trust a man inside my house
anymore than I would trust a man outside my house.

No. In situations like this a woman must rely on herself.
And her sasa broom.
One thing a bad coconut understands is the sasa broom.
You shake it fiercely enough at him, you'll remind him of his mother,
and either shame him or scare him. Away.

A single mother
        is an ABOMINATION
Before the Lord
        of coconuts

                                          Who's single? Who's single?
A single mother   My four year old demands to know,
        and child   interrupting our conversation.
Living in a three bedroom   Your mother, his grandfather
        house   explains.
        is an ABOMINATION   Mama's not single, my son scoffs.
Before the Law   She's got me!
        of coconuts

This little coconut
        went to market
This little coconut
        stayed at home

This little coconut
   had roast pork
This little coconut
   had none
This little coconut
   cried, "We, we, we . . . not afraid! We, we, we not gonna take
this anymore! We, we, we gonna fight back! We, we, we gonna
see just who's the bad coconut here!"
BLOODY BASKET!!

NOTES

1. In the 1960s and 1970s the term coconut was used widely in New Zealand
   to derogatorily refer to migrants from the Pacific Islands. Although this
   poem is set in the multicultural but crime-ridden capital of Fiji in the
   1990s, the word is still used to capture the contrast between its deroga-
   tory potential and its wholesome natural qualities.
2. Fiji-Hindi curse.
3. Fijian swear.

*Teresia Teaiwa is of African American and Kiribati/Banaban heritage. She
was born in Honolulu, Hawai'i, and raised in the Fiji Islands. She currently
resides in Wellington, New Zealand. Her publications include a collection of
poems,* Searching for Nai Nim'anoa, *published by Mana and the South
Pacific Creative Arts Society (1995), and a compact disk of spoken word with
Sia Figiel,* TERENESIA, *produced by 'Elepaio Press and Hawai'i Dub
Machine in 2000.*

Nomadic Tutelage

Meena Aexander

For Audre Lorde

You strike your head against a door
and pluck it back again.

Ancient gesture, ineluctable,
bone bruising wood

and the lyric rears itself,
a silken hood.

Gamba Adisa
you have come to say to me

*Afraid is a country
with no exit visas.*

You taught me to fetch
old meal for fire,

sift through an ash heap.
pick out syllables

molten green,
butting sentences askew.

I try to recall
the color of your face.

Was it lighter than mine?
Or was it the color of the East River

when the sun drops into soil
melting obsidian

and I a child by the wellside
pack my mouth with stones.

Darkness crowns the waters.
The raw resurrection of flesh unsettles sight.

We would journey before light
into a foreign tongue.

I hear you and I am older
than moonlight swallows swim through.

Cries of hawks mark out
four points of the compass.

Nomadic tutelage of cactus and rose.
Blunt rods strike blood,

toss nets of dream
across salt shores.

NOTE
I met Audre Lorde at Hunter College. Gamba Adisa is one of the names by
which she knew herself. The lines in italics are drawn from her poems: the first
from "Diaspora" (32), the second from "From the Cave" (38). Reprinted from
Our Dead Behind Us by Audre Lorde, copyright ©1986 by Audre Lorde. With
permission of the publisher, W. W. Norton & Company, Inc.

Meena Alexander *is Distinguished Professor of English and Women's Studies*
at Hunter College and the Graduate Center of the City University of New York.
Her new volume of poems, Illiterate Heart, *is the winner of a PEN Open Book*
Award. An edition of her memoir, Fault Lines, *with a newly composed coda,*
is forthcoming from the Feminist Press.

On Why I Continue to Write Poetry

Shirley Geok-lin Lim

For Adrienne Rich

I think of Anna Akhmatova,
grieving, awkward,
writing on cigarette paper,
toilet paper, the backs
of bills and envelopes,
in her mind, at night, when
it's a blackout, when she knows
there are watchers
at her window. Writing
in her ear, her voice,
on skin, her body a sheet
of paper for words she cannot
put down. Carrying her fear,
love, hatred, those words
written down on her life.
She's nobody, a woman
without a husband, they'd
shot him at midnight,
and she cannot cry yet.
But see, here are her poems,
here is her cry
fifty years later,
a hundred years later
Anna Akhmatova
is still writing,
and Stalin is dead.

Shirley Geok-lin Lim is professor of English at the University of California, Santa Barbara. Her first novel, Joss and Gold *(Feminist Press) appeared in 2001. Recipient of the Commonwealth Poetry Prize in 1981, she has published four volumes of poetry.* What the Fortune Teller Didn't Say *(1998) was featured in the Bill Moyers PBS special on American poetry, "Fooling with Words."*

She is also author of three books of short stories and the American Book Award–winning memoir, Among the White Moon Faces *(Feminist Press, 1996). Her critical work has appeared in numerous journals.*

Copyright © 2002 by Shirley Geok-Lin Lim

Teaching Motherhood in History

Jodi Vandenberg-Daves

When I tell people that I regularly teach a course on the history of motherhood, there is almost always a flicker of genuine interest and surprise, not only from academics but from neighbors, friends, acquaintances, and relatives, especially the mothers. Do mothers have a history? This seems to be the usually politely unspoken question. It stems from a larger one that has plagued women's history since the second-wave feminists put the field on the map in the 1970s: Do women have a history? Recently, one of the students in my general survey course on modern U.S. women's history told me of her experiences as a student teacher in one of the local schools: A young male colleague of hers, when told about this class, commented, "Must be a short course!"

As this essay will show, the founding mothers of the modern field of U.S. women's history clearly identified the larger possibilities of their enterprise: the prospect of uncovering women's "private" experience in the past, as well as women's untold contributions to the record of "public" human achievements, from invention to diplomacy. But an examination of the challenges of understanding and teaching the history of motherhood provides a particularly useful angle on the extent to which the promise of uncovering private experience has yet to be realized. I base this examination especially on my two most recent experiences teaching a course called History of Motherhood in the United States at the University of Wisconsin–La Crosse (in 1999 and 2001), as well as on my broader experience teaching various women's history courses since 1995. Part of what follows is an explanation of key obstacles to examining the private dimensions of women's history. Through a review of historiographic traditions, I will show how male-centered assumptions about history, as well as feminist ambivalence about motherhood, have complicated the enterprise of searching for mothers in history. The legacy of these assumptions contributes to students' confusion about the meaning of private life in history. However, I also explain here why my experience with this field of privatized history has convinced me that the enterprise is full of promise and well worth the effort for students, teachers, and scholars.

Historiographic Traditions and the Problems of Locating Mothers and Motherhood in History

As with many aspects of women's history, such as access to male-defined politics in the achievement of suffrage and the "pleasure and danger" of sexuality, in the twentieth century students of the history of motherhood are confronted by paradox (Vance). In this case, they become aware that women's capacity to bear children and their historic responsibility to be primary caregivers have been crucial to the rationales for barring them from public activities and public and private power. Yet too in some cultures, arguably even our own, motherhood has been the basis of particular kinds of female empowerment, both private and public. The Million Mom March of May 2000, for example, had deep historical roots in its use of maternal rhetoric for the empowerment of children, mothers, and families, and in its emphasis on values of nurturing and protection.[1]

The paradox is especially intense in this class because students come to realize that through most of history, cultural sources, across cultures in fact, describe women as made for motherhood, *essentially* mothers by virtue of being born female. And yet the lack of scholarship on and sources about the actual experiences of women doing what they were told to do remind us of how devalued this role has been in our culture, so devalued as to be an utter novelty in a college classroom, especially in a history course. It may sound like a truism but history is still largely what men did, and now, what women did as they fought to achieve access to tools traditionally accessible only to men, such as literacy, formal education, suffrage, and economic power. In short, the history of private life remains somewhat marginalized from a discipline focused on public events, so much so that women's history in general is a kind of curiosity for history majors.

In the 1970s, when the feminist pioneers of modern women's history began envisioning what the study of women in history would mean, they immediately tried to discover history that was hidden not just because it was about women but also because what women did in the home was difficult to find in the public record. Nancy Cott and Elizabeth Pleck, editors of a major early anthology of women's history published in 1979, recognized their debt to the new social history, commenting, "History, the oldest and most tradition-laden scholarly pursuits, was for centuries an art patronized by the rulers of society to ensure their own immortality, and written by members of church and court circles, or learned gentlemen of leisure fascinated by the wars and reigns of the powerful" (10). Cott and Pleck pointed out that more recently, historians had become

interested in ordinary people and everyday life. In trying to find records
about these people, historians had to look beyond traditional sources
such as laws, treaties, or newspapers articles. "Historians had to seek
more popular sources, such as folktales, work songs, and oral histories,
or documents which yielded mass data, such as registers of births and
deaths, censuses, church lists, factory rolls, or records of tax collectors,
courts, prisons, and hospitals" (10).

But women's history as conceived in the 1970s would go beyond
either of these traditions. Cott and Pleck argued that the questions
posed by the women's movement would lead historians of women to
new sources and new interpretations. For example, they credited Betty
Friedan's publication of *The Feminine Mystique* in 1963 with prompting
"historical investigation of the ideology and practice of domesticity"
(Cott and Pleck 14). They also remarked that "the search for information about past sexual ideology and behavior" was encouraged by
"theories of women's liberation asserting women's right to control
their own bodies and sexual practices" (15). While Cott and Pleck and
the talented new group of women historians they represent were interested in politics and economics, they gave significant emphasis in their
widely used women's history volume to "private" issues, with articles
such as "Family Limitation, Sexual Control, and Domestic Feminism
in Victorian America" and "The Female World of Love and Ritual:
Relations Between Women in Nineteenth-Century America." At the
same time, they asserted that "a true history of society . . . should reveal
the sources of and the purposes served by those social constructions
which have hampered women's power and autonomy" (9).

In the climate of the late 1960s and 1970s, it was clear to white feminists in particular that motherhood topped the list of "social constructions which have hampered women's power and autonomy." I use
the term "white feminists" because M. Rivka Polatnick has recently
illustrated the more empowering views of motherhood held by radical
African American feminists of that era. According to Polatnick, however, the typical attitude of radical white women's liberationists was
"that child-bearing dragged you down, that child-care responsibility
was mainly a burden, that having children meant being dependent on
a man" (401). Then, as now, the ideas of white feminists received wider
circulation than those of racial-ethnic minority feminists. For example, Jane Lazarre's memoir, *The Mother Knot*, was recently reprinted
and is still a powerful read about maternal ambivalence and the problems of being a (white) feminist and mother.

Ambivalence toward motherhood and domesticity have continued to influence historical scholarship and current attitudes among

many students. In the words of an otherwise thoughtful white male student in my History of Motherhood course, "I was surprised to see that it was thought that a woman's true happiness is found in the domestic setting. Who made this up? Would anyone like to stay home and take care of household duties? Ooh fun!"[2] To many scholars and students of women's history, motherhood in particular hampered women and rationalized their confinement and subordination in both public and private. Historically, then, it could be viewed primarily as an impediment to liberation, rather than an experience in and of itself.

In the mid-1970s, Adrienne Rich wrote movingly of what feminist inquiry had begun to reveal about motherhood as an institution, while clearly emphasizing the negative. She remarked that

> a central nerve is exposed when motherhood is analyzed as a political institution. This institution—which affects each woman's personal experience—is visible in the male dispensation of birth control and abortion; the guardianship of men over children in the courts and the educational system; the subservience, through most of history, of women and children to the patriarchal father; the economic dominance of the father over the family; the usurpation of the birth process by a male medical establishment. (196)

Rich went on to say, "The experience of motherhood by women—both mothers and daughters—is only beginning to be described by women themselves" (196).

Unfortunately, it seems the same comment could be made today. Currently the fields of the history of women's sexuality, experiences of domestic violence, attitudes toward female bodies, and the history of motherhood are all exciting and burgeoning. But it seems to me that historicizing women's private lives is still a somewhat radical and challenging project. The first generation of (predominantly white) women's historians approached the challenge of women's private histories, especially aspects of domesticity, with a mixture of insight and enthusiasm for history's hidden patterns and deep ambivalence. In the ensuing years, under the influence of established historiographic traditions and the well-known challenges of feminist teachers in general, the ambivalence sometimes turned toward neglect of the private altogether. The slowness of the field of women's history to deliver on the promise of history of private life can no doubt be attributed in part to the attitudes of a male-dominated discipline, passed along to students in what remains a male-dominated undergraduate major. For example, in my survey course on Women in the Modern United States, students began a thoughtful discussion of the "beauty culture" and some of its origins in the makeup industry. But when one male student made the comment that the beauty culture has made women increasingly self-conscious about their appearances, another male student dismissed the entire discussion with the comment, "That's not history." Although he was somewhat more forthright than most, his comment echoed the apathy of many men students (who are required to take a women's history course at my university in order to graduate with a history major). His comment also helped me to contextualize the caution with which women students often approach women's history in general. That semester my students were working with a wonderful anthology of U.S. women's history, one of the most widely used collection in college classrooms. *Women's America: Refocusing the Past*, edited by Linda K. Kerber and Sheron De Hart, does a superb job of helping me enunciate an important and accessible storyline about women in the modern United States. I would sum up that storyline as follows: Women increasingly enter the "public sphere," meaning traditionally male arenas such as politics, education, and the paid labor force. *Women's America* has some excellent articles on the history of private life, including topics ranging from lesbianism to domestic violence. But it focuses primarily on public activism; important legislation that assisted women's entry into the public, such as the Nineteenth Amendment and Title IX of the 1964 Civil Rights Act; and the *ideology* of women's place, usually defined as in the home raising children. In fact, a comparison of Cott and Pleck's major 1979 anthology and Kerber and De Hart's 2000 collection is instructive. In the 1979 volume, articles about women's "private" experiences outnumbered those that focused on such "public" activities as political activism and labor force participation. Surprisingly, twenty-one years later, the reverse is true.

To point out that the history of private life receives proportionally less attention in the current major collection than it did in 1979 is not to criticize *Women's America*. In fact, I would argue that such public markers make teaching easier. Students have concrete events as reference points. Moreover, revealing the fact that women do have an important history of influencing public life is vitally important work. Hopefully such work will help dispel the myth that any course on women's history would have to be "short." My point is that in a general women's history class, students will find more histories of private life than in an average history class but still less than we might imagine. In this context, the challenge of helping students understand that history existed "outside the public spotlight" becomes central to the teaching of the history of motherhood. As one of my students observed of the History of Motherhood class, "It was interesting to take a History course that had no major event." In the words of another, "Topics discussed were very personal and private."[3]

New Questions and New Scholarship: An Emerging Field of Historical Inquiry

Much of my own interest in the history of motherhood stemmed from my "personal and private" experiences as a mother for which I sought historical context: In what ways were these intense feelings I had for my own children part of the social construction of American motherhood in the 1990s? How did women feel and think about their children and their social identities as mothers in the past? How had they disciplined their children? How on earth had they managed to care for the seven or so children women bore on average around 1800 (Woloch 606)? Who, if anyone, helped them? These questions are beginning to be answered but there are still vast gaps in our knowledge.

In the 1970s the work of historians of the family and everyday life and the ambitious and path-breaking study of reproductive rights, *Woman's Body, Woman's Right,* by Linda Gordon, established a framework for the study of the history of motherhood.[4] But it was the growing body of scholarship of the mid-1980s and especially throughout the 1990s that made it possible to teach a course on the subject. In the past decade and a half, feminist scholars have pursued Adrienne Rich's critique of the institution of motherhood through many angles, exploring not only the ideology of motherhood and domesticity but also activism in the name of motherhood, including "maternal" reform and its impact on the state, and the regulation of motherhood by poor laws, welfare states, and physicians.[5] In 1997, the first anthology on U.S. women's history appeared, *Mothers and Motherhood: Readings in American History,* edited by Rima D. Apple and Janet Golden. The collection's range of topics included the themes above, as well as the now burgeoning scholarship on the more private experiences of mothers and potential mothers.[6] For example, using this collection my students and I examined emergent scholarship on women's attitudes toward childbirth and breastfeeding, the range of documented experiences of enslaved and immigrant mothers, expressions of maternal grief in popular magazines directed at working-class women, historically specific experiences of infertility, and the meaning of women's often private but nonetheless collectively significant decisions to limit their fertility.

And yet, even with such excellent work, it is difficult to help students truly evaluate continuity and change, the staples of historical inquiry, in the private experience of mothering. For example, from an article that skillfully used oral history analysis, we learned about mother-daughter relationships among Jewish immigrants in the early twentieth century (Weinberg). But we had little information about these relationships in other racial or ethnic groups, or for the period before the twentieth century, since most advice literature for mothers had focused on the moral education of sons.

Adding continuity to topics that lie in the domestic realm is challenging because of the discipline of history's reliance on written, often publicly available, sources. Despite the surge in the study of the history of everyday life since the 1960s, historians remain somewhat wedded to public events, both as a matter of disciplinary tradition and because of the problem of sources. The vast majority of written documents, the staple of traditional history, are public records in which the semiprivate/semipublic experience of motherhood (as well as other kinds of caretaking, friendships, sexuality, and relational patterns in general) are often lost.

Historians of mothers and motherhood continue to search for new sources that reveal facets of private life. The most exclusively "private" are journals, diaries, and letters, often the province of relatively privileged women and frequently scant on details. Marylynn Salmon examined a wonderful, previously hidden source, medicinal recipes using breast milk, for her research into seventeenth- and eighteenth-century mores. Some of the richest semipublic/semiprivate sources available, anthologized by Molly Ladd-Taylor, are the letters written by predominantly rural women to the U.S. Children's Bureau in the early part of the twentieth century (*Raising a Baby*). In those letters, women, sometimes barely literate, asked the advice of the women working at the Children's Bureau on topics ranging from breastfeeding to sex during and after pregnancy to teething babies. Women even asked these total strangers how they might go about convincing their husbands that their prenatal health was important. My students are always captivated by these letters. If only we had such gold-mines of information for earlier periods, but in those times, there was less literacy and no public storehouse of maternal wisdom such as the Children's Bureau.

I use the terms *semiprivate* and *semipublic* because in the letters to the Children's Bureau, as in most historical sources about mothers, the documents lie on the line between public and private. Mainstream American ideology, the most widely circulated public

ideas, have formulated motherhood as a "private" experience, especially since the industrial revolution placed a wedge between the
home and the workplace and marked out the former for women and
the latter for men. In reality, mothers have interacted with the public in countless ways. And interestingly, the more mothers have devi-
ated from the white, middle-class motherhood ideal that emerged in
the nineteenth century of the intensive mother, devoted to her children's education within the confines of "the home," the more they
have been regulated and intruded upon. Examples range from the
interference of market capitalism into the lives of nineteenth-century enslaved women and of paid wet nurses who often left their own
infants in orphanages (Golden), to the intrusions of the regulatory
twentieth-century state in the form of welfare, educational, and medical policies.

There was no shortage of public discussion *about* mothers, no
shortage of advice *to* mothers, and by the late nineteenth century,
there were even a growing number of "helping" agencies designed
specifically *for* mothers. So, on the line between the private and public mother, we find historical sources including popular magazines;
the records of increasingly formalized mother's clubs or maternal
associations, beginning in the nineteenth century and eventually
turning into the National Congress of Mothers; and the records of
the agencies (often run by well-meaning women) that helped or hin-
dered mothers in finding child care or obtaining public assistance
or medical care. We also see mothers' activities crossing into the public sphere in court records, religious advice, and, in the twentieth
century, in the advice of psychologists. Such material formed the
backbone of Julia Grant's major study of the education of mothers,
Raising Baby by the Book: The Education of American Mothers. Still, even
with a twentieth-century focus, Grant had available less information
than she would have liked on how ordinary mothers responded to
such advice.

In summary, we know more about what well-meaning maternal
reformers thought good mothers could do for society and what
prominent segments of society (such as ministers, doctors, and psychologists) told mothers to do, than what they actually did, felt, or
thought. As Marilyn Blackwell wrote of her investigation of one
mother's writings about child-rearing in the post-Revolutionary
"republican motherhood" era, "[t]he term 'republican mother' has
become commonplace in historiography on early nineteenth-century
women, yet scholars have rarely explained how real women adapted
this public ideal in private life" (32).

Helping Students to Confront and Expand the Confines of Historical Scholarship

Given these problems, how do we engage students in analysis of the private, as well as the public/private intersections of motherhood? How do we find, and help students find, new sources? How do we ask new questions that might lead us to new sources? And how do we use the consciousness and concerns of this generation of students (as well as their non-traditional-age fellow students) to make the history of motherhood and other semiprivate experiences meaningful?

Moreover, how do we help students contextualize experiences they encounter in their own investigations? This has become a particularly compelling question for me as I have required students to explore often neglected sources, especially oral history but also literary memoir, fiction, films, letters, and images. For example, when I required students to conduct oral history interviews in my 1999 History of Motherhood course, one student interviewed a woman who received an involuntary tubal ligation operation from her family physician and continued seeing this physician. The young woman who interviewed her was amazed, appalled, and clueless as to how to think about this woman's feelings about her fertility. While Linda Gordon had shown fascinating evidence of the movement toward "voluntary motherhood," and by extension, some control in the bedroom on the part of late nineteenth-century elite women, was it actually possible that a woman a generation and a half older than my student did not have a sense of ownership of her body (Gordon, "Voluntary Motherhood")? When, how, and to what extent did most women obtain some sense of ownership over their bodies and their reproductive capacities? Clearly a chronology of the legalization of birth control and abortion, and even data on the availability of contraceptives, cannot tell us the answer to this very private question.

Similarly, during a semester when I did not require oral histories, one student took it upon himself to regularly share course material with his mother and grandmother, and to collect stories from them. We had read nothing to help him contextualize his grandmother's account of pressuring her daughter into giving a child up for adoption in 1971: "My grandmother confessed to me that she kicks herself every day for this. My aunt has never had another child, and my grandmother knows that it was a mistake."[7] How can we get beyond the silences in the historical record that makes us mystified by such examples?

Another question raised by my students' work is how to contextualize the ambivalence many young women today feel about motherhood, perhaps in part because they do have some choice in the matter. There are interesting expressions of this ambivalence but also a remarkable openness in my students' work: I remember a student who pondered whether her pleasure in seeing other people happy contradicted feminist principles, and how having children in the future would affect her ambition and creativity. Another student said she noticed a theme in her readings on nineteenth-century motherhood: "how women felt empowered through their restrictive roles." This student, like a number of others, thought retrospectively about the past and simultaneously forward toward her own future role. Some weeks later, after reading about the history of La Leche League, she wrote,

> I see the argument about the special bond you feel by breast-feeding and the closeness and protectivensss you feel. And I want that. . . . [But] the thought of a woman breast-feeding for a YEAR astounds me! First of all, I plan on having a professional career so breast-feeding would be the way to go while on maternity leave, but then maybe formula or a breast pump would be handy. Second, the League seems to really fantasize and glorify this image of breast-feeding as a wonderful and voluntary thing, but when I think of being handy round the clock to breast-feed my baby, it doesn't sound like it would stay wonderfully gratifying for long! . . . Why shouldn't the father be allowed a similar joy in being able to have a quiet, serene moment with his baby while he feeds it?[8]

Three themes are evident in this passage: the student's attraction for a motherhood ideal based on intense mother-child bonding, her ambivalence about motherhood as culturally defined, and her embrace of a gender equity ideal in child-rearing. These three themes strike me as representative of this generation of students as they approach this topic.

This student also had thoughtful questions about the historical patterns of care-taking generally, and how the meaning of caring work has changed over time:

> Children were not only additional caretakers, but became an extension of a woman's caregiving ability and range. Young girls were raised to become caregivers. It seems almost sad that the care for the sick and dying has fallen over to professional strangers; yet, in this modern lifestyle, it would be next to impossible to have a network such as [in the past].

And she wondered about what it was like to care for babies in industrializing America in a small tenement full of boarders, children, and sometimes a husband:

> I can't believe all the work these women did for their boarders. I wonder how much these boarders appreciated their stay with these poor families. . . . It is said that tending to boarders gives little time to spend with babies—I bet there were plenty of people around to give them attention though. How would you view your children when they had to be raised in this environment? Would they be seen more as a burden than a blessing?[9]

My students also wondered about cultural diversity in shaping the feelings mothers experienced. Many were fascinated with the contradictions inherent in the conditions of enslaved mothers and were able to see echoes of those contradictions in more recent experiences of African American mothers, such as those reflected upon in Maya Angelou's *I Know Why the Caged Bird Sings*. In the musings of one student, "Black women: apprehension, socialization of fighting discrimination / White women: joy, socialization of accepting society."[10] Others pondered the dilemmas of immigrant mothers after reading articles in Apple and Golden's edited collection about Jewish immigrants and Japanese American mothers: "Why would the Japanese American families WANT to conform . . . to a lifestyle that had been unjust, unfair, and unaware that they were Americans too?"[11] Another student related the dilemmas of Jewish immigrant mothers to those of Chinese American mothers as portrayed in the film *The Joy Luck Club*.[12]

In this course, my students raise fascinating questions about the role of motherhood in private life, while also learning a great deal about the way the ideology of motherhood has been used in the public. They learn about mothers' growing entry into public workplaces and about the public regulation of poor, working-class, racial and ethnic minority mothers, especially with the expanding power of the state in the twentieth century. I attempt to facilitate this wide angle on motherhood in history by incorporating sources that illuminate private relationships. These sources are not entirely new, but the intensity of focus on relatively unconventional sources, especially the use of oral history, is one way in which the course differs from most. While in 1999 I assigned the students oral history projects, in 2001 I brought the oral history to them, in panels of mothers who talked about how they responded to advice literature, how they juggled family and work, and how they confronted discrimination, such as on the basis of sexual orientation. A final panel brought in stay-at-home fathers and posed a question about "fathers as mothers." As evidenced in the students' journals, it was the oral history panels and memoirs that often moved them most deeply, in part because this was not what was expected in a history class.

While I have by no means found satisfying answers to the questions I raise above about the sources for and contextualizing of "private" history, I do believe we owe our students a commitment to a continual investigation of both sides of the story of women's history, even if the private dimensions are harder to find. And we owe them a greater understanding of the fluidity of private and public lives. I would like to see feminist historians reinvigorate discussions of this fluid line and its meaning. I am heartened to witness the growing body of interdisciplinary work on motherhood, exemplified by the Association for Research on Mothering and its journal (*Journal of the Association for Research on Mothering*), for it is this kind of creative investigation that leads to the discovery of new historical—and current—sources.

When I was a graduate student between the late 1980s and mid-1990s, I remember thinking that the generation of women's historians whose work we were reading (essentially the work of the founding mothers) showed us primarily how women struggled to enter the public. While we read Cott and Pleck's anthology, I remember being most struck by the focus of books like Nancy Cott's *The Grounding of Modern Feminism*, Paula Giddings's *When and Where I Enter: The Impact of Black Women on Race and Sex in America*, and Cynthia Harrison's *On Account of Sex: The Politics of Women's Issues, 1945–1968*. All of these major works focused on women organizing to gain a public voice.

Our generation's contribution, I believed at the time, would be somewhat different. I remember the projects in which we were engaged: one friend's study of women's popular music in East Africa, another examining lesbian sexuality, another acquaintance exploring the history of menopause, and my own work on working-class women's identities outside of standard institutions such as labor unions. It seemed to me that we were going to research private dimensions of women's lives as yet unexplored. After all, many of us were of a generation that, thanks to these same foremothers, could take for granted access to the public and now wanted to sort out other complexities in women's lives. This, then, would be the ground we would break.

But my view was too narrow. Feminists had already been working that ground—and are still working it today. Private histories have just proven more difficult to unearth than any of us imagined. Yet in the early 1970s, when a generation of feminist historians set out to discover women in history, they were often told that the sources just were not available to study women in the past, period. The explosion of the field of women's history in the past quarter-century has clearly proved the skeptics wrong. Perhaps the questions of today's students can lead us to investigate as yet unexplored remnants from the past, from oral history to material culture to forgotten images, literature, folktales, music, and recipes. New sources and new interpretations will undoubtedly tell us more than we ever thought possible about the history of motherhood and other aspects of history still apparently "hidden."Only as we come to understand continuity and change in those hidden worlds inhabited by most women through much of history can we transform the meaning of studying the past in a way that is truly inclusive.

NOTES

1. See Jetter et al. This collection of essays on maternal activism is both historical and contemporary, and it is international in scope. See also Naples and Orleck.
2. Student journal, December 2001, used by permission, in possession of author.
3. Student survey, December 2001, used by permission, in possession of author.
4. Besides Gordon, see, for example, Degler, Demos, and Ulrich.
5. See, for example, Berry; Dill; Gordon, *Women, the State, and Welfare;* Jetter et al.; Ladd-Taylor, *Mother-Work; Mink; Naples; Orleck; Rose; and Skocpol.*
6. Major works that focus on more private dimensions of mothering and/or advice literature concerning mothers in the home include Grant; Hoffert; Ladd-Taylor, *Raising a Baby;* Ladd-Taylor and Umansky; and Leavitt.
7. Student journal, December 2001, used by permission, in possession of author. Rickie Solinger in *Wake up Little Susie* has skillfully explored issues of adoption in this period, but her study is of limited utility in illuminating the lasting impact of such a decision on mothers of daughters with unwanted pregnancies.
8. Student journal, May 1999, used by permission, in possession of author.
9. Student journal, May 1999, used by permission, in possession of author.
10. Student journal, May 1999, used by permission, in possession of author.
11. Student journal, December 2001, used by permission, in possession of author.
12. Student journal, December 2001, used by permission, in possession of author.

WORKS CITED

Angelou, Maya. *I Know Why the Caged Bird Sings.* New York: Bantam, 1983.
Apple, Rima D., and Janet Golden, eds. *Mothers and Motherhood: Readings in American History.* Columbus: Ohio State UP, 1997.

Berry, Mary Frances. *The Politics of Parenthood: Child Care, Women's Rights, and the Myth of the Good Mother.* New York: Viking, 1993.

Blackwell, Marilyn S. "The Republican Vision of Mary Tyler Palmer." *Mothers and Motherhood: Readings in American History.* Ed. Rima D. Apple and Janet Golden. Columbus: Ohio State UP, 1997. 31–51.

Cott, Nancy F. *The Grounding of Modern Feminism.* New Haven, CT: Yale UP, 1987.

Cott, Nancy F., and Elizabeth H. Pleck, eds. *A Heritage of Her Own: Toward a New History of American Women.* New York: Simon, 1979.

Degler, Carl. *At Odds: Women and the Family in America from the Revolution to the Present.* New York: Oxford UP, 1980.

Demos, John. *A Little Commonwealth: Family Life in Plymouth Colony.* New York: Oxford UP, 1970.

Dill, Bonnie Thornton. "Our Mothers' Grief: Racial Ethnic Women and the Maintenance of Families." *Journal of Family History* 13 (1988): 415–31.

Friedan, Betty. *The Feminine Mystique.* New York: Norton, 1963.

Giddings, Paula. *When and Where I Enter: The Impact of Black Women on Race and Sex in America.* New York: Bantam, 1984.

Golden, Janet. "The New Motherhood and the View of Wet Nurses, 1780–1865." *Mothers and Motherhood: Readings in American History.* Ed. Rima D. Apple and Janet Golden. Columbus: Ohio State UP, 1997. 72–89.

Gordon, Linda. "Voluntary Motherhood: The Beginnings of Feminist Birth Control Ideas in the United States." *Mothers and Motherhood: Readings in American History.* Ed. Rima D. Apple and Janet Golden. Columbus: Ohio State UP, 1997. 423–43.

————. *Woman's Body, Woman's Right: A Social History of Birth Control in America.* New York: Grossman, 1976; New York: Penguin, 1990.

————, ed. *Women, the State, and Welfare.* Madison: U of Wisconsin P, 1990.

Grant, Julia. *Raising Baby by the Book: The Education of American Mothers.* New Haven, CT: Yale UP, 1998.

Harrison, Cynthia. *On Account of Sex: The Politics of Women's Issues, 1945–1968.* Berkeley: U of California P, 1988.

Hoffert, Sylvia D. *Private Matters: American Attitudes Toward Childbearing and Infant Nurture in the Urban North, 1800–1860.* Urbana: U of Illinois P, 1989.

Jetter, Alexis, Annelise Orleck, and Diana Taylor, eds. *The Politics of Motherhood: Activist Voices from Left to Right.* Hanover, NH: UP of New England, 1997.

Kerber, Linda K., and Sherron De Hart, eds. *Women's America: Refocusing the Past.* 5th ed. New York: Oxford UP, 2000.

Ladd-Taylor, Molly. *Mother-Work: Women, Child Welfare, and the State, 1890–1930.* Urbana: U of Illinois P, 1995.

————, ed. *Raising a Baby the Government Way: Mothers' Letters to the Children's Bureau, 1915–1932.* New Brunswick, NJ: Rutgers UP, 1986.

Ladd-Taylor, Molly, and Lauri Umansky, eds. *"Bad" Mothers: The Politics of Blame in Twentiety-Century America.* New York: New York UP, 1998.

Lazarre, Jane. *The Mother Knot.* New York: McGraw, 1976.

Leavitt, Judith Walzer. *Brought to Bed: Childbearing in America, 1750–1950.* New York: Oxford UP, 1986.

Mink, Gwendolyn. *The Wages of Motherhood: Inequality in the Welfare State, 1917–1942.* Ithaca: Cornell UP, 1995.

Naples, Nancy A. *Grassroots Warriors: Activist Mothering, Community Work, and the War on Poverty.* New York: Routledge, 1998.

Orleck, Annelise. "'We Are that Mythical Thing Called the Public': Militant Housewives During the Great Depression." *Feminist Studies* 19.1 (1993): 147–72.

Polatnick, M. Rivka. "Diversity in Women's Liberation Ideology: How a Black and a White Group of the 1960s Viewed Motherhood." *Mothers and Motherhood: Readings in American History.* Ed. Rima D. Apple and Janet Golden. Columbus: Ohio State UP, 1997. 389–416.

Rich, Adrienne. "Motherhood in Bondage." *On Lies, Secrets, and Silence: Selected Prose, 1966–1978.* New York: Norton, 1979. 195–97.

Rose, Elizabeth. *A Mother's Job: The History of Day Care, 1890–1960.* New York: Oxford UP, 1999.

Salmon, Marylynn. "The Cultural Significance of Breast-Feeding and Infant Care in Early Modern England and America." *Mothers and Motherhood: Readings in American History.* Ed. Rima D. Apple and Janet Golden. Columbus: Ohio State UP, 1997. 5–30.

Skocpol, Theda. *Protecting Mothers and Soldiers: The Political Origins of Social Policy in the U.S.* Cambridge, MA: Belknap, 1992.

Solinger, Rickie. *Wake up Little Susie: Single Pregnancy and Race Before Roe v. Wade.* New York: Routledge, 1993.

Ulrich, Laurel Thatcher. *Good Wives: Image and Reality in the Lives of Women in Northern New England, 1650–1750.* New York: Knopf, 1982.

Vance, Carole. *Pleasure and Danger: Exploring Female Sexuality.* Boston: Routledge, 1984.

Weinberg, Sydney Stahl. "Jewish Mothers and Immigrant Daughters: Positive and Negative Role Models." *Mothers and Motherhood: Readings in American History.* Ed. Rima D. Apple and Janet Golden. Columbus: Ohio State UP, 1997. 334–50.

Woloch, Nancy. *Women and the American Experience.* 3rd ed. New York: McGraw, 2000.

HISTORY OF MOTHERHOOD IN THE UNITED STATES

Course Description

This course considers motherhood in American history from a variety of perspectives. We will explore women's lived experiences as mothers across lines of class, race, and relationship status. We will consider both the restrictive and empowering dimensions of motherhood in history, and we will examine the larger social, cultural, political, and economic forces that shaped the experience and ideology of motherhood.

Required Readings

Main Texts

Rima Apple and Janet Golden, eds., *Mothers and Motherhood: Readings in American History*, Columbus: Ohio State University Press, 1997 (appears as *M&M*);

Alexis Jetter, Annelise Orleck, and Diane Taylor, eds., *The Politics of Motherhood: Activist Voices from Left to Right*, Hanover, NH: University of New England, 1997 (*P of M*)

Additional Readings

Angelou, Maya, excerpt from *I Know Why the Caged Bird Sings*, in *The Norton Anthology of Literature by Women*, Sandra M. Gilbert and Susan Gubar, eds., New York: W. W. Norton, 1985, 2001–2007.

Barry, Melanie, "Is Martha Stewart Our Role Model? *www.womenconnect.com*, Dec. 12, 1998.

Brent, Linda, *Incidents in the Life of a Slave Girl*, New York: AMS Press, 1973, 78–87.

Dill, Bonnie Thornton, "Our Mothers' Grief: Racial Ethnic Women and the Maintenance of Families," *Journal of Family History* (1988): 415–431.

Ehrenreich, Barbara, *The Worst Years of Our Lives: Irreverent Notes from a Decade of Greed*, New York: Harper Perennial, 1990, 172–175, 145–149, 159–163.

Ginsburg, Faye, "Women Divided: Abortion and What It Means to Be Female," in *Women's America: Refocusing the Past*, 5th ed., L. Kerber and J. DeHart, eds., New York: Oxford University Press, 2000, 553–563.

Gordon, Linda, "Single Mothers and the Contradictions of Child-Protection Policy," from Gordon, *Heroes of Their Own Lives: The Politics and History of Family Violence*, New York: Penguin Books, 1988, 82–115.

Grant, Julia, *Raising Baby by the Book: The Education of American Mothers*, New Haven, Conn.: Yale University Press, 1998.

Hewlett, Sylvia, and West, Cornell, "Parents and National Survival," from Hewlett and West, *The War Against Parents: What We Can Do for America's Beleaguered Moms and Dads*, New York: Houghton Mifflin, 1998, 26–53.

Hochman, Andee, "Mothers and Others: New Links to the Next Generation," from Hochman, *Everyday Acts and Small Subversions: Women Reinventing Family, Community, and Home*, Portland, Ore.: The Eighth Mountain Press, 1994, 103–110.

Hoffert, Sylvia, "Attitudes Toward Infant Nurture," from Hoffert, *Private Matters: Attitudes Toward Childbearing and Infant Nurture in the Urban North, 1800–1860*, Urbana, Ill.: University of Illinois Press, 1989, 142–168.

Ladd-Taylor, Molly, "The Work of Mothering," from Ladd-Taylor, *Mother-Work: Women, Child Welfare, and the State, 1890–1930*, Urbana, Ill.: University of Illinois Press, 1995, 17–42.

Lerner, Gerda, *Black Women in White America: A Documentary History*, New York: Vintage Books, 1973, 10–13, 34–41, 46–51.

Le Seur, Meridel, "Annunciation," in *The Norton Anthology of Literature by Women*, Sandra M. Gilbert and Susan Gubar, eds., New York: W. W. Norton, 1985, 1627–1637.

May, Elaine, "Baby Boom and Birth Control: The Reproductive Consensus," from May, *Homeward Bound: American Families in the Cold War Era*, New York: Basic Books, 1988, 135–161.

Moynihan, Ruth Barnes, et al., eds., *Second to None: A Documentary History of American Women, Volume II: From 1865 to Present*, Lincoln, Neb.: University of Nebraska Press, 1993, 173–175, 285–287, 341–347, 350–353.

Orleck, Annelise, "'We Are that Mythical Thing Called the Public': Militant Housewives During the Great Depression," *Feminist Studies* (1993): 147–172.

Rowbatham, Sheila, *A Century of Women: The History of Women in Britain and in the United States in the Twentieth Century*, New York: Penguin Books, 1997, 524–532.

Scheinfeld, Amram, "Are American Moms a Menace?" *Ladies' Home Journal*, November 1945, 36.

Silko, Leslie Marmon, "Lullaby," in *The Norton Anthology of Literature by Women*, Sandra M. Gilbert and Susan Gubar, eds., New York: W. W. Norton, 1985, 2382–3290.

Swerdlow, Amy, "Ladies' Day at the Capitol: Women Strike for Peace Versus HUAC," in *Women's America: Refocusing the Past*, 5th ed., L. Kerber and J. DeHart, eds., New York: Oxford University Press, 2000, 471–486.

Wesley, Susannah, "Evangelical Childrearing," in *Early American Women: A Documentary History, 1600–1900*, Nancy Woloch, ed., Belmont, Calif.: Wadswoth Publishing, 1992, 39–43.

Course Requirements

Outline for First Analytical Essay (10 points)

The outline is due one week before the paper. Outlines should include a tentative thesis, topic titles for each major portion of the paper, and a brief overview of sources you will use to develop your argument. (e.g., I will use quotes from Margaret Sanger's The Woman Rebel to illustrate her rationale for legalizing contraceptives.) Outlines will be graded on the basis of completeness; a good grade will not necessarily translate into a good grade on your paper.

Analytical Essays (60 points and 70 points)

In these 6–8 page essays, you will analyze major historical themes in modern U.S. women's history based on *in-class readings*. The papers must address historical issues pertaining to the history of motherhood and must be based on assigned readings. (Additional readings may of course be brought in to supplement your evidence.) Suggested topics will be discussed in class. *Please note: Your essay topic may not be the same as the project you researched for your research presentation.*

Assignment Options (70 points)

Option A: Intellectual Journal (35 points) and Film Review (35 points)

Journal Guidelines: This journal provides you with the opportunity to reflect on both readings and class discussions in a way that is meaningful to you. Hopefully, you will see connections between current issues and historical patterns, and write creatively about those connections. This is an intellectual journal because it is both creative AND rigorous. I expect at least one entry per week, approximately one to two pages, that *directly engages the week's readings* as well as class discussions. In addition, I will ask you to brainstorm in your journals within and outside the classroom. Journals will be collected and evaluated at mid-semester and at the end of the term. I will evaluate journals on the basis of critical engagement with readings and class discussion, completeness of entries, and evidence of thinking that draws connections among issues.

Film Review Guidelines: Watch two popular films from different eras that depict mothers. Prepare a brief summary of each film (one paragraph each). Write a brief essay (2–3 pages) that compares and contrasts the assumptions about and/or images of mothers in these films and relates them to historical patterns discussed in class. Make a clear argument about what changes and/or does not change over time and why. Strong essays will place the film in historical context through references to material read in class.

Option B: Group Research Presentation (70 points)

You will work in groups of three or four to prepare a presentation on a topic assigned to you early in the semester. You and your group will research information pertaining to the day's topic and present it to the class in any way you think is appropriate; the presentations will be 40–45 minutes long—approximately half the class period on the assigned day. See examples of presentation formats below.

Requirements:

- Meet with me as a group at least once to talk over your presentation.
- Provide the instructor with a pre-presentation synopsis five days before your presentation day.
- Presentation needs to be accompanied by a bibliography of major works consulted and used, including Web sites, music, films, etc., as well as books.

Failure to provide a pre-presentation synopsis and/or to hand in a bibliography will result in point deductions.

Evaluation: Presentations will be evaluated by the instructor (40 points), by the rest of the class (15 points), and by your group members (15 points). The audience and I will look for organization, knowledge, creativity, clarity of presentation, and ability to engage and clearly respond to the audience.

Final Exam (90 points)

This will be a take-home exam, in essay form, that will ask you to develop a response to broad questions related to the history of motherhood and tie together themes of the course. Details will be provided toward the end of the semester.

Total Points: 300

Schedule

Week 1: Introduction / Cultural Norms: Caring for Children, Infants in the Preindustrial U.S.: Document—Wesley, "Evangelical Childrearing"; Hoffert, "Attitudes Toward Infant Nurture."

Week 2: Development of Motherhood Ideals and Mothers' Political Roles: *M&M*, "The Republican Vision of Mary Palmer Taylor," "The Cultural Significance of Breast-Feeding and Infant Care."
Motherhood and Slavery: *M&M*, "Mothering under Slavery in the Antebellum North"; Brent, *Incidents in the Life*; Selections from Lerner, *Black Women*.

Week 3: Motherhood, Service, and Female Occupations in the Preindustrial U.S.: *M&M*, "The New Motherhood and the New View of Wetnurses," "'The Living Mother of a Living Child': Midwifery and Mortality."
Nineteenth Century Motherhood Ideals Revisited: *M&M* "Mother's Love: The Construction of an Emotion," "Motherhood Denied: Women and Infertility in Historical Perspective."

Week 4: Mothers' Lives in the Transition to Industrialization: Ladd-Taylor, "The Work of Mothering."
Mothers' New Relationships to the State in the Progressive Era: *M&M*, "'When the Birds Have Flown the Nest, the Mother-Work May Still Go On': Sentimental Maternalism and the National Congress of Mothers."

Week 5: ESSAY OUTLINE DUE.
Single Motherhood: Perceptions and Reality in the Progressive Era: Gordon, "Single Mothers and the Contradictions."
Women's New Relationships to Reproduction and Reproductive Health Care: *M&M*, "Voluntary Motherhood: The Beginnings of Feminist Birth Control Ideas," "African-American Women and Abortion, 1800–1970."

Week 6: ANALYTICAL ESSAY NO. 1 DUE.
The Struggle for Birth Control: Document: Sanger, "For the Children's Sake," in Moynihan et al., eds.; Le Seur, "Annunciation."
Issues for Racial-Ethnic Minority Mothers in the Modern Era, I: Dill, "Our Mothers' Grief"; Silko, "Lullaby."

Week 7: JOURNALS DUE FOR FIRST EVALUATION.
Issues for Racial-Ethnic Minority Women in the Modern Era, II: *M&M*, "'Go

after the Women': Americanization and the Mexican Immigrant Women," "Jewish Mothers and Immigrant Daughters." *P of M*, "Mothers in Race-Hate Movements."

Working-Class Mothers: Political Mobilization and Cultural Contradictions: Orleck, "'We Are that Mythical Thing'"; *M&M*, "Regulating Industrial Homework: The Triumph of 'Sacred Motherhood.'"

Week 8: Twentieth Century Ideals of Motherlove: *M&M*, "Constructing Mothers: Scientific Motherhood," "Confessions of Loss: Maternal Grief in *True Story*, 1920–1985"; Grant, *Raising Baby*, chapter 2 (to page 54) and chapter 5. Document: Scheinfeld, "Are American Moms a Menace?"

Week 9: Mothers in the 1940s and 1950s: Cultural Norms and Cultural Contradictions: May, "Baby Boom and Birth Control"; *M&M*, "Social, Historical, Political, and Cultural Settings of Japanese-American Motherhood, 1940–1990," "'I Wanted the Whole World to See': Race, Gender, and Constructions of Motherhood in the Death of Emmett Till"; Angelou, *I Know Why the Caged Bird Sings*.

Week 10: Organized Activism in the Name of Motherhood since the 1960s: Swerdlow, "Ladies' Day at the Capitol"; *P of M*, "A Mother's Battle for Environmental Justice" *and* "Motherhood and the Politics of Sustaining Community, An Interview with Winona LaDuke"; *M&M*, "'Employable Mothers' and 'Suitable Work': A Reevaluation of Welfare and Wage Earning for Women in the Twentieth-Century United States"; *P of M*, "A Spontaneous Welfare Rights Protest by Politically Inactive Mothers: A Daughter's Reflections" *and* "'If it Wasn't for You, I'd Have Shoes for My Children': The Political Education of Las Vegas Welfare Mothers."

Week 11: Reclaiming Maternal Bodies in the Age of Science: *M&M*, "Reconstructing Motherhood: The La Leche League in Postwar America," "The Alternative Birth Movement in the United States."

Motherhood and the Second Wave of Feminism: *M&M*, "Diversity in Women's Liberation Ideology: How a Black and White Group of the 1960s Viewed Motherhood"; *P of M*, "Overview: The Uneasy Relationship Between Motherhood and Feminism" *and* "Feminism at the Maternal Divide: A Diary."

Week 12: *ANALYTICAL ESSAY NO. 2 DUE.*
Abortion and the "Maternal Divide": Ginsburg, "Women Divided." Documents: "I Would Not Be Doing the Child a Favor," "Abortion

Is Not Immoral," "Postmodern Patriarchy Loves Abortion," in Moynihan et al., eds.
Work, Motherhood, and the Culture Wars: Rowbotham, "Work" (in the 1980s). Document: Schlafley, "A Flight from the Nature of Woman," in Moynihan et al, eds.; B. Ehrenreich, "The Mommy Test" *and* "Stop Ironing the Diapers"; Barry, "Is Martha Stewart Our Role Model?" Document: Schroeder, "Family Medical Leave Act," in Moynihan et al., eds.

Week 13: FILM REVIEWS DUE.
Panel: Motherhood, Paid Work and Professional Development in Women's Lives.
New Issues: The War Against Parents? New Maternal Politics? Hewlett and West, "Parents and National Survival"; *P of M*, "Rethinking 'Maternal' Politics."*

Week 14: HAND IN JOURNALS FOR FINAL EVALUATION.
New Issues: Reconfiguring the Family: *P of M*, "Lesbian Motherhood and Other Small Acts of Resistance"; Ehrenreich, "The Lesson of Mary Beth," in Ehrenreich, *Worst Years*; Hochman, "Mothers and Others"; Fathers as "Mothers"? (not a reading, but a question addressed by panelists). *Review.*

Jodi Vandenberg-Daves is assistant professor of history at the University of Wisconsin–La Crosse. She is the author of several journal articles in her fields of interest, which include working-class women in the recent past, history of education, history of motherhood, and the history of masculinity; and she has published numerous secondary school curriculum guides for National History Day.

'I Don't Know Where This Will Take Me'

Rethinking Study/Work Relationships for Women's Studies Students

Maryanne Dever

The specific relationship between women's studies programs and students' postgraduation career and employment aspirations is an under-researched issue. While some attention has been given to graduate tracking,[1] the career aspirations of students entering women's studies classrooms have received little consideration.[2] Two factors suggest the need to examine this issue in more detail. First, current shifts in educational, fiscal, and political priorities throughout the western academy arguably make it increasingly difficult for teachers and researchers, especially those in public institutions, to continue fostering women's studies programs without clear understandings of students' career aspirations, their postgraduation experiences, and the changing environment in which important educational and employment decisions are negotiated. The new consumerist logic within higher education, together with growing rates of unemployment and underemployment among university graduates in many western societies, means that not only administrators but students (and their families) are placing a new emphasis upon the so-called "vocational relevance" and the long-term "rewards" of particular majors (Skeggs 477).[3]

A second and related factor is the rapidly changing nature of the contemporary labor market. The vision of life-long career progression within a single position, occupation, or industry is no longer a viable one and the current pace of technological change dictates that many of the jobs for which our graduates are destined have yet to be imagined. Further, in the new deregulated and "flexible" employment marketplace, direct relationships between qualifications and careers have also been radically destabilized, along with the notion of education as providing a guaranteed "gateway" to secure employment. So while the dominant messages higher education institutions continue to offer students on the pathways from study to work promote predictable outcomes and seamless, linear transitions, the reality is that we now live in a world where "even the highly qualified are entering into a radically restructured labor market in which greater flexibility and contingency are at play, and for whom a dilemma arises because the meaning of career has changed" (Wyn and Dwyer, "New Patterns" 150).

It would seem timely, therefore, to inquire into the attitudes and expectations of students participating in women's studies programs and to explore how they understand the relationship between that enrollment decision and their anticipated career paths. This article reviews findings of an extensive survey of women's studies undergraduate students in Australia, the United Kingdom, and the United States designed to learn whether—or to what extent—these students view the skills and knowledge learned through women's studies as building toward their subsequent career plans. The findings may assist women's studies practitioners in developing a more textured understanding of what brings students into our classrooms, what they find there, and the visions they have for their lives beyond graduation.

Method

The original data analyzed here was obtained through surveys conducted across 2000 and 2001. Following a pilot study in 1998, a forty-two-question survey was distributed to two designated student cohorts: (1) those enrolled in entry-level women's studies subjects and (2) advanced-level students with a women's studies concentration who were approaching graduation. These cohorts were selected to contrast the views of those in the process of weighing their options for majoring with those close to completing their major (and therefore actively considering their postgraduation directions). The survey focused on the following questions: Do career and employment issues influence students' initial enrollment in women's studies? Or do they look to their other subjects for these types of outcomes? How do women's studies students negotiate the prevailing discourses of "vocationalism"? What relationship, if any, do they see between women's studies and their future employment pathways? What do they think we're offering them? What do they imagine they'll be getting?

The project quite deliberately shifted the emphasis away from the question "what do you do with women's studies?" to "what do you *think* you can do with it?" and "what do you *want* to do with it?" I hoped the data gathered would provide avenues for problematizing prevailing understandings of the relationship between specific educational programs and labor market outcomes and for engaging in an informed dialogue about these issues, not just with our students but also with those who argue with seemingly axiomatic force that women's studies holds little or no vocational potential for its students.

Surveys were distributed to four campuses in Australia (Flinders University, Monash University, University of Sydney, Victoria University), three in the United Kingdom (University of Hull; Lancaster University; University of Surrey, Roehampton), and five in the United States (Duke University; Ohio State University; University of California, Irvine; University of Southern Maine; and Washington State University). These programs were geographically dispersed, represented both large and small, research-focused and teaching-focused institutions, and, in the United States, a mix of public and private institutions. Surveys first asked students about their reasons for enrolling in women's studies and their levels of satisfaction with the program, before moving to questions about career plans and the relationship between those plans and their enrollment in women's studies. They concluded by asking respondents basic demographic questions. Responses were received from a total of 781 women's studies students (639 entry level and 142 advanced level).[4] In order to gain a keener sense of how the career attitudes and aspirations expressed by women's studies students compared with those of other students enrolled in generalist degrees, parallel surveys were distributed to control groups of entry-level and advanced-level undergraduates across a range of arts and social science disciplines at Monash University.

Respondents represented a cross-section of students taking women's studies across the different national domains. In the U.S. cohort, for example, of the advanced-level, majoring students approximately 45.9 percent were aged twenty-one or under, and a further 52.7 percent were twenty-two to twenty-nine years old, with only 1.4 percent aged thirty or over. Nearly 72 percent had entered their current program of study straight from high school. Taking the advanced-level cohorts for Australia and the U.K. together, larger proportions of mature-age students were reported, with only 36.8 percent of respondents proceeding to their current degree studies directly from high school. Racial and ethnic minorities comprised slightly more than 50 percent of entry-level students and slightly more than 28 percent of advanced-level students in the United States (see Figure 1).

Racial and ethnic minorities comprised slightly more than 50 percent of entry-level students and slightly more than 28 percent of advanced-level students in the United States (see figure 1).

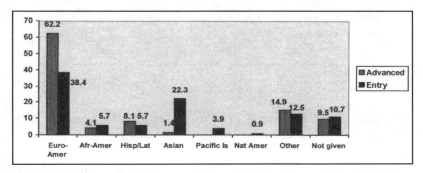

Figure 1
Ethnic/Racial Breakdown: U.S. students

By contrast, the U.K. and Australian samples were considerably less diverse as figures 2 and 3 show.

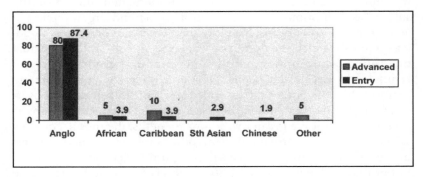

Figure 2
Ethnic/Racial Breakdown: U.K. students

Just over 90 percent of the U.S. majors were studying full time, compared to 100 percent at the same level in the U.K. but only 66.7 percent in Australia. Among the U.S. respondents, just over 66 percent at the advanced level and 61 percent at the entry level recorded at least one parent with postsecondary educational qualifications, compared to 55 percent at the advanced level and 45 percent at the entry level in the

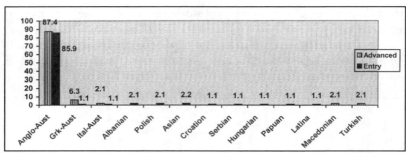

Figure 3
Ethnic/Racial Breakdown: Australia students

U.K., and 41 percent and 40 percent, respectively, in Australia. This paper is devoted to an analysis of the results of these surveys.

Career Issues in Initial Enrollment and Subsequent Choice of Major

As the original pilot study indicated, career and vocational concerns do not feature prominently in students' initial reasons for enrolling in a women's studies unit. With the exception of a single program where women's studies was a compulsory freshman unit, students overwhelmingly (between 70 and 90 percent) nominated "interest in the subject" as their primary reason for enrolling, a trend largely replicated among the control groups. No more than 5 percent of women's studies students selected the option of "career prospects" as the principal motivating factor in their enrollment, with most groups returning results in the range of 1–2 percent. However, while women's studies students both at the entry and advanced levels of study indicated overwhelmingly that they viewed their second subject concentrations as potentially providing greater vocational benefits, the most frequently selected reason for enrollment in this other subject remained "interest in the subject." This pattern of selecting units according to interest rather than with a view to career prospects is not an uncommon one among students enrolled in generalist degrees. Still, it was thrown into relief here by the finding that—depending on the campus—anywhere between 14 and 60 percent of the same students indicated that they were "somewhat anxious" or "highly anxious" about their prospects of "securing satisfactory employment and establishing a career following graduation," figures that were considerably higher than those found among the control groups and that suggest a heightened sensitivity to employment-related issues among the women's studies cohorts.[5]

Career issues emerged more visibly among the entry-level students' reasons for selecting their majors. The numbers of students enrolled in a first-year women's studies unit who planned to major in the field varied from campus to campus. Among U.S. campuses, 7–13 percent answered "yes" to majoring in women's studies, with a further 20–22 percent undecided; in Australia and the United Kingdom, 29 percent of students at the same level planned majors, with 25–41 percent undecided. Students selecting "yes" generally related their decisions to major directly to their satisfaction with the unit in which they were currently enrolled, writing of their "passion" and "fascination" for the material. In contrast, while some of those who selected "no" or "unde-cided" with respect to majoring also sought to explain their decisions in terms of their relative satisfaction levels with the program, a signif-icant minority couched their responses explicitly in terms of either see-ing "no career prospects" flowing from women's studies or of being unable to discern what "career options" the major might offer. As one such student observed, "I don't know where this will take me." While it should be noted here that the capacity of entry-level students to assess the longer term vocational benefits of any program of study may be limited, it is nevertheless worth considering the impact that the mere perception of the relative vocational potential of different sub-jects might ultimately have on students' likelihood of continuing within a program. And the data here seem to suggest that while career issues may not be crucial for those opting to major, they could be a fac-tor for those deciding not to.

Families, Friends, and the Discourse of Vocationalism

As higher education systems throughout the western world are transformed by the discourses of economic rationalism, the notion of education as a public investment in a wider social good is giving way to one of education as an investment individuals make in them-selves and their futures. This investment is frequently characterized as an intergenerational one where "education becomes a kind of bargain between parents and their children, and failure means not just personal failure, but letting the family down" (Wyn 67). It was interesting, therefore, to consider how students represented their families' attitudes to their enrollment in women's studies, particularly as 50 percent or more of respondents across all domains were under-taking their studies with significant financial support from families or partners. Students rated their families' responses to their enrollment on a scale from "supportive" to "hostile." In the U.S. cohorts, almost

95 percent of students at both entry and advanced levels selected the options of "supportive," "curious," or "neutral," with those reporting "supportive" family responses increasing from 31 percent at the entry level to over 50 percent in higher years. Similar results appeared in the Australian and U.K. cohorts where over 90 percent of students reported "supportive," "curious," or "neutral" attitudes, with 48–50 percent of both entry- and advanced-level students indicating "supportive" family responses.

Despite these approval levels, the question nevertheless elicited illuminating comments concerning perceptions of the subject's "usefulness," "credibility," and overall career "value." While some students offered responses like "[my family is] supportive of any decision I make" and "they trust me to study whatever I value as important," others obviously experienced pressure to explain and/or justify their enrollment. "They thought of it as an interesting subject but compared it to 'basket-weaving'," one student reported, while another wrote that "My father wouldn't pay for my education any longer, so I transferred to where I could pay for it myself." Responses such as these were commonplace: "Women's studies is regarded by them as not a 'proper' subject"; "psychology . . . is regarded more highly academically"; "since dropping pre-med, they're very interested in the job I'm going to get with a women's studies degree."

Friends and peers, by contrast, were reported as more likely to be "hostile" or "ridiculing" toward women's studies. Although criticisms and remarks, particularly from male peers, were generally addressed to the perceived political or lifestyle aspects of the program ("a lot of them rolled their eyes"; "are you a lesbian?"), career-value questions were raised here too, with reported comments such as "when do you plan to get a 'real' or 'normal' major?" and "[the field is] worthless in relation to income."

These attitudes were frequently linked to perceptions of the field as "esoteric," "narrow," or "separatist": a poor, perverse, or risky choice with respect to their futures. The core assumption was that women's studies was not "real" (or as "real" as other possible majors) and was unable to "provide a good background and basis for [a] career." While many students appeared keen to resist these particular constructions of women's studies, some nevertheless harbored their own related concerns. A small number of students indicated frustration that the subject which interested them passionately was generally not "highly regarded" and, in their experience, did not appear to share the same status—either inside or outside of the academy—as other arts and social science subjects. A few wished the field had a more "impressive"

title, while others worried that it did not appear regularly in the job
advertisements they saw. ("All the workplaces I have looked at don't
include women's studies as a subject area requested.")

The picture that emerges is of a body of students who exhibit a general sensitivity to career and employment issues and experience pal-
pable pressures concerning the desirability of selecting potentially
"rewarding" study pathways. Nevertheless, the majority seemed content to establish their own priorities for their degree studies. One
indicative response from students was that their enrollment in
women's studies was "something I am doing for myself." On the one
hand, these responses accord with the findings of Manuela du Bois-
Reymond on young people's growing reluctance to commit themselves
in a world where they have multiple options available to them but
remain unwilling or feel they are unable to make a "good choice" (66).
As du Bois-Reymond observes, unlike their parents' generation who
valued predictability of actions and developments within the life
course, these young people prefer to shape their personal biographies
around "contingency and openness," viewing their futures as constantly evolving "project[s]" to be managed, adapted, or perhaps abandoned in favor of alternative ones (66). On the other hand, given that
there is "a growing mismatch [in the contemporary labor market]
between actual credentials and employment outcomes" (Wyn and
Dwyer, "New Patterns" 151), what might seem to their parents and
peers to be risky or willful decisions could well turn out to be more
strategic and rewarding—both personally and professionally—than
the strictly vocational selections they are counseled to make. This
strategic element in the students' approach to their studies becomes
even more apparent in their assessments of the benefits they derived
from their women's studies enrollment.

Skills Versus Knowledge

Despite their anxieties, the majority of students appeared to hold quite
firm opinions about the broader professional and workplace applications of a women's studies major. While they clearly understood that
women's studies would not necessarily "qualify" them or alone provide
for their entry into particular professions, they nevertheless readily
named a wide range of employment destinations where they believed
"a women's studies education would be an advantage." These included
social work, welfare, criminology, policing/correction services, and
law; education, academe, and research; government, policy, and politics; media, advertising, marketing, and journalism; human resources;

and the health care professions. A common perception among those surveyed was that women's studies provided them with more of the "how" than the "what" when it came to career and workplace issues: It offered them important ways to read and negotiate systems, ideologies, and power structures. As one student so aptly phrased it, women's studies gave her the "ability to see through bullshit."

Further, in response to specific questions, these students showed that they were capable of identifying potential career benefits derived from women's studies and of devising their own understandings of what might constitute "vocational" returns from the field. The most frequently listed were general knowledge and specific knowledge of feminism and women's issues, together with a range of important applied and process skills such as critical analysis, research, and writing. However, another commonly reported quality was that of increased "confidence," "assertiveness," or "self-worth," occasionally expressed quite specifically as "confidence as a woman in the workplace." Positive attitudinal change (e.g., increased open-mindedness) also rated highly. This particular finding complements trends identified in other research which indicates that women's studies programs and students place a high emphasis on personal transformation as an outcome of both curriculum and pedagogy (Griffin; Lovejoy). But it also suggests that one benefit might be the fostering—among teachers and students—of a more detailed understanding of how the personal is also vocational. After all, "one of the key determinants of early success in a graduate career and indeed, for that matter, throughout a career, is confidence" (Perkins 29).

Beyond the specific knowledge gained from their studies, the women's studies students placed emphasis on a collection of transferable personal and professional skills (i.e., confidence, communication skills, team work, creativity, verbal reasoning) as holding key career benefits. This mode of interpreting their studies is significant given that labor market analysts suggest that in the future it will be broad sets of competencies like these rather than training for a specific job or vocation that will be the key determinant of many young people's employment pathways (Australian Council of Social Services 15). These findings intersect productively with those of Barbara Luebke and Mary Ellen Reilly in *Women's Studies Graduates: The First Generation.* The accounts offered there of the diverse career pathways of women's studies graduates clearly show that they engaged with ideas and concepts drawn from women's studies in ways that were strategically useful to them. And those graduates believed that women's studies "made them better at what they have done since graduation" (199).

Career Aspirations and the Feminist Question

Where then do these students see themselves going after graduation? When faculty offer advice on career opportunities emerging from women's studies, this routinely means listing occupations or employment settings that they believe could or should accommodate graduates with competence in feminist and gender issues. The caring, nurturing, and teaching professions, together with those involving social and rights issues, tend to predominate. This pattern is repeated on numerous program Web sites where pages outlining "what to do with women's studies" encourage students to consider futures in activism or advocacy, social work, and family therapy, where they can "make a difference in women's lives." It was interesting, therefore, to examine whether these students imagined their own futures in these terms or whether we need to revise our career advice to reflect the different life-patterns (and political subjectivities) that young people today are shaping for themselves. Students were asked to predict their preferred career destinations and rate the significance of the skills and knowledge fostered in women's studies for those fields. Entry-level students clearly found this a challenge, but advanced-level students demonstrated considerable focus here.

Asked to nominate up to three potential destinations, nearly 50 percent of the U.S. majoring cohort selected "a women's organization" from the list offered them, compared with only 7 percent of the entry-level students. Significant numbers also selected the legal field (37.5%), education (34.4%), and the arts, culture, and entertainment sectors (25%), with slightly lower numbers nominating social work or welfare (18.8%), public service or administration (18.8%), and business or commerce (14.1%). Interestingly, community organizations scored much lower (7.8%) as did the health and caring professions (6.3%). Of the U.K. and Australian majors, nearly 30 percent selected "a women's organization," with similar or greater percentages nominating education, community work, social welfare, or the arts and entertainment areas, and significant numbers also selecting "media" and "further study." Of the U.S. majors, 73.4 percent rated the skills and knowledge developed in women's studies as "central" to their career plans, with a further 23.4 percent rating them "of some importance." This compares with the Australian and U.K. majors where 48.5 percent considered them to be "central" to their career plans and a further 44 percent rated them "of some importance." The appended comments of those who selected "of some importance" suggest this answer was often chosen where students felt women's studies would "enhance" but not be "pivotal" to their careers. Others appeared to select this response when they were undecided about career direction but believed a "knowledge of gender relations is always useful to have." These figures contrast markedly with those of the entry-level students where, for example, only 10.9 percent of the U.S. cohort considered the knowledge and skills developed in women's studies as "central" to their career plans, suggesting that those who progressed to majors developed a greater sense both of their own career pathways and of the application of women's studies to those tracks.

The broad range of career destinations these students nominated, combined with the relatively high rating for the significance of the knowledge and skills developed in women's studies in relation to those careers, suggests that these students understand their futures as taking them beyond any simple one-to-one fit between the political content of these programs and the types of career and employment pathways they hope to forge—away from what we might think of as an "employment-as-activism" scenario. While program Web sites lean toward the view that women's studies majors can or will lead with their "gender edge" as they move into postgraduation employment, the data here would seem to indicate that students do not necessarily construct their career aspirations along the same lines, instead seeing the transferable personal and professional skills developed in women's studies programs as having equal or greater significance for their future careers as the political/structural insights. Although a significant number demonstrate an interest in women's organizations as one possible employment option, it would appear that these students equally see themselves potentially moving into a wide variety of mainstream employment sectors. It is probably necessary for us as practitioners to recognize that the notion that women's studies might inspire graduates to seek employment in areas which offer specific opportunities for making a material difference to women's lives is underpinned by an investment in a definition of feminism and of feminist political engagement that these students may well not share. Chilla Bulbeck, for example, contends that her women's studies students do not necessarily see questions of structural disadvantage or constraint as central to their understandings of feminism and of the status of women in society, preferring to negotiate for themselves more individualistic or "do-it-yourself" feminist agendas (141). Her findings mesh with those of Johanna Wyn and Peter Dwyer who identify a tendency among young people to downplay the relationship between structure and individual agency and to discount the influence of the structural factors that still deter-

mine many of their life choices ("New Directions" 14). In short, we
need to be careful not to endlessly re-inscribe our own particular
experiences of education, employment, feminism, and women's studies as normative where our students are concerned. We need to recognize that today's students inhabit very different subjectivities and
their life course transitions, including their transitions into the paid
labor force, have become "more extended and complex" (Looker and
Magee 74).

Lessons to Consider

I am interested in the long-term viability of women's studies and
believe that its future is intimately tied to its ability to engage actively
with the rapid transformations currently taking place both within and
beyond our institutions of higher education. This research reveals a
keen sensitivity among women's studies students to general perceptions of how the field rates, particularly with respect to its longer term
"rewards." In confronting this as practitioners we need to challenge
prevailing definitions of the "vocational," particularly those definitions
that exclude broader understandings of the relationships between
career success and the types of generic skills and attributes developed
in programs such as women's studies. This would not simply entail
pushing the boundaries of current definitions of the "vocational" by
invoking research on the changing nature of the labor market and the
increasingly uncertain relationship between higher education and specific employment outcomes. We also need to learn more about the
processes by which students themselves come to understand different
fields as "vocational," "useful," or "applied," because it is clear that our
newly enrolled students are arriving in our classrooms already
equipped with sets of convictions with which we must actively engage.

Further, as it is possible that uncertainty about the field's immediate and longer term vocational rewards figures in at least some students' decisions to continue or discontinue their concentrations in
women's studies, I suggest we need to begin discussing postgraduation
outcomes earlier rather than later in our programs. Luebke and
Reilly's research demonstrates that the women's studies major is an
enabling qualification that opens up rather than closes off opportunities for its graduates. The testimonies of graduates offered in that
project admirably demonstrate the flexible nature of a women's studies qualification and the extent to which women's studies' ethic of
empowerment readily translates from classroom or campus to the
workplace. Indeed, something very telling about the nature of a

women's studies qualification is demonstrated in the diverse range of careers those respondents were pursuing, including graduate studies, journalism, public relations and the media, the health care industry, education, social work and social policy, and so forth. These actual graduate destinations differ little from the preferred career destinations nominated by students in the current survey. This should give us the confidence to open discussions with our students and to stress the genuinely transferable nature of the knowledge, skills, and competencies acquired as part of the major, while recognizing that our graduates may seek employment pathways that diverge from the political imperatives toward activism and social change that have been so central to our programs.

We may also need to become conversant with a whole new language for talking about our field and engaging systematically with some of the more extreme stereotypes that beset women's studies. In this way we will hopefully begin to shift people's thinking away from the narrower perceptions of the field as pertaining solely to women and women's issues toward an understanding of its broader significance and application. In this way I believe we can engage with some of our students' pressing needs and anxieties, as well as open dialogues with those both inside and outside of our institutions who currently have difficulty understanding and valuing our work in terms other than these. After all, it is only by remaining cognizant of the shifting educational and social contexts in which we operate that women's studies programs can remain relevant to the present (and future) lives and aspirations of our students.

NOTES

This project is indebted to the cooperation of teaching staff and students in each participating institution. I acknowledge the assistance of Sue Jackson (formerly University of Surrey, Roehampton, now Birkbeck College, London), Luisa Deprez (University of Southern Maine), and Deborah Rosenfelt and Laura Nichols (University of Maryland), together with research assistants Xiaomei Ma, Lisa Star, and Sara Williams.

1. See Luebke and Reilly, and Stearns.
2. For a discussion of why these issues have not been widely considered see Dever et al. 102–6.
3. With the rise of economic rationalism—particularly in Australia and the United Kingdom—the discourse of "vocationalism" traditionally associated with programs of training for non–college graduates and employment pathways in non-white-collar sectors has entered higher education. I use the term "vocational" here to refer to the knowledge, skills, and attributes acquired by graduates in the course of their studies that are deemed to have future workplace utility.

4. The difference in the size of the survey pools at each level is not indicative of different response rates but of the enrollment "pyramid" that is common to women's studies programs. Despite large numbers of students "sampling" women's studies at the entry level, the numbers of students continuing on to majors is often comparatively small, approximately 10–20 percent of the original cohort. As the survey was mainly administered during class time response rates were generally high for both groups.

5. Anxiety levels were higher in Australia and the United Kingdom than in the United States, which has known strong economic growth and comparatively low levels of unemployment over the last decade.

WORKS CITED

Australian Council of Social Service (ACOSS). *The Future of Work and Young People's Pathways to Adulthood.* Sydney: ACOSS, 1996.

Bulbeck, Chilla. "Articulating Structure and Agency: How Women's Studies Students Express Their Relationships with Feminism." *Women's Studies International Forum* 24.2 (2001): 141–56.

Dever, Maryanne, Denise Cuthbert, and Anna Dacre. "Women's Studies Graduates and the Labour Market: New Thoughts and New Questions." *Atlantis: A Women's Studies Journal* 23.2 (1999): 102–10.

du Bois-Reymond, Manuela. "'I Don't Want to Commit Myself Yet': Young People's Life Concepts." *Journal of Youth Studies* 1.1 (1998): 63–79.

Griffin, Gabriele. "Uneven Developments—Women's Studies in Higher Education in the 1990s." *Surviving the Academy: Feminist Perspectives.* Ed. Danusia Malina and Sian Maslin-Prothero. London: Falmer, 1998. 136–45.

Looker, E. Dianne, and Pamela A. Magee. "Gender and Work: The Occupational Expectations of Young Women and Men in the 1990s." *Gender Issues* 18.2 (2000): 74–88.

Lovejoy, Meg. "'You Can't Go Home Again': The Impact of Women's Studies on Intellectual and Personal Development." *NWSA Journal* 10.1 (1998): 119–38.

Luebke, Barbara F., and Mary Ellen Reilly. *Women's Studies Graduates: The First Generation.* New York: Teachers College, 1995.

Perkins, Helen. "Association of Graduate Recruiters." *Arts Graduates, Their Skills and Their Employment: Perspectives for Change.* Ed. Heather Eggins. London: Falmer, 1992. 27–35.

Skeggs, Beverley. "Women's Studies in Britain in the 1990s: Entitlement Cultures and Institutional Constraints." *Women's Studies International Forum* 18.4 (1995): 475–85.

Stearns, Chris. "Is There Life after Women's Studies: An Update to the Original Inquiry." *Women's Studies im internationalen Vergleich.* Ed. H. Flessner, M. Kriszio, R. Kurth, and L. Potts. Pfaffenweiler: Centaurus-Verlagsgesellschaft, 1994. 65–69.

Wyn, Johanna. "The Postmodern Girl: Education, 'Success' and the Construction of Girls' Identities." *Researching Youth.* Ed. Julie McLeod and

Karen Malone. Hobart: Australian Clearinghouse for Youth Studies, 2000.
59–70.

Wyn, Johanna, and Peter Dwyer. "New Directions in Research on Youth in Transition." *Journal of Youth Studies* 2.1 (1999): 5–21.

————. "New Patterns of Youth Transition in Education." *International Social Science Journal* 164 (2000): 147–59.

Maryanne Dever is director of the Centre for Women's Studies and Gender Research at Monash University in Melbourne, Australia. She researches on feminist pedagogy and women's writing.

Teaching as Healing at Ground Zero

Karla Jay

11 May 2002: We New Yorkers like to think that we're at the center of it all, but when the rest of the world believes that, too—though with entirely negative connotations—we're shocked and outraged. Luckily, New Yorkers also tend to spring back from adversity with defiance and incredible pluck. How else could the 1993 bombing of the World Trade Center have sunk so completely out of sight?

Although Pace University's Civic Center campus is just two blocks from where the Twin Towers stood, we have never thought of ourselves as the epicenter of anything. We are usually a footnote to New York University or Columbia. If I ask a taxi driver to take me to Pace, I have to be careful not to wind up at Pratt in Brooklyn. Our students aren't polled to find out what's happening in education. Indeed, to read the media after 11 September, one might have thought that New York University was the closest school to ground zero; actually, Pace and the Borough of Manhattan Community College (BMCC) were both right there, BMCC to the north and Pace to the east.

Thus it was a great surprise to find ourselves at the center of something so horrific, a tragedy from which none of us will ever recover and from which, I fear, many of us will eventually die. Who knows what it is that we have been inhaling downtown since the world as we knew it changed? Not surprisingly, I have developed asthma this spring.

But my story—and Pace's—isn't just about life near a construction site where the tallest buildings in the city once stood. My experiences would be meaningless if what I learned about teaching, about my love for students, and about the larger role of women's studies in the curriculum didn't have universal applications. Looking back now, I wonder why it was ever possible for me to become distant from students on my large urban campus or to allow teaching ever to become just a job, even though everyone said I was and am very good at what I do.

And so this essay revisits that horrific day that changed my life forever but gave me an opportunity to re-evaluate what it means to be a teacher.

11 September 2001: Getting dressed for the second class of the semester, I, like millions of other Americans, was riveted by the breaking television story that a plane had hit the World Trade Center. Then another one. In addition to disbelief, shock, anger, and sadness I had another thought: "Oh no, not us, not again!" Pace University's downtown campus, where I have taught English and Women's Studies for twenty-seven years, is just two blocks from where the towers stood.

Where were my students, colleagues, and the many Pace alums who work in the Trade Center? Some of the dorms were in the hot zone; many students lived on or near West Street in the shadows of the towers. How could I contact them since phone lines and our e-mail system were knocked out?

Luckily, I had had students fill out profile sheets that provided me with their e-mail addresses and home phone numbers. I managed to reach all but one. They were terrified and shaken, most with tales of being evacuated from the dormitories or classrooms, of huddling in basements, classrooms, or windowless bathrooms while the buildings shook. Others saw the towers implode, watched smoking bodies and body parts tumble from the sky. Singing "Amazing Grace," students ran down seventeen flights of stairs only to emerge onto streets covered with inches of dust and concrete as well as a confetti of travel itineraries, stock transactions, checks, and memos. One former student, whom I had frequently chewed out for being tardy, proudly e-mailed me that she was late to class that day as well. Four less fortunate Pace students were killed in the disaster. We lost forty alums; a chunk of concrete clobbered one faculty member on his head. Many of us lost friends or relatives as well.

As the administration, led by President David A. Caputo, valiantly tried to reassure the Pace community, find out who was missing, and get the New York City campus back up and running, I wondered what was the best course to take with my students. I remembered that when I was an undergraduate I had been caught up in the April 1968 Columbia University student uprisings, which shut down the campus for at least ten pivotal days before final exams. Several faculty members invited us into their homes to continue with our work. It gave us some continuity and also some assurance that our semester wouldn't be a washout.

Taking a page from history, I suggested that my literature students try to turn off the television for a while and read Mary Shelley's *Frankenstein*. In some ways, there couldn't be a more apt literary text—a work that deals with good and evil, creation and destruction, the desire for control over human destiny, the failure to take responsibility for one's acts. If the university were closed more than a week or two, we could meet at my home. Almost every student wrote me a thank-you note. One student said that she couldn't read at all; later, she said she was reading an hour every day and was only up to page twenty-seven. I put her in touch with another student in the class who agreed to read with her.

On Wednesday, 19 September, Pace finally reopened two buildings with the help of electric generator trucks. I never wanted to see lower Manhattan again. In 1993, I had avoided a bombing when a last-minute call canceled an appointment that would have put me in the Trade Center at the moment the explosion occurred. I had also narrowly survived another tragedy that affected me even more personally. In 1977 I was trapped in a burning building. My cat, jumping up and down on my chest, had awakened me to the blaze that started in my next-door neighbor's apartment. The flames shot through the roof, two stories above the fire. Several hours later, the firefighters led the stunned tenants down a smoldering staircase as ash and water cascaded on us. I saved only my dissertation and my cat, but he died shortly afterward from heart failure.

The events of the past overlapped in an all-too Proustian way with the current catastrophe. Although at first I couldn't name my pain, I shook uncontrollably, was unable to sleep, and suffered from an upset stomach. I had been metaphorically thrown from the horse more than twice. Each time it was harder to go on with "life as normal" as politicians encouraged us to do in the teeth of such tragedy. I am no hero, only a fragile survivor. How could I hope to be the strong arm around my students when I could not conquer my own terror?

By Thursday I felt braver. I packed my new standard "teaching accessories"—two small flashlights, a bottle of water, a tiny portable radio, a new cell phone, a respirator mask, and construction goggles. I felt as if I had finally won a Fullbright Fellowship to Beirut. I headed downtown on the A line. As we passed below Fourteenth Street, I broke into a cold sweat. Then the conductor announced that the train wasn't stopping near Pace as promised but would be going nonstop from Canal Street to Brooklyn. I exited at Canal Street, the edge of the "hot zone," and showed the National Guard my Pace identification. Hopscotching around shut or closely guarded buildings, I meandered toward Pace. It had started to rain and the dense air smelled like a wet ashtray. I fitted the respirator mask over my nose and mouth, hoisted my umbrella, and trudged onward. I had wondered why footage of the rescue operation showed workers with their protective masks dangling around their necks. Now I knew why. Perspiration poured into my mouth and down my neck. Smoke smoldered from sewer covers and grates; steam rose from the wet pavement as the rain splashed on it—I was walking through Dante's

Inferno. By the time I got to school, I was so wet from exertion that my colleagues assumed that I had forgotten my umbrella.

We had electricity but we were told that the phones might be out for weeks and that the mainframe would work only sporadically. As soon as our computer system was up and running, a virus knocked it out. The day's instructions were printed on yellow forms; Wednesday's had been blue. Would Friday bring a pink slip? I attended a workshop on how to help students cope. Although we were told that a range of emotions from shock and hysteria to anger were normal, we left without a clue about what to do if a student ran screaming from the room. For the first time in my teaching career, I went home and had a stiff drink.

Despite the failure of the well-intended effort, the presence of my colleagues comforted me. I realized how much I would miss this slightly dysfunctional family were I never to see them again. I hugged my friends and former students, no longer afraid that I would be sued for sexual harassment if I touched anyone.

Talking with my colleagues in the group session and individually, I realized there could not be a single approach to recuperation. I contacted last spring's Creative Nonfiction students and reminded them of their anxiety that they had nothing to write about. Now, I pointed out, for better or worse, they had had a front row seat to history. I encouraged them to write about the event in journals or any form they wanted to use.

I realized that women's and gender studies classes were in a unique position to help students better comprehend the events around them. Students heard of the Taliban in our Gender, Race, and Class courses, which discussed the ways that women in Afghanistan were forbidden to leave their homes or work in contact with men. Despite the footage of men fleeing Afghanistan for Pakistan, our students knew that most of the refugees in the world are women and children. The service learning course that I developed last spring placed students in the surrounding communities as volunteers working with the children of battered women, the elderly, the ill, and the homeless. After the class ended, more than half of them continued to work regularly in these programs. "Women are still being battered; the poor are still hungry; the guys you helped out still have AIDS," I wrote the students. "But they will have fewer resources as many Americans donate to the Red Cross instead of to local organizations not connected to the events of September 11th. Therefore, I'm urging you to continue your community participation. The less fortunate in our community need you more than ever." Students quickly contacted me, some offering to escort Arab American women to and from classes. I had no idea how prescient my message was. By Christmas, the food pantries in the area had about one third of their normal supplies. Everybody Wins!—a reading program for elementary school children—lost 115 of its 150 local volunteers because they had lost nearby jobs or their companies had relocated out of lower Manhattan. In December, I signed up as a reader and began working every Tuesday with a nine-year-old girl.

But as classes resumed at the end of September, I found it hard to shake off the fugue state I was in and turn to the only class I was teaching—a sophomore-level honors literature course of writing about women from the Middle Ages until 1900. Typically, I would approach Shelley's *Frankenstein* from a feminist perspective and discuss issues like the gender of both Frankenstein and his Creature, the equation of female sexuality with death, and Shelley's ambiguity toward creation. But I didn't feel that I could go into the class with a Marshall plan for education nor could I reduce their education to a semester in therapy. I would steer a middle ground. I would have to see what shape the students were in and try to reach for issues that related to the events at large.

On 29 September, the first day of classes, my thirty-minute subway ride was transformed into a two-hour nightmare of rerouted subway lines and an anthrax scare. (All too soon these "police activities"—not reported in the newspapers to make the tourists feel safe—became regular events.) I emerged shaking again onto smoky streets that now had the sharp, rancid odor of death.

I gathered my books from my office and started my class. Much to my joy and amazement, almost all of the students were there. They had been debriefed to the bone, and they wanted to get back to work. The largest constituency, students from the former Soviet Union, were used to adversity. I started by giving them a feminist perspective on the events and on the language used to describe the terrorists. No one spoke of "white terrorists" after Timothy McVeigh bombed a building in Oklahoma, nor did they suggest profiling Caucasians with crewcuts in red pickup trucks. I also drew an analogy to the AIDS epidemic: In the mid-1980s, dentists and airlines wanted to refuse service to gay men, Haitians, and others suspected of having HIV. But making sure that everyone was safe took precedent over taking away the civil liberties of some. Finally, I was concerned by the gendered portrayal of the events in the media. Watching the fundraising telethon, which billed itself as a "Tribute to Heroes," I noticed that all the individualized stories were about male rescuers. While the New York Fire Department is overwhelmingly white and male, many female doctors, emergency technicians, police officers, and nurses were first responders. I know two female police officers who dug tirelessly in the rubble, one of them looking for her brother. As late as May 2002, one of the officers was still sifting rubble on a conveyor belt in Staten Island in the hopes of finding additional human remains and personal belongings. Some body parts that she picked up—including a decapitated head—made Dr. Frankenstein seem even more an amateur than he was.

Frankenstein ties in neatly to discussions about judging people by their appearances. When Victor's brother William is murdered, Victor concludes that the Creature must be the guilty party. "No sooner did that idea cross my imagination than I became convinced of its truth" (60). People long for clear-cut visions of guilt and innocence. Some of my students disliked my complicated analysis—they longed for an obvious villain.

The very discussion of the text drew us back into the world of literature that was meant to be our common bond in the first place. But soon our roles shifted. I became the strong one—though I hardly felt that way—while many of my students faltered. Miraculously, all of my students eventually returned to class. But as the days passed, some of them sat dazed and speechless, others coughed or slept openly, and two stopped coming altogether. Some continued having problems concentrating so we spent more time than usual reading poems and parts of books out loud.

Large-scale disasters provoke us to fight or flee. Women, in particular, have been conditioned to flee rather than fight, and I had only one male student this semester. From time to time, we would interrupt the coursework for a "check-up" on how everyone was doing. I would remind them of the availability of our crisis counselors, but I also understood that some of the many cultures represented in the class view therapy, however well-intended, with suspicion. When a student was absent for more than one class, I would tell the others the general reason for the absence if I knew it. Ordinarily, I wouldn't comment at all on such matters but I noticed a quiet panic when a classmate was inexplicably missing. The greatest pain was felt by the dorm students. They rightly pointed out that even if they turned off the television, all they had to do was look out their dorm windows at the ruins of the Trade Center to have it all come back to them. They felt that they could not flee reminders of the catastrophic event—from the foul winds that blew our way to the armed police officers and barricades almost everywhere.

The words *college* and *campus* are almost synonymous, but for urban schools like Pace, our "quad" is a small square of light and trees sandwiched between two towers of classrooms and dorms. New York City is usually a glorious canvas to experiment on, but after 11 September, life near Wall Street was like being pecked to death by pigeons. The Starbucks served only uniformed officers and then closed altogether until mid-December. The Egyptian street vendors from whose carts I bought breakfast every day were chased from the area for about six weeks. One day I counted fifteen stores in a row that had closed on nearby Nassau Street. How could a university survive when McDonalds had gone under? Across the street from Pace, Mayor Rudolph Guiliani shut City Hall Park, cutting us off from the few stores that remained on the western side of the park. Then when the streets started to reopen, we found ourselves surrounded by gaping tourists who wanted to hug us and hear our stories.

I tried to remind my students of New York's riches by taking them to the theater to see *Hedda Gabler*, which we read in class. I also rounded up some tickets to *Urinetown*, a play that had no connection to our course or to feminism. It was, however, very funny, and the plot dealt with surviving through a difficult and unusual ordeal. I tried not to mind when a few overslept and didn't show up even though other students would have enjoyed the thirty-dollar tickets we gave them for free.

Despite my efforts, I was unable to console them about the alienation that they experienced when they tried to socialize beyond the college. When they went to local bars, the guys they met didn't understand why they were still concerned with "yesterday's news," something no longer interesting or important. Why couldn't they simply "lighten up and have a good time"? I was not surprised that a number of my students asked me to assist them in their attempts to leave Pace. While I applaud students' desire to study abroad and wish I had had such an opportunity when I was their age, I found myself filling out recommendation forms in record numbers. Other students approached me with essays that they had written in preparation to transfer to other institutions. Some of them had quixotic Ivy League aspirations: One did get into Cornell while another will start at Smith in the fall. Others had more prosaic goals and moved on to local colleges. It pained me to think I was losing our best students, especially those who knew me well enough to ask for recommendations in the first place. Nevertheless, their crisis was not about me and, though I know some of my colleagues would disagree with me, I believe that my mission as a professor is to help students realize their dreams. In the end I was pleased that other colleges agreed with me that Pace has some incredibly smart students. In the fall, sitting there with a stack of blank recommendation forms, I felt that they were abandoning me. "What about me?" I thought one day. "I want to go to Spain and France, too!" By December, more than three hundred students had left Pace.

I continued to worry more about how these students would perform if they studied elsewhere. Although my colleagues at other institutions complained that their students were more forgetful than usual about appointments and assignments, they didn't see the same level of malaise. Since I had been through the same experience, I could not only sympathize but empathize. I wouldn't claim that I was functioning at my highest level either. Even now, some days the only thing my brain holds is water: I feel as if I've dashed through my midlife changes to embrace senior moments.

It's hard in the midst of such common despair to keep the curriculum running. I revised the course outline so that we all knew where we were at. Had I known that the students would be surrounded by tragedy, I don't think I would have chosen three texts—*Hedda Gabler*, *The Awakening*, and *Anna Karenina*—in which the protagonist kills herself. I thought of renaming the course Women on the Edge, though it would be unclear whether I was referring to the texts or the students. Although the students noticed that our protagonists, like the women in Afghanistan, were enclosed within their homes, ironically, some students expressed a bit of nostalgia for the limited but seemingly safe worlds of Edna Pontellier and Hedda Gabler. I knew what they meant: In my spare time I was soothed by old-fashioned mysteries in which people were murdered one at a time. We made our way through the texts as usual, though I spent more time recapping the plot and repeating some of the salient points of previous days' work. We somehow finished before Christmas, even though my students had to rewrite everything, including in-class essays, which were far below typical honors level.

In a sense, current events became our most salient text. Although nothing excuses the barbarism of the terrorists who destroyed the World Trade Center and part of the Pentagon, at least those of us who are older can put the events into the context of Vietnam and other wars. For today's adolescents who have no memory of any war, such events are totally without a frame of reference. Understanding how terrorism operates in the world can only help young adults get through recent horrors.

I reminded the students that as women, they probably all understand terror. We are like Robin Morgan's Everywoman, looking over our shoulders as we hurry along:

> Suddenly there are footsteps behind her. Heavy, rapid. A man's footsteps. She knows this immediately, just as she knows that she must

not look around. . . . She is afraid. He could be a rapist. He could be
a soldier, a harasser, a robber, a killer. He could be none of these. He
could be a man in a hurry. He could be a man merely walking at his
normal pace. But she fears him. She fears him because he is a man.
She has reason to fear. . . .
   This moment she shares with every human being who is female.
This is the democratization of fear. (23–24)

Morgan is right in that fear is a great equalizer. Interestingly enough,
Leon Botstein, the president of Bard College, expressed a similar
notion of terrorism as a democratizing force in an address to faculty
at Pace during our convocation on 7 October. If terrorism is the great
equalizer, then the equation has it that the terrorist attacks on America
have been thwarted in a sense because out of the rubble we emerged
united as we have never been before. In a sense this belief is true,
except that we probably felt that same cohesion after Pearl Harbor was
attacked. But a close analysis illustrates that not all people were treated
equally in the aftermath of the attacks. The firemen were singled out
as especially heroic for going into the World Trade Center as it
burned. Yet, commentators refrained from noting that among the photographs of the over three hundred lost, there were no women and
only four people of color. Were the fire department more diverse, I
have no doubt that others would have been equally heroic, but not
everyone is given an equal opportunity, even for heroism.[1]
   When attention was turned to taking care of the surviving spouses
and children, members of Congress and local charities rushed to
exclude partners and children of lesbian and gay parents, a move later
reversed by the New York State legislature. If there was a call to
exclude the children of heterosexual domestic partners, I haven't
heard it, but perhaps they, too, will have limited benefits because of
their lifestyle choice. But at the end of 2001, complicated charts
released by the government indicate that the value of every life is not
the same. Single people are worth less than married people; those
without children are worth less than "traditional" families. Those who
earned more in life will receive more in death, too (Henriques).
Although juries generally weigh a person's value when assessing
claims in civil suits, the disparity in the proposed settlements under-
cuts politicians rhetoric about "unity."[2] The families of illegal aliens—
often working under false names and social security numbers—will
likely receive nothing. The rush to cut off homosexual families is chill-
ing and appalling because it signals a willingness to ostracize some
victims. In fact, the first person to die in the disaster, Father Mychal

Judge, was well-known within the gay male community (and apparently within parts of the Catholic church) for having gay sensibilities. Yet he was not named a "gay priest" until he was posthumously "outed" first in the *Advocate* and then in the *New Yorker.* Mark Bingham, one of the men who tackled the hijackers on United Airlines Flight 93, was openly gay, but the widows of two other heroes were paraded on television instead.

The second group that feminist analysis speaks to is the postal workers. It is shameful that the Hart Building, which houses congressional offices, was shut down at the first hint of anthrax while postal workers were told to continue their work at many facilities. While some congressional office buildings were evacuated for months as the government attempted to remove all traces of anthrax, postal employees continued to work at Morgan Station in New York City, even after successive tests found anthrax on sorting machinery. It should be shocking that one Washington-area postal worker was sent home from a hospital emergency room with Tylenol when he appeared with symptoms of anthrax. But the most distressing fact of all is that the American public hasn't rallied to support the postal workers, hasn't created vast funds to take care of their spouses and children, and hasn't hailed them as heroes for going back into post offices knowing full well that anthrax was found within. And when stories emerged on the news that involve the postal workers, we finally saw many people of color who have sought blue-collar civil service jobs because of so-called equal treatment and benefits. And now we have told them—as if they didn't know already—how little they are worth.

Apparently, anthrax is horrible when it shows up in the offices of television anchors and members of Congress but is barely newsworthy when family planning clinics receive hundreds of anthrax threats every year. Since 11 September, abortion clinics have had hundreds of anthrax scares. According to the *New York Times,* in October "about 200 clinics and abortion rights groups were sent Federal Express packages containing a powdery substance and, in some cases, a letter signed by the Army of [G]od indicating that the substance was anthrax." The article went on to note, "Because there have been so many anthrax threats against abortion clinics in the last three years, abortion rights groups have developed routines for notifying all clinics of the threats that have been received and most are careful to screen their mail" (Lewin). Yet not only did the government at first decline to meet with these groups to learn from them about safely handling mail, but it also failed to pursue the many forms of terrorism that abortion clinics face daily, including harassment of workers and patients and the murder of several providers. No national guard troops have been sent to protect the clinics though their procedures are legal. The Federal Bureau of Investigation hasn't put these anthrax terrorists on their priority list. According to their own logic, whether or not it supports the right to abortion, the government should certainly oppose and hunt down the terrorists who threaten democratic choice. If this is a war in which you are either for terrorism or against it, which side is our government on when it comes to the lives of women and their supporters? Like Afghanistan, our government is harboring and supporting terrorists because it is doing nothing to drive them and their supporters out.

We also discussed the role of women in much of the Islamic world. That a hundred million women have had cliterodectomies and/or infibulation in Africa, the Middle East, Indonesia, and even the United States, and that more women die from this every month than all who perished in the World Trade Center, is of little interest to our government. The government funded the Taliban in May 2001 with over forty million dollars. They imprisoned women in their homes, prohibited education for women, and allowed women to die without proper medical treatment. But so long as the Taliban claimed, however falsely, that they were destroying poppy fields, we were willing to support them, just as we support the oil-rich Saudis despite their corruption and persecution of women and religious minorities. We demand that the world be for us or against us, yet when the Indian Parliament was bombed in December 2001, the U.S. government did everything in its power to prevent India from pursuing the perpetrators. Terrorism is a daily occurrence in Ireland, Israel, and Palestine; people have their arms hacked off in Sierre Leone and other war-torn African nations. Which side are we on?

Like the bodies two blocks from our campus, the world seems to be decomposing right in front of my students' eyes. At nineteen, it's hard for them to think anyone is suffering more than they are. At the same time they are angry with themselves for not being able to get on with their lives, and they are furious with those professors who insensitively try to go on with their lives by cramming fourteen weeks' work into ten. Some of them would like to blow up an Afghan city or country to avenge their own suffering; feminism makes life more complicated, not simpler.

By December, I felt one-dimensional, crushed under the weight of my students' grief and the drumbeat of committee meetings. I realized that in taking care of my students I had neglected myself. Generally cheerful and unflappable, I found it difficult to cope with petty annoyances. Finally, I had to let myself feel my own pain, my own fears, my own losses. And I realized that since my students never inquired how I was doing, I was going to have to tell them myself.

Perhaps letting the students know how hard a time I was having was the best thing I could share with them. My pretense of bravery made them feel weaker. My global concerns sounded as if I didn't care about their suffering or my own. Admitting that this struggle to survive was *our* problem allowed us to go forward together, to understand that sometimes reality dwarfs art in its poignant tragedy. And so, on the last day of class, most of us had lunch together at a pizzeria at the South Street Seaport. This once bustling tourist hub of trendy shops was quiet now except for the squawking seagulls. We teased each other and drank from each other's glasses like family members. At the end of the meal, the students decided that the dorm students, who had to eat cafeteria food, deserved the leftovers. I saw that we had all bonded in a way that we never could before, that we never would again. I felt sorry for those who would leave a place like Pace.

These students had lost their adolescence and whatever remained of their innocence, but they had finished the semester. The very eagerness of my students to learn, their determination not to allow terrorism to deprive them of an education, their courage in attending class although some of them looked stressed and exhausted, reminded me of how much I love teaching these gritty, first-generation college students. I felt whole again, and I learned a valuable lesson: I thought I would have to hold them together; instead, they healed my soul.

NOTES

A much shorter version of this essay was originally published in the 12 October 2001 issue of the *Chronicle of Higher Education*, B20.

1. According to the *New York Times,* there are only six black female firefighters. They account for .06 percent of the force (Newman).
2. An explanation of each person's "worth" can be found at *www.usdoj.gov/victimcompensation/loss-calc.html.*

WORKS CITED

Henriques, Diana B. "In Death's Shadow, Valuing Each Life." *New York Times* 30 December 2001, sec. 4: 10.

Lewin, Tamar. "Anthrax Scare Hits Groups Backing Right to Abortion." *New York Times* 9 November 2001: A24.

Morgan, Robin. *The Demon Lover: The Roots of Terrorism.* New York: Washington Square, 2001.

Newman, Andy. "First for Fire Department: A Black Female Lieutenant." *New York Times* 30 January 2002: B2.

Shelley, Mary. *Frankenstein.* New York: Bantam, 1983.

Karla Jay *is Distinguished Professor of English at Pace University. An award-winning author and editor of ten books, she is currently completing a collection of satirical and serious essays entitled* Migrant Laborers in the Fields of Academe, *to be published by University of Wisconsin Press.*

Women and Work

Class Within the Classroom

Barbara Omolade

The increased numbers of working women in the college classroom provide scholars and instructors with unique opportunities to develop new scholarship and theories about the working class and its connection to gender and race and ethnicity. Previous theories that focused on the social relationships among industrial workers and their employers at the site of production led to a whitened and masculinized analysis of class. However, sociologist Rose Brewer asserts, "The conceptual anchor of recent Black feminist theorizing is the understanding that race, class and gender are simultaneous forces" (16). Economists Teresa Amott and Julie Matthaei agree, adding that these forces are "interconnected, interdetermining historical processes, rather than separate systems" (13). These systems are not experienced separately nor can they be adequately examined as discrete phenomena. Examining any one system, however, can become a lens for understanding the interconnections among all three and especially their collective impact on social actors. For example, the sexism that marginalized European American women workers operated in tandem with racist treatment of workers who were men and women of color. The experiences of both groups in the labor market fostered a sexual and racial division of labor that, in turn, reinforced distorted theories about the relationship of all women to the working class.

One such distorted theory was able to dismiss women's class by assuming that the husband's position in the labor market was the sole determinant of his wife's class position. Yet since the onset of the industrial revolution, most working-class women whether married or single have worked for wages. Wives of male workers usually earned money to supplement their husband's earnings.

Nonetheless, the places and forms of women's wage earning differed from that of men. When unable to work in factories because of child care responsibilities, dangerous conditions, or male bias, women earned money by working as servants or washerwomen. They worked out of their homes and cared for boarders in order to earn money.

They augmented their low wages by engaging in mutual support efforts with women kin and friends. Indeed, wage earning could be considered a reliable indicator of a woman's working-class position, for only the wealthiest families could afford an unemployed wife or daughter.

In addition, unlike men, the home has been as much a work site for women workers as the office or factory. Women must balance and juggle the demands of the public world of wage earning with unpaid work in the private sphere of the household and family. Therefore, rather than experiencing a single and dominant social relationship to class based on wage earning at industrial sites, working-class women have simultaneously occupied multiple sites of production involving paid and unpaid labor. These multiple sites are connected to complex social relations sustained by women's emotional as well as physical and mental labor.

This article examines the significance of this multiplicity and complexity for the development of a class analysis. It argues that beginning with the experiences and voices of social subjects such as working women, rather than with ideology or a structural analysis, reveals the many dimensions of class. Most importantly, studying the "authentic chronicles" created by working-class women college students of diverse racial and ethnic backgrounds about their work lives, enables theorists to better understand the connections among race, class, and gender.

The analysis of class described in this article was based on teaching Women and Work, a course developed to bridge the pragmatic issues of contemporary urban working women students with the pedagogy and scholarship of women's studies. The course was taught four times at the City College of New York Center for Worker Education, an evening college program especially designed for working adults.[1] Nearly all the students in the course, as in the program, are African American and Latina; many are immigrants or the children of immigrants from the Caribbean.

Most of the African American women workers in the course were in their late thirties and forties and had worked for at least a decade as administrators in public sector government agencies and hospitals. Younger mainly Latina workers who were in their twenties and early thirties had begun working during and after high school in supermarkets, fast food chains, and department stores. They were now mostly employed as secretaries and clerks in banks, companies, and corporations. Immigrant women from the English-speaking Caribbean usually had begun working in the United States as nannies or factory workers, and then followed the patterns of African American women.

Some women from all groups, including immigrants from the Spanish-speaking Caribbean, worked in child care centers or as paraprofessionals in the public schools. Also, a few women from all groups were employed in nontraditional jobs such as court clerk, prison guard, or restaurant maître d'.

The employment patterns of students in the Women and Work course reflect those described by sociologist Rosalie Cohen about women workers across the country:

> According to 1989 and 1990 U.S. Bureau of Labor Statistics, the range of jobs held by women has been relatively narrow, falling predominantly into clerical and service fields. For instance, 80 percent of clerical workers are women, and from 95 to 99 percent of service workers are women, totally dominating such occupations as secretary, typist, receptionist, dental hygienist or assistant, pre-school teacher and teacher's aide, and child-care worker and practical nurse. (144)

Rose Brewer notes also that "Black women's clerical work reflects the partial collapsing of a racial/gender division of labor. Both Black and white women do the same work in most places in the USA" (21). However, the experiences of students in the Women and Work course revealed that race and ethnicity continue to impact the kinds of service jobs women hold.

The persistent division of labor by gender and race and ethnicity has not deterred the long-term, direct, and primary relationship of these women workers to the labor market. Like most contemporary women, wage work is central to their lives and identities as "grown women" who are economically competent to take care of themselves, irrespective of familial connections to men and male workers. In addition, while those in the past tended to be poorly educated and informed, most contemporary working-class women have a wide range of skills and knowledge about business and the economy. Today's working-class women are literate public citizens with economic and political authority of their own.

Moreover, these women know firsthand what sociologists Barbara Reskin and Irene Padavic have concluded about the importance of education: "The amount of schooling people have is important. It affects whether one is in the labor force, the jobs they hold, their authority, and their earnings" (40). Many working-class women believe that their positions in the labor market will improve only when they have college degrees. So they make great personal, familial, and financial sacrifices to attend school. In their view, a college degree is not an option but the most reliable means for upward mobility, increased wages, and job security.

Once enrolled in college, the women are highly motivated and practical students who focus on courses and majors most directly associated with occupations and jobs. However, their academic progress is often slow and difficult, in part because of work and family obligations. Few students realize that their educational progress is also affected by the clash between their working-class backgrounds and the academy's "culture of power." However, most students view themselves—incorrectly—as members of the middle class because they are neither poor nor rich.

Educator Lisa Delpit uses the term "culture of power" to discuss the influence and impact of "the culture of those who have power" on working-class students (24). She points out that "The upper and middle classes send their children to school with all the accoutrements of the culture of power; children from other kinds of families operate within perfectly wonderful and viable cultures but not cultures that carry codes or rules of power" (25). In many college programs, working-class women, not their children, confront the class-bound "culture of power" that, for example, privileges intellectualism and professionalism over other forms of social activity, such as wage work. The emphasis on standard English expression, critical analysis of written texts, and a rigid organization of learning reflects the rules of the culture of the intellectually powerful in the same ways that rules governing the behavior and performance on the job reflect the economic elite. Most significantly, schooling is "intimately related to power because of its role in determining the preparation and kind of job people can hold" (Delpit 25). Working-class women students learn of this connection between power and schooling every day at work. However, the academy does not make it easy to transfer or translate the worker's workplace knowledge about power arrangements into its academic requirements and demands.

College instructors reflect the culture of power in their classrooms by organizing information and knowledge, framing discussion and discourse through assignments and texts, and then evaluating and measuring the intelligence and ability of their students. Students are expected to master "the codes or rules" for participating in the culture of power "especially linguistic forms, communicative strategies and presentation of self" (Delpit 25).

Women's studies programs in colleges and universities were initiated in order to examine and produce scholarship about women's lives. The scholarship emerging from these programs has produced a gendered critique of the "culture of power" in the academy, the political economy, and the family. The relationship between class and gender or a gendered understanding of class, however, has been less developed. The experiences of contemporary working-class women, especially college students, are for example virtually absent from women's studies textbooks and course syllabi.

Although many women's studies faculty, particularly in public colleges, have working-class backgrounds and empathize with working-class students, they often uncritically reproduce the rules and assumptions of the culture of power. As members of the intelligentsia and the professorate, these faculty members like "those with power [who] are frequently least aware of—or least willing to acknowledge—its existence" (Delpit 24).

Still, the very authority of college instructors enables them to either reinforce the cultural and social supremacy of the powerful or give voice to those students without class or cultural power. If the instructor is aware and forthright in interrogating and critiquing the class dimensions of the academy and the class divisions between herself and the students, then the classroom can become an effective site for learning and teaching about class. Again Delpit provides useful insights to educators: "We must keep the perspective that people are experts on their own lives. There are certainly aspects of the outside world of which they may not be aware, but they can be the only authentic chroniclers of their own experience" (47).

Several strategies in the Women and Work course were used to enable women students to become "authentic chroniclers of their own experiences" about work. First, students were required to read and write research papers about the history of working women and contemporary employment and workplace issues. This requirement provided students with links between their personal experiences in the labor force and the history and structure of work and the economy. Second, students were assigned to prepare extended resumes with information about all the jobs that they had ever held. This project allowed both the instructor and the students to discover and reflect on the individual and collective employment patterns of the lives of working women students in the class. Third, in another project students were asked to keep journals describing daily tensions and stress on the job and at home.

Developing and discussing the journals revealed the frustrations, anxieties, and anger of women workers about overwork. The journals described the tremendous emotional labor required by working-class women to perform tasks and roles at their jobs and at home. One student writes, "It seems like I always end up doing the dirty work around work and home. . . . Sometimes I think I function best under stress, although that is not healthy. My biggest problem is that I try to help everyone and always end up getting too involved."

The concept of "emotional labor" was analyzed by sociologist Arlie Hochschild in her 1983 classic *The Managed Heart*. In their analysis of the impact of the concept, sociologists Ronnie Steinberg and Deborah Figart indicate that "Emotional labor emphasizes the relational rather than task-based aspect of work found primarily but not exclusively in the service economy. It is labor-intensive work; it is skilled, effort-intensive, and productive labor. It creates value, affects productivity, and generates profit" (9).

They describe the "characteristics of jobs with emotional labor" as first "requiring contact with other people external to or within the organization, usually involving face-to-face or voice-to-voice interaction, especially in service work" (13). Workers who perform emotional labor are expected to manage their own emotions in order to impact the emotions of others regardless of whether their feelings are genuine.

These characteristics seemed to fit the jobs of nearly all the students in the Women and Work course. As a child care worker indicated, even before learning about the concept, emotional labor was an integral part of her job: "I don't think most people realize how emotionally draining my job is. Those children can really suck it out of me. In addition, I constantly have to submerge my real feelings of frustration or anger, and present a very non-aggressive and simple explanation or admonishment." Another worker described masking her feelings and knowledge in order to assuage her bosses' feelings: "Work has gotten to be too exasperating. I have not told my boss, I am graduating this semester. My reasons are clearer each passing day. She is too competitive. My boss expects me to do everything and look like I need help. That is, it is fine I have knowledge of what I do, but I should not act as if I know more than my boss."

For many other women emotional labor was needed to manage racial or ethnic cultural code switching on the job. These workers constantly had to monitor their language, demeanor, and social interactions in order to make the bosses and clients feel comfortable and assured that they are competent workers. In addition, displays of stereotypical female behaviors, especially in anticipating and meeting the personal needs of superiors, were job requirements. Rather than being evaluated for their ability to do the job, women workers were also evaluated for "acting right."

While emotional labor at work involves attempting to please others irrespective of their real feelings, caring for family and kin at home was no act. In fact, many were frustrated by the demands of work and school that encroached on their desire to better mother their children, help their parents and siblings, and enjoy their partners. However, family members also demanded allegiance, attention, and time from these women workers.

Kin work involves much more than emotional labor but requires other forms of work. Sociologist Micaela Di Leonardo describes kin work as "The conception, maintenance, and ritual celebration of cross household kin ties, including visits, letters, telephone calls, presents and cards to kin; the organization of holiday gatherings; the creation and maintenance of quasi kin relations; the decision to neglect or intensify particularities; the mental work of reflection about all these activities" (442–43).

Working-class women are essential to maintaining kin in still other ways. Their steady employment assures financial help for unemployed and less secure members of their families. They are expected to help parents and kin who are not fluent in English or familiar with the educational, health care, and other systems in the United States. Ethnic kin work by immigrant women or their children often straddles two countries, the United States and the homeland, in order to support families.

While women work and attend school in multi-ethnic and racially diverse settings, most in New York City live among their own groups in racial or ethnic enclaves and neighborhoods. Their labor also contributes to maintaining ethnic group cohesion and survival by preserving linguistic, culinary, musical, religious, and other cultural traditions. In addition, women of color experience and witness racial violence, discrimination, and inequities and consequently must also frequently undertake activities such as political meetings, protests, and mobilizations to advocate and protect their family members and their community. Since so much kin work and family and community emotional labor occurs in racial or ethnic enclaves and neighborhoods, it is not surprising that racial and ethnic identity is often more salient for working-class women students than gender or class.

Religious beliefs and activities further intensify the racial and ethnic identities of working-class women. Most of the students in the Women and Work class were Christians who were active members in the churches in their neighborhoods. Although quite devout and learned—many had enrolled in Bible study courses or attended religious-focused seminars—students rarely shared theological or religious views in class. Still, their journal entries frequently described a reliance on prayers and regular habits of Bible reading. The journals also offered a way for students to discuss more explicitly the role of faith in their interpretations of society and in their personal and family lives.

In conclusion, teaching and learning from the "authentic chronicles of working class women" suggests an expansive notion of class. Class distinctions are necessarily related to the structural issues of economic organization and the unequal distribution of wealth and status in the society that is especially expressed in schooling and employment. However, these relations are not sufficient for addressing the standpoint of the working class or accounting for the experiences of women workers.

First of all, we learn from the experiences of working women students that the way that class operates is tied to the way race and gender is organized in the society. These inextricable links imply that class division does not have greater significance for explaining inequity and stratification in society than gender or race and ethnicity. It also implies that class division and struggle among owners and individual workers is only one manifestation of class conflict, for racial conflict between workers and gender competition between male and female workers are essential elements of class struggles as well.

Second, the theoretical process for understanding gender and race and ethnicity privileged the voices and experiences of people of color and women rather than structural analyses. Their standpoint revealed that racial oppression was only one feature of racial and ethnic group life and racial dynamics in the society and that sexism and patriarchy were not the sole determinants of women's lives and worldviews. The experiences of working women students similarly reveal that class conflict and exploitation are only one aspect of the standpoints and worldviews of the working class.

Lastly, class is a complex social dynamic that begins with the perspective of workers engaged in many forms of labor (physical, mental, emotional) that occur in multiple sites (home, job, ethnic enclave, and homeland) involving social relations with various groups at the job (employer, coworker, and client) and at home with family members, kin groups, and ethnic or racial groups. Emotional labor is the lynchpin of women's work because it is essential for mediating and attending to these disparate forms of work and social relations. And it is an unstated but necessary requirement of service sector jobs where most women are employed. Many of these gender-specific issues of class are ignored at the wage-earning work site; in contradictory fashion women workers continue to be penalized by the gendered division of labor.

As college instructors accurately critique their relationship to the culture of power and elitism within the academy, the voice and stand-point of working women college students can be developed. Then rather than merely theorize *about* them, scholars could produce knowledge and theories about class with workers. When the working-class women's voice is privileged then both theorists and workers can understand and confront the structures of economic power that shapes both their lives.

NOTE

1. The first Women and Work course, offered in spring 1995, was organized around three modules: history and economics of work, analyzing women's work, and contemporary topics in women's work. The required text was Natalie Sokoloff's *Black Women and White Women in the Professions.*

In spring 1997, the Women and Work course was offered again, with a focus on the experiences and issues facing contemporary working women as part of the overall history of working women. The main text was *America's Working Women: A Documentary History 1600 to the Present* by Rosalyn Baxandall, Linda Gordon, and Susan Reverby. Also effective was a showing of the classic film, *Salt of the Earth,* depicting the interaction between gender, labor, family, and ethnicity in a community of Chicano miners and their families in the southwest during the 1940s.

The next version of the course was taught in fall 1999 and included a textbook that provided a more scholarly examination of issues such as pay equity, gender relations on the job, and tensions between work and family. *Workplace/Women's Place,* an interdisciplinary anthology by Dana Dunn, offers the "big picture—trends in segregation and the sex gap in pay, explanations for both, and employer or governmental policies that could reduce inequality." It also "explores links between employment and other institutions . . . job and family links and between gender, race, and class" (ix). The text was supplemented by *Puerto Rican Women and Work,* a volume of essays edited by Altagracia Ortiz that introduced issues of migration and ethnicity into the course.

In fall 2001, the Dunn text was assigned along with another reader, *Women and Work,* edited by Paula Dubeck and Kathryn Borman. This text consists of 150 short articles that describe the latest research, theories, and data on a myriad of subjects involving occupational histories, workplace equity issues, family-work tensions, and the work of various racial and ethnic groups including a section on women workers around the world.

WORKS CITED

Amott, Teresa, and Julie Matthaei. *Race, Gender and Work: A Multicultural Economic History of Women in the United States.* Boston: South End, 1991.

Baxandall, Rosalyn, Linda Gordon, and Susan Reverby, eds. *America's Working Women: A Documentary History 1600 to the Present.* New York: Norton, 1995.

Brewer, Rose. "Theorizing Race, Class and Gender: The New Scholarship of

Black Feminist Intellectuals and Black Women's Labor." *Theorizing Black Feminisms: The Visionary Pragmatism of Black Women.* Ed. Stanlie James and Abena Busia. New York: Routledge, 1993. 13–30.

Cohen, Rosalie. "Women in the Service Occupation Sector." *Women and Work.* Ed. Paula Dubeck and Kathryn Borman. New Brunswick, NJ: Rutgers UP, 1996. 143–47..

Delpit, Lisa. *Other People's Children: Cultural Conflict in the Classroom.* New York: New, 1996.

Di Leonardo, Micaela. "The Female World of Cards and Holidays: Women, Families, and the Work of Kinship." *Signs: Journal of Women in Culture and Society* 12:3 (1987): 440–53.

Dubeck, Paula, and Kathryn Borman, eds. *Women and Work: A Reader.* New Brunswick, NJ: Rutgers UP, 1996.

Dunn, Dana, ed. *Workplace/Women's Place, An Anthology.* Los Angeles: Roxbury, 1997.

Hochschild, Arlie Russell. *The Managed Heart: Commercialization of Human Feeling.* Berkeley: U of California P, 1983.

Ortiz, Altagracia, ed. *Puerto Rican Women and Work.* Philadelphia: Temple UP, 1996.

Reskin, Barbara, and Irene Padavic. *Women and Men at Work.* Thousand Oaks, CA: Pine Forge, 1994.

Sokoloff, Natalie. *Black Women and White Women in the Professions.* New York: Routledge, 1992.

Steinberg, Ronnie, and Deborah Figart, eds. "Emotional Labor since the Managed Heart." *The Annals of the American Academy of Political and Social Science* 561 (1999): 8–38.

Barbara Omolade *is a founding staff member and current associate professor of sociology of the City College Center for Worker Education, where she teaches courses about sociological theory, women, African Americans, and race. She has published a collection of essays addressing historical, political, and education issues,* The Rising Song of African American Women, *(Routledge 1995).*

Women's Studies in the 'Women's Professions'

Berenice Malka Fisher

At the height of the women's liberation movement of the early 1970s, Margaret Adams, a leading social worker, wrote a searing indictment of how the women's "helping professions" perpetuated women's oppression and how women themselves collaborated in this oppression. Adams called this pattern "the compassion trap." She argued that professionals in these fields should break out of their bondage through militant thought and action, challenging the prevailing belief that women were by nature responsible for fulfilling the caring needs of society.

Adams's call could have been heard as a timely invitation to integrate feminist teaching and research in the women-predominant fields into the burgeoning mainstream of women's studies. If so, few answered the call. The field of women's studies was born, and remained, deeply rooted in the liberal arts arena of higher education. The long-standing gap between the liberal arts and professional education—in particular the women-predominant professions that are stigmatized by class (relatively low pay) and gender ("women's work")—was not easily bridged through creating the discipline of women's studies. Thus, with few exceptions, the story of women's studies in the women-predominant fields has remained an untold part of women's studies history.[1]

In this brief essay, I am going to tell that story from the perspective of my twenty-five years in organizing and teaching women's studies in the School of Education at New York University. This school, with its own faculty of over two hundred, includes a wide range of women-predominant professions: educational fields, psychological services, nursing specialties, health disciplines, and arts-based therapies. In the late 1970s, I co-organized a faculty group that eventually became the Women's Studies Commission—an interdepartmental committee dedicated to promoting women's studies in our school.[2] Most of our original group had been active in or strongly influenced by recent social justice movements, including the civil rights movement, the new left, and the women's movement. In this respect, we had a lot in common with feminists who had pioneered women's studies courses and programs in the liberal arts and conceived of this new field as "an academic arm of women's liberation" (Boxer 676). Yet even when we faced similar issues, our project differed from liberal arts–based women's studies in significant ways. Our main concerns focused around activism, interdisciplinarity, pedagogy, difference, research, and the deconstruction of the "women's professions." In this essay, I will touch on each of them in turn.

In education for the professions, "activism" entails, among other things, addressing the problem of how to integrate feminism into professional fields. Theory and research are critical to this process, but their meaning is shaped through interaction with practice. Thus, while women's studies based in the liberal arts has had to develop modes of connecting classroom work to feminist practices of different kinds, those of us in professional schools have sought to connect feminist theories and research to professional practices. Practical questions inform teaching and research in education and the human services: How can a teacher respond to the sexism and racism she encounters in texts she is required to use? How can a counselor help a woman who is too poor to take advantage of available services? How can a nurse promote advocacy for women patients? How can a sexuality educator deal with community outrage at her sex-positive course content? These are not merely technical questions; they go to the heart of feminist thinking about social change. In this activist spirit, our commission wanted to discover how we could support such thinking in our school and in the professions it represents.

The women's studies commitment to interdisciplinarity was an important factor in our effort, because the vision of feminist faculty converging from a wide variety of fields inspired us to come together in the first place. But feminists in the liberal arts long have disagreed about the nature of this kind of collaboration—whether it involves providing a gathering place in which feminists from various disciplines can share their research with each other and students or whether it requires creating an entirely new field with its unique forms of research and teaching. For a professional school such as ours, the outcome of this debate was determined largely by the fact that many programs prepare students for different kinds of state licensure. Dissolving the boundaries between such professional fields would pose a massive problem and not necessarily lead to desirable results. Student schedules often were packed to meet program requirements, leaving little space for electives let alone women's studies courses linked to their fields.

In the face of these facts, our Women's Studies Commission opted for the gathering place model of interdisciplinarity, complemented by a strategy of working from within the established structures. The best way to increase feminist consciousness in these fields, we decided, was to make our presence felt in as many ways as possible: to create a greater number of feminist courses for students who were able to take them, to promote attention to feminist issues in programs where this was possible, to support doctoral research on women, and to offer seminars and other events to both faculty and students in order to stimulate feminist thought and discussion.

In lieu of a formal program, the commission decided to group and publicize our feminist courses under the rubric of Women in the Human Services. In 1982–83, for example, we offered Women in the Human Services: History and Theory, Women and Mental Health, Contemporary Perspectives on Women's Development, Women as Human Service Consumers, A Theoretical and Experiential Approach to Body-Mind Interaction, and Feminist Philosophies of Education. That spring semester, we presented a day-long conference for professionals entitled "Women in the Human Services: Dilemmas of Caring," at which guest speakers talked about the economic and social conditions in women-predominant fields, participants addressed common problems in small-group discussions, and faculty described strategies for dealing with burnout.

Teaching the kinds of students who enroll in our programs also poses a challenge. For much of the commission's twenty-year history, our school offered mostly graduate degrees and attracted many older women students who had years of experience in and commitment to their chosen fields. Our gradually increasing proportion of undergraduates was also, in general, very serious about professional education. Both graduates and undergraduates often worked full time and many had family responsibilities. Their schooling was purchased at a high price, and they expected concrete outcomes. At worst, this pressure toward practicality could lead to a refusal to engage in studying anything that did not have immediate application. But in teaching graduate courses like Feminist Philosophies of Education or the undergraduate course Gender and Professional Life, I found that most students already perceived contradictions within their chosen professions and wanted help in thinking about them. Why are these occupations so gender-stratified? What does it mean to "care" for others, and how should such activities be organized? What is the relation between caring, teaching, or healing work in the private and public spheres? What are the costs as well as benefits of professional organizations or unionization?

These students and this subject matter had a strong impact on my understanding of feminist pedagogy. A given class might

include elementary school teachers, nurses, occupational therapists, college administrators, high school history teachers, counselors, art therapists, and sexuality educators, or student interns in
any of these fields. Comparing their experiences in the light of feminist theory and research could lead toward valuable, collective
thinking about social injustice and social change. I could facilitate
these discussions but could not offer neat answers to the complex
questions students faced in their different work settings. I could
only insist that both the personal and the professional were political—that professional life involved political choices that could not
be evaded. This image of guiding the students through a process
of feminist political discussion became the heart of my own feminist pedagogy. Eventually, I spelled out this thinking in a book that
I somewhat wryly titled *No Angel in the Classroom* (Fisher).

As that title implies, I discovered through my teaching that—like
Margaret Adams, who admitted her own complicity in perpetuating
"the compassion trap"—I shared with many of my students a struggle
with the stereotype of "the good woman." On the one hand, I wanted
to distance myself from the association between my professional work
and the assumption that women were "naturally" caring. Similarly, in
their drive to acquire professional status, leaders of the women-predominant professions often have tried to downplay any association
with women's nurturing work. On the other hand, I was drawn to
teaching in part because of its caring component. In the same way,
despite the threat that the association with caring poses to their claims
to be professionals, students generally come to these fields with strong
commitments to helping others.

This motivation to "care" is both necessary and dangerous. It
plays an especially problematic role in relation to the feminist project of dealing with "differences" among women and in women's
studies classes that address racism. For a white woman teacher, counselor, or nurse to acknowledge that she is complicit in racism simultaneously threatens her sense of personal and professional worth.
The attempt by white students to preserve a belief in their own altruism contributes to deep denial of such complicity, understandably
angering many students of color. Feminist criticism of ideals such
as "the angel in the house" or "the lady with the lamp" may show students the racial and class assumptions underlying many of our gendered interpretations of altruism. But, even with these insights, we
are all still faced with the problem of how to organize and practice
caring in ways that do not perpetuate gender, racial, and other kinds
of injustice.

Our commission made a number of good-faith efforts to integrate critiques of racism into our work. We invited speakers to address such topics as confronting racism in the training of mental health professionals and integrating gender and race into disciplinary perspectives. We organized faculty presentations of research on race and ethnicity, and we honored the work of a number of doctoral students whose research dealt with racial inequities. Faculty assigned texts that related to racism in the women-predominant professions, and our offerings eventually included a class entitled Contemporary Issues in Science and Mathematics Education: Gender and Ethnicity. Yet we often found it difficult to talk about racism and to conceptualize the role of antiracist critiques in our collective work. In the end, the women of color on the commission continued to carry the major burden for keeping racism on the agenda, and I found myself wondering whether the pattern that I encountered in my teaching—of white women in the women-predominant professions wanting to preserve belief in their own altruism—kept us from going more deeply into this problem.

Sexual orientation raises a different but perhaps related problem for education in the women-predominant professions. These fields involve a great deal of intimate contact with the bodies, minds, and psyches of vulnerable individuals and populations. Feelings of heterosexual attraction can pose a threat to relationships of teaching, caring, and healing, but within certain limits (depending on the ages and degrees of dependency involved), such reactions are normalized—both validated by the broader heteronormative society and held in check through professional cultures and codes of ethics. For instance, a female occupational therapist may be attracted to a male patient, which is seen as normal, but she is expected to restrain herself from acting on her impulses. In contrast, homoerotic desires are still commonly erased or stigmatized, and there is very little discussion of their meaning for professional education.

In my workplace, the silence has been deafening. In more than thirty years, I have encountered only two other out lesbians on our school faculty, both of whom eventually left the institution. I believe that the status anxiety that pervades women-predominant fields contributes to this silence. If the "women's professions" are suspect claimants to the title of "profession," then acknowledging that the field includes lesbians poses an additional danger. (Gay men may be less threatening because many people in women-predominant fields think that increasing the proportion of men will improve their professional standing.) This does not mean that progress is impossible. Lesbian and gay groups within professional associations stimulate discussion and change, as does the inclusion of lesbian, gay, bisexual, and transgender texts in classes within professional schools. Members of the commission have incorporated such readings in a number of courses. I look forward to a time in which a critical mass of lesbians will be able to raise these issues through more collective efforts.

The question of economic inequity is also extremely difficult to deal with in the context of the women-predominant professions. Like all professions, these fields are highly stratified in terms of class. The structure of higher education simultaneously reinforces and obscures such hierarchies. A nursing student from a working-class background attends a community college and ends up on the floor of a large hospital. Another from a middle-class family goes to a four-year private university and, after getting her doctorate, ends up directing research at that same hospital. Their economic access to education fragments their profession and makes it hard for them to talk across class boundaries. The division of labor within many higher educational institutions reinforces this difficulty. Students and faculty have their own work to pursue, while time and space further highlight social class distinctions.[3] Maintenance workers often clean buildings at night. Much of the clerical staff that keeps an institution going may be housed in back offices. The richer, better endowed disciplines are likely to have their own quarters, while poorer ones are squeezed into the remaining space. Under these conditions, little cross-class conversation occurs.

In my women's studies courses, the most vital discussions of the meaning of class difference for the women-predominant professions have taken place when students are willing to talk and think critically about their class backgrounds. For example, we do an exercise in which the students have to identify certain class-associated characteristics in their own backgrounds, and they are surprised to discover what a wide range of meanings "middle class" has within this one room. Students from poor and working-class backgrounds become more willing to talk about how they perceive their educations differently. We can talk, then, about how gender compounds this picture: What does "class" mean for an underpaid teacher or health worker?

The topic of class has entered commission discussions on occasion, but it is especially difficult to address within the context of an expensive, private school. Commission members have helped students garner institutional and other resources to pursue their degrees, but it has not been possible to take a collective stand on class issues like the unionization of the clerical staff or of graduate teaching assistants. (Some of us have actively supported such union drives while others have not.)

At some points, however, the work of the commission cross-cuts the class lines that permeate the institution. In the early 1990s, in the wake of the Clarence Thomas confirmation hearings and the resulting national debate on sexual harassment, our group planned an afternoon of practical activities to complement a university-sponsored morning that featured lectures by experts. We held workshops and offered guidance to those experiencing sexual harassment. Together with a graduate student in educational theater, I worked with members of the clerical union to improvise and perform a problem play based on their experiences. I was especially pleased with this activity, but I was also gratified to see our commission making use of its greatest strength: the ability of its members to connect theory with practice and to use this knowledge to affect the wider world.

As my earlier remarks suggest, this orientation toward connecting theory and practice constitutes a distinctive feature of women's studies in the women-predominant professions. Our commission provided the opportunity to demonstrate the importance of this connection by instituting awards to doctoral students for outstanding research in women's studies. Over a ten-year period, we gave awards for dissertations that focused on topics such as the classroom writing of women students; competing theories and practices in the counseling of battered women; the sexual abuse of girls; the family and career issues faced by black professional women; the problems of rural women with HIV/AIDS; teacher education in relation to lesbian, gay, bisexual, and transgender sexualities; and educational opportunities for girls in central Africa. Such research often grew out of years of professional practice in teaching, counseling, or healing as well as years of study. Part of what has always motivated such doctoral work is the vision of improving practices that the researchers know from the inside as well as from an academic perspective.

In the realm of research, there are long-standing tensions between liberal arts disciplines and education for the women-predominant professions. Faculty based in the liberal arts still frequently assume that educational, health, applied psychological, and similar research fails to meet their standards of scholarship. In response, faculty based in women-predominant professions may strike back with charges of educational elitism. Very little attention is paid to the gender, race, and class dimensions of this conflict or to the ways in which feminist researchers located in distant parts of the academy might learn from each other.

Doctoral research in women's studies contains the potential for bridging this gap because of the shared commitment to generating knowledge for and through the liberation of women. Of course, feminists conceive of this liberation in many ways, and arguments about which kind of research best serves this end are bound to continue. But these arguments need not deepen the theory-practice split—a binary opposition that itself has done much to perpetuate the oppression of women. Rather, they could broaden the arena of feminist academic discourse, helping to link it to a wider range of situations and social worlds.

In the past decade, another binary—that between women and men—has been subject to such intense academic scrutiny that the very notions of "women's studies research" or of "women's studies in the women-predominant professions" are open to serious question. This questioning played a significant role in a process of redefining our Women's Studies Commission that took place as it passed its twentieth anniversary. By the latter part of the 1990s, we had exhausted the impulse behind our group. Our original collective structure had given way to bureaucratic pressures toward hierarchy. I had become the virtually permanent chair. Senior faculty were overburdened with responsibilities, junior faculty with the increased demands for achieving tenure. A number of us agreed that if we did not transform we would simply fade away.

Through a process of outreach and discussion with a larger group of faculty, we revised our mission statement and renamed ourselves the Commission on Gender, Race, and Social Justice. Many people preferred this language because they considered it more inclusive—and, indeed, for the first time in our history several men joined the group. The new name also conveyed the commitment to place greater emphasis on issues of race. I was happy that we could find a fresh formulation to support feminist, antiracist efforts in our school. But it saddened me to let go of our earlier name. My own academic identity remained rooted in women's studies as an intellectual and political home.

The current feminist engagement in postcolonial, racial-ethnic, and queer studies has complex implications for women's studies in the "women's professions." What does the deconstruction of categories like "women" mean for our understanding of the women-predominant professions? What does a critical analysis of how various people have conceived of the human body offer for the practices concerned with health and healing? How have racism and colonialism helped to construct our notions of teaching, healing, and caring? As always in the realms of professional education, such theoretical concerns are shaped in interaction with practice, and the practical problems remain massive. Gender, race, class, and other forms of occupational segregation still profoundly mark these professional fields. Large-scale privatization of educational and human service activities and the pressures toward deskilling of professionals worsen the conditions of women and undermine claims to professional autonomy: Teachers and nurses often find themselves fighting losing battles over the value of their professional training and whether they have the professional skills to make important decisions about their work. Persisting patterns of homophobia still ignite public debates, silencing practitioners and those they seek to serve. Dilemmas of caring, both public and private, continue to shape women's lives in massive and subtle ways. There are few easy answers.

To the extent that it is possible to hope in the current world, however, I believe that we can make progress in these areas. Problems associated with teaching, healing, and caring have long plagued the human species. They are not unsolvable but they call out for fair and imaginative solutions. There is a lot of important feminist work to be done here, and willing minds and hands to do it.

NOTES

1. Occasionally, "women's studies" is conceptualized as including "women in the professions." In 1993, the *Women's Review of Books* devoted a special section of their annual issue on feminism and women's studies in the academy to "Women who Teach with the Wolves," a group of articles on professional education in about a dozen areas, all of which, except nursing, were male-predominant. In locating the mainstream of women's studies in the liberal arts, I do not mean to understate the difficulties that have been and continue to be faced by faculty within liberal arts fields who also identify with women's studies. Nor do I want to suggest that connections never have been made between faculty in the women-predominant fields and those in the liberal arts (as, for example, when a faculty member from a department of education or nursing is included in a school's women's studies program or committee). But a discourse on women's studies that crosses the boundaries between the liberal arts and the women-predominant professions has still to develop. This may happen eventually as liberal arts–based women's studies faculty increasingly make connections with higher prestige professional fields such as law. For instance, in her review of women's studies at the turn of the millennium, Barrie Thorne confines her overview to which of the liberal arts fields have been receptive and which have been hostile to feminist reformulation, but she also mentions coteaching a course with a colleague in their law school (Thorne).

2. The following New York University faculty were members of the Women's Studies Commission of the School of Education (now the Steinhardt School of Education) for significant periods of time during its twenty-year history: Judith Alpert, Patricia Carey, Cynthia Caroselli, Vivian Clarke, Nancy Esibill, Iris Fodor, Pamela Frazer-Abder, Marcia Leventhal,

Carla Mariano, Mary McRae, Rosalie Miller, Mary Sue Richardson, Lisa Suzuki, and Emily Wughalter. Nancy Allen, Joanne Griffin, and Patricia Moccia also contributed at its early stages. I deeply appreciate having had the opportunity to work with these colleagues over the years. However, they are in no way responsible for my interpretations here, which are entirely my own.

3. This rough picture is drawn from the middle-class institutions in which I have taught and does not take into account, for example, the patterns of communication in a community college where the majority of students are working class or poor. Nor does it reflect the sense of shared racial or ethnic, sexual, or political culture that may support cross-class communication (for example, bonding between lesbian faculty members and lesbian security guards or between socialist faculty and clerical union activists).

WORKS CITED

Adams, Margaret. "The Compassion Trap." *Woman in Sexist Society: Studies on Power and Powerlessness.* Ed. Vivian Gornick and Barbara K. Moran. New York: New American Library, 1971. 555–75.

Boxer, Marilyn J. "For and About Women: The Theory and Practice of Women's Studies in the United States." *Signs: Journal of Women in Culture and Society.* 7.4 ((182): 661–95.

Fisher, Berenice Malka. *No Angel in the Classroom: Teaching Through Feminist Discourse.* Lanham, MD: Rowan and Littlefield, 2001.

Thorne, Barrie. "A Telling Time for Women's Studies." *Signs: Journal of Women in Culture and Society* 25.4 (2000): 1183–87.

Women's Review of Books 10.5 (1993).

Berenice Malka Fisher is professor of educational philosophy at New York University. She has published articles and essays on feminist topics since the late 1970s and in the past eight years has served as a consultant on teaching women's studies and other subjects in higher education.

Theory and Activism in a Core Course

Beyond Service Learning

Lynne Derbyshire

The interaction between feminist theory and practice is a challenging concept in contemporary women's studies courses. Although feminism is historically rooted in activism, students sometimes lack familiarity with the activism that was deeply woven into the lives of earlier generations of women, and the subsequent understanding that women's studies courses and programs were developed as an expression of that activism (Fox 230). Feminism: Theory and Practice attempts to provide the opportunity for students actively to engage contemporary theory through group action as a reiteration of the activism inherent in feminist theoretical perspectives across disciplines. Familiarity with the lives of nineteenth-century activists enriches student studies of twentieth-century activism and provides both models and inspiration for student actions.

The course is composed of three major requirements: a group action project that runs simultaneously with the other assignments throughout the course, individual student presentations on the lives and work of nineteenth-century activists, and student-led discussions of contemporary scholarly articles that introduce feminist theory to other academic disciplines. The combination of these assignments provides students with the opportunity to appreciate the need for theory in understanding experience, and the need for practice in order to clarify theory.

Group Action Project

The core of this course is a group action project. As I co-taught the capstone course in women's studies at the University of Rhode Island with a more experienced colleague (Dana Shugar), we talked about the pedagogical challenge of helping students to make the connection between activism and theory. Service learning, a traditional approach, offers one possibility for learning outside the classroom, but students in service-learning placements often fail to make the connection between the work they do and the theory they study (Boss 185). Service learning (or community service learning) is defined as "an instructional strategy in which students are involved in experiential education in real-life settings and where they apply academic knowledge and previous experience to meet real community needs" (Boss 20). Frequently, service learning involves the placement of students on an ongoing community project or agency and ideally includes some structured opportunities to reflect on their experiences, although this does not always happen. The goals, activity, and need for the activity are predetermined. Our group action project is intended to accomplish goals different from those traditionally associated with service learning.

The group action project differs from service-learning experiences in that it is embedded in a context of theory. Not only do the students study theory simultaneously with conceptualizing and planning the group action, but they must conduct the necessary research to write a proposal and plan for the group action. Their research and proposal is consequently used to evaluate the process and results of their group action. Another important distinction between service learning and group action is that rather than working alone in preexisting agencies or projects, students must work together as a group in the conceptualization, research, planning, implementation, and evaluation of the group action. The students must identify the issues, consider what is significant in their immediate community, and then document their assertions regarding what is significant. They must determine what is a useful and possible approach to addressing the need they have identified. And finally, they must collaborate.

The process of group decision-making regarding all aspects of the action project becomes a critical part of the discussion of theory. Also, once there is a tangible action and potential outcome, students think more critically about the topics being researched and discussed. In my experience the students became invested in truly looking at the issues from personal perspectives, and understanding the perspectives of others, rather than simply viewing it from an objective academic perspective. Students find that agreement with alternative points of view is especially challenging when their work and credibility are on the line. They recognize, too, that they need to do more than show up and put in time. They do not all have to be involved in every step, but they must all coordinate and collaborate each step of the way.

The class usually begins by brainstorming topics they believe to be significant. Each topic problem is discussed in terms of significance and practicality of action. Student must consider the time limitations of a semester course, as well as realistic expectations of their time and other hidden costs. The class then narrows down the possible projects and how they might be addressed in terms of an action. Two examples of class group action projects demonstrate the range possible.

The spring 1999 class decided to write a proposal for the institution of a Commission on the Status of Women at our institution. They researched the need for a commission on our campus and the existence and function of commissions on other campuses. They presented their findings and sought letters of support from students, faculty, staff, and administration. They wrote a proposal for the commission, including mission, functions, structure, and budget, and made appointments to meet with the president, provost, and vice president for student affairs. They prepared a PowerPoint presentation of their findings and proposal. Subsequently, the proposal was approved, and the commission appointed.

The spring 2000 class (taught by Judith Anderson) chose to focus on breast cancer and the environment. A breast cancer cluster had been identified on the campus, and it appeared to be environmentally related (though this has not been definitively determined). The students researched breast cancer and environmental issues and created a newsletter that included information about potential environmental carcinogens, research results, and local sources of potential environmental carcinogens. It also contained information on breast cancer prevention, early detection, and an article on the politics of breast cancer, discussing the funding of Breast Cancer Awareness Month by Imperical Chemical Industries (Zeneca Pharmaceuticals), and their control of all related advertising with its emphasis on lifestyle factors (Brennan 14). Finally, the newsletter lists local polluters, local resources and support groups, and information on how to take political action.

The process of selecting an area of focus and determining what the action should be involves engaging in group process, exploring theory, and conducting the necessary research. In the best of circumstances students forgot there was a grade involved because they became so personally invested in the work they chose to do and the project they created.

Nineteenth-Century Activists: Biography/Autobiography

For their presentations on the biography, autobiography, or collected letters, essays, and/or speeches of a nineteenth-century woman's rights activist, I encourage students to select an activist from the earlier part of the century. Students discover that nineteenth-century feminists "organized campaigns for the right of married women to control their property, the right of women to an education and suitable employment opportunities, and the right of women to vote" (LeGates 502). After all of the students have completed their presentations, we have a class discussion addressing why and how each of the women became activists and the theoretical basis for their actions. The woman's rights activists from the early part of the nineteenth century tended to be involved in at least two or three different social movements, including abolition, temperance, moral reform, property rights for women, and suffrage for women (Derbyshire 117), and it is easy to direct a discussion that looks at the heuristic value of the theory of one movement for another. Studying the lives of women involved in these multiple issues also leads students to readily see the intersections of race, class, and gender. Finally, the assignment provides students with models to guide a concrete understanding of the role of theory and activism in one's life.

Academic Disciplines and Feminist Theory

At our university, women's studies majors usually have a second major and/or a minor in another academic discipline. The interdisciplinary nature of twentieth-century feminism arose from activism across a wide range of concerns. Feminists' work to achieve equal opportunity in employment, to secure reproductive rights, to establish women's health clinics, and to organize "Take Back the Night" marches, rape crisis centers, and shelters for women seeking to escape domestic violence generated theory that has permeated academia at every level in every discipline (Freeman 513–17). The third assignment in this course is for each student to research and select an article in his or her non–women's studies academic major that represents the introduction of feminist theory to that discipline, or a feminist challenge to the theory of that discipline. Students must lead class discussions on the readings they have selected and distributed. Additional required readings from Domna Stanton and Abigail Stewart or Beverly Guy-Sheftall make our examination of the disciplines more inclusive.

Asking the students to research articles from their disciplines and lead class discussions of the readings accomplishes two goals. In searching for their articles they often develop a much better sense of how feminist theory relates to or exists in their disciplines, and they discover the processes by which a feminist perspective or theory evolved. Also, in finding the articles and leading the discussions, they develop a sense of connection with and responsibility to feminist theory in those disciplines. This does not occur when they are simply assigned to read and discuss a series of articles in a range of disciplines.

Conclusion

The assignments at the center of this course provide connections between contemporary theory and action and historical activism as well. This combination of assignments, when successful, helps students discover the value theory holds for better understanding of lived experience, and the value of lived experience in testing and validating theory. Sometimes it provides the incentive for students to make feminist activism an ongoing part of their lives.

WORKS CITED

Boss, Judith A. "The Effect of Community Service Work on the Moral Development of College Ethics Students." *Journal of Moral Education* 23.2 (1994): 183–98.

Brennan, Casey. "Breast Cancer and the Environment: The Real Story." Ed. Judith Anderson, Lauren Holt, Sara Conway, Lynn Morelli, Brie Pendleton, and Casey Brennan. Unpublished ms., 2000.

Derbyshire, Lynne. "'Living, Energetic Beings': The Rhetorical Constitution of Woman's Rights Advocates." Diss. U of Maryland, 1997.

Fox, Mary Frank. "Women and Higher Education: Differences in the Status of Students and Scholars." *Women: A Feminist Perspective.* 5th ed. Ed. Jo Freeman. Mountain View, CA: Mayfield, 1995. 220–37.

Freeman, Jo. "From Suffrage to Women's Liberation: Feminism in Twentieth-Century America." *Women: A Feminist Perspective.* 5th ed. Ed. Jo Freeman. Mountain View, CA: Mayfield, 1995. 509–28.

LeGates, Marlene. "Feminists Before Feminism: Origins and Varieties of Women's Protest in Europe and North America Before the Twentieth Century." *Women: A Feminist Perspective.* 5th ed. Ed. Jo Freeman. Mountain View, CA: Mayfield, 1995. 494–508.

FEMINISM: THEORY AND PRACTICE

Course Description

This course examines feminist theory and feminist activism. We will examine feminist analyses through a range of disciplines such as philosophy, science, anthropology, African American studies, literature, history, communication, and psychology. We will explore these disciplines through a variety of feminist approaches. To understand the ways theory interacts with practice, we will also examine woman's rights activism of the nineteenth century and feminist activism of the twentieth century. The class will theorize, design, implement, and critique a specific community (campus or larger) action. Students should gain an understanding of feminist theory as both a critique that has been applied in a variety of traditional fields as well as a discipline in and of itself, and of the inherent connections between feminist theory and feminist practice.

Texts

Stanton, Domna, and Abigail Stewart, eds. *Feminism in the Academy.* Ann Arbor: U of Michigan P, 1995.

Butler, Judith, and Joan W. Scott, eds. *Feminists Theorize the Political.* New York: Routledge, 1992.

Guy-Sheftall, Beverly, ed. *Words of Fire: An Anthology of African-American Feminist Thought.* New York: Norton, 1995.

Requirements

Class Participation

Active discussion is critical to the success of this class. You are required to read all assigned material before each class and come prepared to participate in a thoughtful, analytical, and lively discussion. Punctual attendance is therefore necessary.

Group Action

Throughout the semester we will set aside at least one hour of class time per week to decide upon, plan, theorize, implement, and critique a specific community action, preferably geared to the campus community. Once we have agreed upon an area of concern, the class will be responsible for identifying, gathering, and reading a body of feminist theory relevant to the issue. Based upon those readings, the group will determine the plan of action then carry it out. After the action, each student will write a final evaluation of the work. This group action will require several assignments due throughout the semester: (1) an annotated bibliography; (2) an outline of the detailed plan of action (the class will be graded as a group for the plan); (3) the action itself (this is ungraded); and (4) individual written evaluations of the preparation and action. The evaluation should address the process of deciding on an issue/need, the research, the process of putting the action together, and the mechanics of implementation. Consider both long- and short-term outcomes of your action for the community, for individuals in the community, members of the class, and yourself. The evaluation should also address your assessment of your experience in selecting, planning, and implementing the action. This should include what you have learned from the process and how that confirms or contradicts class readings and discussions. Each student will be graded individually on her or his evaluation of the action.

Biography/Autobiography Presentation

Each student will select and read a biography or autobiography of a nineteenth-century woman's rights activist and will prepare a fifteen-minute presentation for the class. As an alternative to a biography, you may select the collected letters, essays, speeches, and so on, of an activist.

Academic Discipline Article

Each student will select an article from their second (or non–women's studies) major or their minor that represents a feminist challenge to that discipline or the introduction of a feminist theoretical perspective. Everyone will read the articles selected and participate in a class discussion lead by the student who selected the article.

Discussion Questions

You are to formulate one considered, thoughtful question developed from each of your assigned readings. The questions should go beyond simple factual questions that one might ask of the author and should instead focus on analytical questions of larger implications that the essay raises for you. We will pose some of these questions for each class discussion, attempting to ensure that each person gets about the same amount of time for his or her questions over the course of the semester.

Schedule

Week One. Introduction: Discussion—What is feminism? What is theory? What is feminist theory?

I. Nineteenth-Century Theory and Activism

Week Two. Brief history of the evolution of early nineteenth-century women's activism and the development of the woman's rights movement.

Weeks Three, Four, and Five. Biography/autobiography presentations: discussion of why and how women engaged in public activity related to women's lives. (Week Five: Annotated bibliography for group action due.)

II: Feminism and Academic Disciplines

Weeks Six, Seven, Eight, and Nine. Discussion of articles selected by students as well as additional readings from Stanton and Stewart and Guy-Sheftall (selected to fill in disciplines not covered by student selections). Possible choices:

Philosophy: Longino, Helen E. "To See Feelingly: Reason, Passion, and Dialogue in Feminist Philosophy." In Stanton and Stewart, 19–45.

Art History: Kampen, Natalie Boymel. "Looking at Gender: The Column of Trojan and Roman Historical Relief." In Stanton and Stewart, 46–73.

Literature: McKay, Nellie Y. "The Narrative Self: Race, Politics, and Culture in Black American Women's Autobiography." In Stanton and Stewart, 74–100.

History: Pomeroy, Sarah B. "The Contribution of Women to the Greek Domestic Economy: Rereading Xebiphon's *Oeconomicus.*" In Stanton and Stewart, 180–98.

Archaeology: Conkey, Margaret W., and Ruth E. Tringham. "Archaeology and the Goddess: Exploring the Contours of Feminist Archaeology." In Stanton and Stewart, 199–247.

Psychology: Marecek, Jeanne. "Psychology and Feminism: Can This Relationship Be Saved?" In Stanton and Stewart, 101–34.

Political Science: Sapiro, Virginia. "Feminist Studies and Political Science—and Vice Versa." In Stanton and Stewart, 291–310.

Science, Engineering: Hughes, Donna M. "Scientific, Feminist and Personal Epistemologies: Conflicts and Opportunities." *Women's Studies Quarterly* 28.1–2 (2000): 305–12.

Natural Sciences: Hughes, Donna M. "Women and the Natural Sciences." *Women's Studies Quarterly* 28.1–2 (2000): 203–6.

Week Seven: Outline of group action plan due.

Week Ten. Discussion integrating feminism in the various academic disciplines: What are the similarities and differences in theory and practice? What are the similarities and differences in how and when feminist theory emerged in the various disciplines? What are the implications?

III. Feminist Theory Beyond the Disciplines

Week Eleven. What is theory? What are the implications of theorizing? Butler and Scott: Introduction, xiii.

Contesting Grounds: Butler, Judith. "Contingent Foundations: Feminism and the Question of Postmodernism." In Butler and Scott, 3. Scott, Joan W. "Experience." In Butler and Scott, 22. Spivak, Gayatri Chakravorty. "French Feminism Revisited: Ethics and Politics." In Butler and Scott, 54. Haraway, Donna. "Ecce Homo, Ain't (Ar'n't) I a Woman, and Inappropriate/d Others: The Humanist in a Post-Humanist Landscape." In Butler and Scott, 86. Signifying Identity: Crosby, Christina. "Dealing with Differences." In Butler and Scott, 130.

Week Twelve. Law.
Poovey, Mary. "The Abortion Question and the Death of Man." In Butler and Scott, 239. Cornell, Drucilla A. "Gender, Sex, and Equivalent Rights." In Butler and Scott, 280. Schultz, Vicki. "Women 'Before' the Law: Judicial Stories about Women, Work, and Sex Segregation on the Job." In Butler and Scott, 297.

Week Thirteen. Critical Practices.
McClure, Kirstie. "The Issues of Foundations: Scientized Politics, Politicized Science, and Feminist Critical Practices." In Butler and Scott, 341. Marcus, Sharon. "Fighting Bodies, Fighting Words: A Theory and Practice of Rape Prevention." In Butler and Scott, 385. Pathak, Zakia. "A Pedagogy for Postcolonial Feminists." In Butler and Scott, 426. Flax, Jane. "The End of Innocence." In Butler and Scott, 445. Singer, Linda. "Feminism and Postmodernism." In Butler and Scott, 464.
Wrap up.

Week Fourteen. Discussion of theory and activism integrating the semester's reading and work. Evaluation of the group action and the planning and research on which it was based. Written evaluations of the group action due.

Suggested Readings in Biography and Autobiography

Anthony, Katherine. *Susan B. Anthony: Her Personal History and Her Era.* Garden City, NY: Doubleday, 1954.
Bacon, Margaret Hope. *Valiant Friend: The Life of Lucretia Mott.* New York: Walker, 1980.

Banner, Lois L. *Elizabeth Cady Stanton: A Radical for Woman's Rights.* Boston: Little, 1980.

Barry, Kathleen. *Susan B. Anthony: A Biography of a Singular Feminist.* New York: New York UP, 1988.

Birney, Catherine H. *The Grimké Sisters: Sarah and Angelina Grimké: The First American Women Advocates of Abolition and Woman's Rights.* New York: Haskell, 1970.

Blackwell, Alice Stone. *Lucy Stone: Pioneer of Woman's Rights.* Melrose, MA: Alice Stone Blackwell Committee, 1930.

Bloomer, D. C. *The Life and Writings of Amelia Bloomer.* New York: Schocken, 1975.

Boydston, Jeanne, Mary Kelley, and Anne Margolis. *The Limits of Sisterhood: The Beecher Sisters on Woman's Rights and Woman's Sphere.* Chapel Hill: U of North Carolina P, 1988.

Cazden, Elizabeth. *Antoinette Brown Blackwell: A Biography.* Old Westbury, NY: Feminist, 1983.

Ceplair, Larry, ed. *The Public Years of Sarah and Angelina Grimké: Selected Writings, 1835–1839.* New York: Columbia UP, 1989.

Coon, Anne C., ed. *Hear Me Patiently: The Reform Speeches of Amelia Jenks Bloomer.* Westport, CT: Greenwood, 1994.

Cromwell, Otelia. *Lucretia Mott.* Cambridge, MA: Harvard UP, 1958.

D'Arusmont, Francis Wright. *Life, Letters and Lectures, 1834–1844 (Including Course of Popular Lectures).* 1829. New York: Arno, 1972.

DuBois, Ellen C., ed. *Elizabeth Cady Stanton/Susan B. Anthony: Correspondence, Writings, Speeches.* New York: Schocken, 1981.

Eckhardt, Celia Morris. *Fanny Wright: Rebel in America.* Cambridge, MA: Harvard UP, 1984.

Flexner, Eleanor. *Mary Wollstonecraft: A Biography.* Baltimore: Penguin, 1972.

Griffith, Elisabeth. *In Her Own Right: The Life of Elizabeth Cady Stanton.* New York: Oxford UP, 1984.

Hare, Lloyd C. M. *The Greatest American Woman: Lucretia Mott.* New York: American Historical Society, 1937.

Harper, Ida Husted. *The Life and Work of Susan B. Anthony; Including Public Addresses, Her Own Letters and Many from Her Contemporaries.* Vols. 1, 2, and 3. Indianapolis: Hollenbeck, 1898.

Hayes, Elinor Rice. *Morning Star: A Biography of Lucy Stone, 1818–1893.* New York: Harcourt, 1961.

Kerr, Andrea Moore. *Lucy Stone: Speaking out for Equality.* New Brunswick, NJ: Rutgers UP, 1992.

Lasser, Carol, and Marlene Deahl Merrill, eds. *Friends and Sisters: Letters Between Lucy Stone and Antoinette Brown Blackwell, 1846–1893.* Urbana:

U of Illinois P, 1987.

Lumpkin, Katherine Du Pre. *The Emancipation of Angelina Grimké.* Chapel Hill: U of North Carolina P, 1974.

Lutz, Alma. *Created Equal: A Biography of Elizabeth Cady Stanton, 1815–1902.* New York: John Day, 1940.

Oakley, Mary Ann B. *Elizabeth Cady Stanton.* 2nd ed. Old Westbury, NY: Feminist, 1972.

Painter, Nell Irvin. *Sojourner Truth: A Life, A Symbol.* New York: Norton, 1996.

Stanton, Elizabeth Cady. *Eighty Years and More: Reminiscences 1815–1897.* New York: Schocken, 1971.

Sterling, Dorothy. *Ahead of Her Time: Abby Kelley and the Politics of Antislavery.* New York: Norton, 1991.

Suhl, Yuri. *Ernestine Rose and the Battle for Human Rights.* New York: Reynal, 1959.

Waggenspack, Beth M. *The Search for Self-sovereignty: The Oratory of Elizabeth Cady Stanton.* Westport, CT: Greenwood, 1989.

Lynne Derbyshire *is assistant professor of communication studies and women's studies at the University of Rhode Island. She has a Ph.D. in communication studies from the University of Maryland, College Park.*

Disciplining Feminism: From Social Activism to Academic Discourse by Ellen Messer-Davidow (Durham, NC: Duke University Press, 2002)

Dorothy O. Helly

All stripes of feminists need to read this book, which is written lucidly, compellingly, and in a narrative style that accommodates intellectual analysis. Whether readers agree or disagree with her arguments, they will have to acknowledge that Messer-Davidow writes with feminist passion. As a participant-activist in the earliest years of the second wave of feminism and as a graduate student involved in community and campus activism, she took part in the new feminist caucus at the Modern Language Association (MLA) and spent two years as an administrative assistant to her university president as he tried to make institutional change happen. Having taken part in the feminist determination to change the elitist ways of the academy and transform its disciplines, she asks, "[H]ow did it happen that a bold venture launched thirty years ago to transform academic and social institutions was itself transformed by them?" (1).

Messer-Davidow believes that proponents of "feminist studies" (the term she uses throughout) started out to bridge the academy-community divide but ultimately failed because their efforts to secure a place in the academy ultimately subjected them to the rules of exclusivity and inequality that govern universities. Seeing feminist studies as increasingly "formatted as an academic discipline" (13), she concludes that its initial political agenda for social change has been lost. Academic feminists read, teach, do research, and write about social activism, she laments, but they no longer do it.

Part 1 provides a sharply etched picture of how the disciplines historically edged out women who were not seen to "fit in" to their disciplinary order. It then explores the universities' defense of their traditional exclusionary practices of sex-discrimination.

Part 2 shows that despite the growth of feminist studies, in terms of thousands of courses and hundreds of programs, the wage gap for women faculty persists. They remain clustered in lower prestige disciplines, lower prestige institutions, lower faculty ranks, and part-time positions. Feminist efforts have led to curriculum transformation

projects, the establishment of campus-based feminist research centers, a national association of feminist scholars, and women's cau-
cuses in every disciplinary association. Yet increased numbers of
women faculty and women students have had no radical effect.
Feminist presses and conferences have only made it easier for mainstream disciplinary arenas to resist and ignore feminist scholarship
and to keep feminist studies marginal. Maintained on scant budgets
and usually restricted to offering only introductory and senior
courses, programs have had to rely on discipline-approved crosslisted
courses over which they have minimal control. Instead of sponsor-
ing outreach into the community, feminists in the academy at best
only teach about such issues. Only feminist theory, which continues
to expand, remains truly interdisciplinary. But, in Messer-Davidow's
words, feminist theory only generates "streams of knowledge partic-
ularized according to their identity, disciplinary, and/or political
positions" (212). On top of this, the challenges of poststructuralism
have further reduced social change to the "workings of signification"
(213).

In Part 3, Messer-Davidow compares feminist social change efforts
with those of the new conservative movement that has grown steadily
in America. Well-funded, professionally managed, and using all the
services of modern information technology, conservative organizations by the 1990s had formed tightly networked lines of communication at the national level, offering summer leadership institutes to
train the next generation of young conservatives for future roles in
government and media work. The nearest feminist equivalent
Messer-Davidow found was a statewide curriculum integration effort,
the New Jersey Project, but it focused on the higher education sector within one state. The better-funded conservative organizations
have sought to inculcate a fairly homogeneous set of male and
female students from all over the country with an appreciation of the
"superiority of the American system" (240). And in practice, she
found, the courses are heavily weighted toward conservative economics, ethics, and rhetoric. Meanwhile, on tighter budgets, at feminist centers and in masters-level courses, students who reflect the
diverse and multicultural nature of the country were being trained
with a progressive vision of what American public leadership
"should" be.

Messer-Davidow exhorts feminists to wake up to the real dangers
posed by conservative organizations to programs like affirmative
action. She warns feminists not to become "too engrossed in particu-
larizing identities and issues, and too busy sustaining our organizations

on scant resources to keep the gradually shifting conditions of social change in view" (287). She lays out her own activist agenda to accomplish social justice goals.

Messer-Davidow became a feminist as a returning woman graduate student caught up in the cauldron of community and professional activism. Readers who came to feminism at a different stage in their lives will still understand her fears. This reviewer believes, however, that she does not fully appreciate the accumulated impact of the past thirty years of a feminist revolution in scholarship, particularly in challenging the content and methodology of the traditional disciplines. The continued marginalization of most feminist studies programs in the structures of the academy is indisputable. I have no quarrel with her activist agenda, but it seems to me that she needs to acknowledge that teaching an increasingly inclusive curriculum is a form of activism. Similarly, theorizing about diverse identities and the coalitions that are needed to forge a joint social agenda is far better than ignoring the power of such issues in our daily lives. The thousands of feminist courses have had some effect on the hundreds of thousands of students who have taken them. Universities may still marginalize feminist programs in their budgets, but they can no longer ignore these programs intellectually. From women's studies programs have come the strategies that have won multicultural and gender-conscious core curriculums. Mainstream disciplinary journals and scholarly conferences can no longer ignore feminist scholarship lest they seem "out of touch" and fail to attract a new generation of graduate students and assistant professors.

Interdisciplinary programs of many kinds—from a focus on urban life to new combinations of scientific disciplines to the expansion of ethnic and area studies—have gained in academic prominence and funding, in no small measure due to the explosion of interdisciplinary feminist methodologies (embracing race, ethnicity, class, and sexuality) within the traditional disciplines. New textbooks that fail to include women in all their complexities do so at their peril. Web sites offer this generation of students a readily available source of every kind of information about women. Development studies, and organizations like the World Bank and the International Monetary Fund, have learned not to ignore gender factors. A new emphasis on issues like "human rights" and "human security" reflect not only feminist theory today but also the substantive feminist accomplishments in the international arenas of the recent past.

At the City University of New York, for example, where two thirds of its approximately 200,000 students are women of color, students represent a United Nations array of different communities. If their courses—women's studies courses and courses on gender, race, and class in the disciplines—open students' eyes to issues of social and economic justice (and Messer-Davidow does acknowledge that feminists do "teach" about such issues), these urban university students learn to become change agents in their communities. Second-wave feminists in and out of the academy have brought such issues as reproductive choice out into the open in this country and around the globe, and that change continues to affect women's lives everywhere. Third-wave feminists remain committed to that goal. We can agree with Messer-Davidow that there is much to do, that we need to do it right now, and that feminism has to continue to struggle against being "disciplined" in the traditional exclusionary practices of the academy, but I contend that we have not yet lost that struggle.

Dorothy O. Helly *is professor emerita of history and women's studies at Hunter College and the Graduate Center of the City University of New York.*